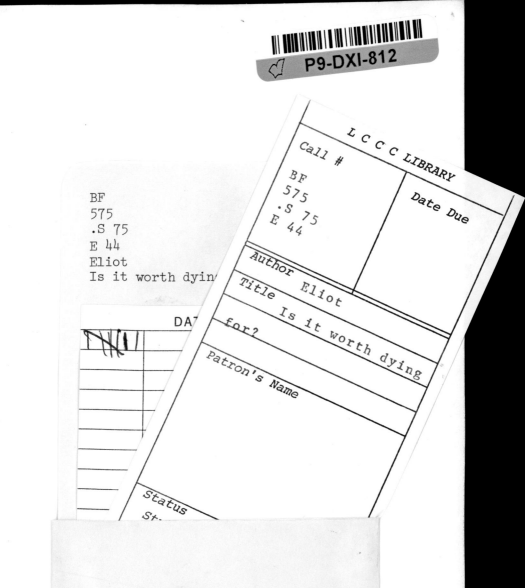

Laramie County Community College
Instructional Resources Center
Cheyenne, Wyoming 82001

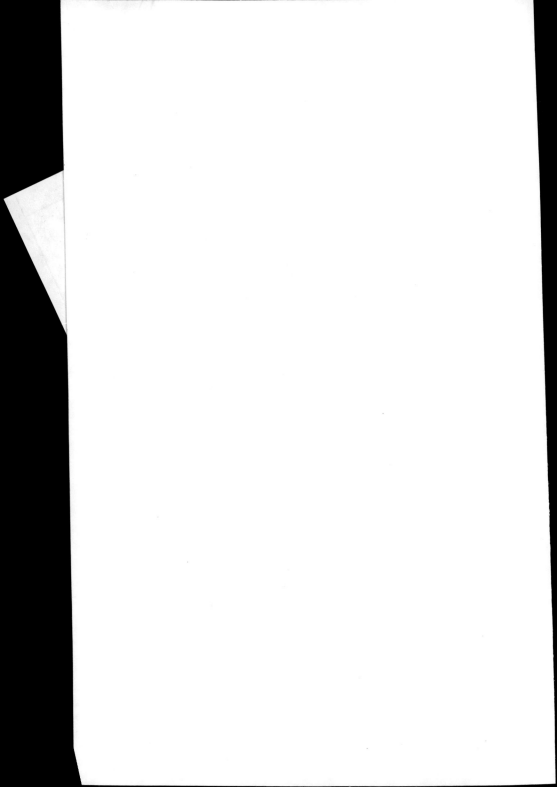

Is It
Worth Dying For?

Is It Worth Dying For?

A Self-Assessment Program
to Make Stress Work for You,
Not against You

Robert S. Eliot, M.D.,
and Dennis L. Breo

BANTAM BOOKS
TORONTO · NEW YORK · LONDON · SYDNEY

IS IT WORTH DYING FOR?

A Bantam Book / May 1984

List of Type A characteristics on page 37 by Jane Brody,
September 1980, copyright © 1980 by The New York Times
Company. Reprinted by permission.

The description of the five stages of burnout in Chapter 13 is
from *The Work/Stress Connection: How to Cope with Job Burnout*
by Robert L. Veninga, Ph.D., and James P. Spradley, Ph.D.,
copyright 1981 by Robert L. Veninga and James Spradley,
reprinted by permission of Little, Brown and Company.

Library of Congress Cataloging in Publication Data

Eliot, Robert S.
  Is it worth dying for?

  Bibliography: p. 233
  Includes index.
  1. Stress (Psychology) 2. Stress (Physiology)
  3. Heart—Infarction—Prevention. I. Breo, Dennis L.,
  1942–   . II. Title.
  BF575.S75E44   1984   616.1'205   83-45986
  ISBN 0-553-05039-7

Published simultaneously in the United States and Canada

Bantam Books are published by Bantam Books, Inc. Its trade-
mark, consisting of the words "Bantam Books" and the portrayal
of a rooster, is Registered in the United States Patent and
Trademark Office and in other countries. Marca Registrada.
Bantam Books, Inc., 666 Fifth Avenue, New York, New York 10103.

PRINTED IN THE UNITED STATES OF AMERICA

FG   0 9 8 7 6 5 4 3 2 1

To those who provided me with something to share.
ROBERT S. ELIOT, M.D.

For my son, David, and my wife, Suzanne.
DENNIS L. BREO

This book was written with the assistance of the following faculty and staff members of the Department of Preventive and Stress Medicine at the University of Nebraska Medical Center:

Judith Timberg, M.S., editor
James C. Buell, M.D.
Tracy Dorheim, B.A.
Phyllis Eliot, R.D.
Helen McIlvain, Ph.D.
Mark McKinney, Ph.D.
Morris Mellion, M.D.
Michael Miner, Ph.D.
Hermann Witte, Ph.D.

Contents

Acknowledgments   xi
Foreword by Michael DeBakey, M.D.   xix
Introduction   1

Part One: Stress and the Hot Reactor
   1   Stress: The Modern Epidemic   13
   2   Stress in Action: How Your Body Responds   22
   3   The Hot Reactors   35
   4   Hot Reacting, High Blood Pressure, and
              Heart Attack   55
   5   Are You a Hot Reactor?   65

Part Two: Learning to Manage Stress
   6   Changing Your Self-Talks   95
   7   Clarifying Your Values   112
   8   Relaxing Your Body   120
   9   Increasing Your Fitness   134
  10   Making the Most of Support and Leisure   152
  11   Eating Right   162
  12   Managing Alcohol, Cigarettes, Caffeine,
              & Pills   187
  13   Relieving Stress on the Job   202
  14   Maintaining a Healthy Heart   215

Epilogue   It's Not Worth Dying For   224

Notes and Sources   227
Recommended Reading   233
Index   237

Acknowledgments

No one person can be an expert in all the fields of knowledge covered by this book; in these times, the Renaissance man is a group. I have been extremely fortunate to work in the Department of Preventive and Stress Medicine with colleagues who have generously shared their expertise. Their ideas and feedback at every stage of this book have played a crucial role in bringing it to life, and their active participation has made it far more comprehensive and helpful.

In many cases these colleagues have allowed me to publish material that they have spent years developing, and the book is much the richer for it. In particular I would like to recognize the contributions of James Buell to all of Part One, to the Epilogue, and to several careful reviews of the entire manuscript. We have worked together for over nine years, and it was his clinical and research genius that set the stage for the mental stress testing outlined in the book.

In addition, *Is It Worth Dying For?* has greatly benefited from the knowledge of Tracy Dorheim on fitness; Phyllis Eliot on nutrition; Helen McIlvain on self-talks and support systems as well as many informative discussions on stress in women; Mark McKinney on selected areas of Part One as well as relaxation and fitness; Morris Mellion on fitness, alcohol, smoking, caffeine, and drugs; Michael Miner on relaxation, alcohol, and drugs; and Hermann Witte on self-talks, relaxation, support, leisure, and clarifying values. I hope I have represented their information clearly and accurately.

Pulling together the vast and diverse wealth of material generated in the writing of this book was the demanding task of my coauthor, Dennis L. Breo. A physician-scientist who produces a book for the public needs to test his message, language, and style with a writer of considerable repute. I was fortunate in collaborating with the award-winning national affairs editor for the *American Medical News* at the American Medical Association. In addition to bringing out the fascination of our material for general readers, Dennis has contributed considerable knowledge of his own, and he has magically bound it all into a whole. His understanding of this field, his felicitous phrasing, and his humanistic touch with the pen have made our collaboration truly a synergistic relationship.

Concurrent with Dennis's efforts were those of our department editor, Judith Timberg, who coordinated the contributions of everyone concerned with *Is It Worth Dying For?* She saw to it that ideas were developed and organized and that the entire book flowed. Her unique touch and thoughtful editing at every stage harmonized the input of many individuals from diverse backgrounds in a way that not only respected them but heightened their contributions. I am grateful for her skilled and dedicated work.

Is It Worth Dying For? has also benefited enormously from editorial assistance at Bantam. Senior editors Charles Bloch and Linda Raglan Cunningham were crucial and highly constructive in shaping the manuscript and shepherding it through many stages of development. Their dedication to this project went beyond the call of duty. In addition, Wendy McCurdy contributed important editing ideas throughout, and Dona Munker's thoughtful and incisive copy editing honed both the form and content of the book.

Many friends and colleagues reviewed the manuscript, including Duane and Phyllis Acklie, Wilbert Aronow, David Blumsohn, Jack Canaday, Joyce Daly, Ellen Davis, Bill James, Bob and Inger Koedt, Bob and Maxine Kouba, Don and Carol

Lowe, William Nelligan, Bill and Marge Raymond, Robert Rosenlof, Ronald Roskens, Norm and Midge Sample, Leo Schamroth, David and Lynda Tews, and Glenda Woscyna. In a special category is Emily James, who worked with me as a medical editor for six years and reviewed the manuscript as well as consulting about specific chapters. I value her continuing interest and thoughtful input.

James Ussery, who has been my administrative assistant for eight years, was essential in helping me to find and structure the time and material to make this book possible. Joyce Slusher was of great assistance in the speed and accuracy of her typing and in her editorial suggestions; she always came through with style and grace under pressure. Dee Nielsen was particularly helpful in all stages of the book's preparation. Patricia Gardels and Russell Montgomery also offered valuable support in the many activities surrounding an effort such as this, as did Jane Henderson at Bantam.

I have developed and tested the ideas for this book in many years of lectures, and I would like to acknowledge here my appreciation for the creative art work for hundreds of slides provided by Phyllis and Don Hanson.

In addition, behind a book that reflects twenty years of research and teaching stand many supporters who have made that work possible. First among these are inspiring medical teachers and researchers, including S. Gilbert Blount, Jr., Jesse E. Edwards, Hans Selye, Wilhelm Raab, Meyer Friedman, Ray Rosenman, Giorgio Baroldi, Michael DeBakey, Lester Gorenstein, and many friends in Finland, especially Pentti Halonen.

A number of colleagues in medicine played critical roles in the early development of our program. Dr. Laurent P. LaRoche, former medical director of the ground support teams at Cape Kennedy (now Cape Canaveral), had remarkable insight into the human aspects of the Cape and opened my mind to the price people pay for twentieth-century stress. Drs. George Warheit and Dick Reynolds were also especially helpful at Cape Canaveral. Within our department, Dr. Gordon Todd was one of the first in this field to describe the destructive effects of adrenaline on the heart muscle, and he continues to amplify his observations in a number of areas that are important for the treatment and prevention of heart disease. Also in our department, Dr. Jimmy Salhany has worked with me for many years in clarifying basic molecular concepts that are relevant to the cardiovascular consequences of stress. The support of Drs. Jerry Cassuto and Lee Grant from the Western Electric Company permitted the development of a pilot study and later an enlarged prospective study that supplied a data base for the concept of hot reacting. At the national level are Dr. Stephen Weiss, chief of the Behavioral Medicine Branch at the National Heart, Lung, and Blood Institute (NHLBI), Dr. James Shields at NHLBI, and Dr. Harrison Owen. Journal editors Dr. Sylvan Weinberg of *Heart and Lung* and Dr. Simon Dack of the *Journal of the American College of Cardiology* also offered significant input at the early phases of our development. And we received encouragement from Drs. David Blumsohn and Leo Schamroth of South Africa; Drs. Bruce and Evenlyn Munro of Dallas; and in particular Drs. Robert Rosenlof of Kearney, Nebraska, and Helen Starke of the University of Nebraska Medical Center, who combined the art and science of medicine to give the author a second chance post heart attack.

Other leaders who showed early support for our work are William Nelligan, executive vice president of the American College of Cardiology, Roger Tusken, executive vice president of the American Academy of Family Physicians, and members of the board of the International Stress Foundation, in particular Duane Acklie, Don Lowe, and Dave Tews. I am grateful also for the early support of John Delich, Gen. Russell E. Dougherty, Heidi and Daryl Jones, Bob and Maxine Kouba, Mrs. E. Louis Meyer, Mary Elaine O'Neal, William, Robert, Roy, and Howard Monsour, Lou and Roe Somberg, and Norm and Midge Sample.

Colleagues who influenced the later development of the program include Drs. John Burns, Joe Brady, Ken Cooper, Ted Dembroski, Ed Langdon, Marianne Frankenhaeuser, David Glass, Jim Henry, Alan Herd, Jim Kelsey, Jim MacDougall,

Ed Magee, Heinz Rueddel, Neil Schneiderman, and many others.

Among those who opened critical administrative doors at the University of Nebraska Medical Center are former chancellor Robert D. Sparks; vice-chancellor James Griesen; University of Nebraska president Ronald Roskens; Michael F. Sorrell, chairman of Internal Medicine; and Philip Hofschire, chief of Pediatric Cardiology. Above all, I want to acknowledge Alastair M. Connell, dean of the College of Medicine, whose courage, counsel, and leadership have been fundamental to the inception of the first program of its kind in any medical school.

Nebraska state senators Jules Burbach, Robert Clark, Glenn Goodrich, Roland Luedtke, Richard Marvel, John Savage, and Jerome Warner helped to make special funding possible through a legislative act that was essential to the developments leading to our new program. In addition, our research has been supported by private grants from the Western Electric Foundation, the Meyer-Ceco Foundation, Mary Elaine O'Neal, Dr. David Halbersleben, and Duane and Phyllis Acklie.

Institutions and professional associations that have responded helpfully to our work include the American Society of Association Executives, the American Association of Medical Society Executives, the American Medical Association, the American College of Cardiology, the American Heart Association, and the National Institutes of Health.

I have also spoken to a number of corporate groups that have helped to establish the importance of stress and preventive medicine in the corporate setting and have played a large role in inspiring the writing of this book. Among them are the Million Dollar Roundtable, Top of the Table, the American Concrete Pipe Manufacturers, New England Life, Ralston Purina, National Association of Refrigerated Warehouses, and Pepsi-Cola Bottling Group. In addition, several individual corporations and their chief executive officers were critical in the development of our program. These include John Woods, president of the Omaha National Bank; Sam Segnar, chairman of the board, InterNorth; Willis Strauss, formerly chief executive officer of Northern Natural Gas; Robert Daugherty, chairman of the board, Valmont Industries; V. J. Skutt, president and chairman of the board, Mutual of Omaha; Jack MacAllister, chief executive officer designate, Western Region of Mountain Bell; Richard McCormick, president of Northwestern Bell; and Bill Kizer, president and chief executive officer of Central States Life Insurance and founder of the Wellness Council of the Midlands.

The analysis and accuracy in reporting of the communications media have been much appreciated, particularly the work of ABC's Tom Jarriel, Bernie Cohen, and Mark Goldman; Joyce Daly; Teletronics; Jane Brody of *The New York Times*; and Jerry Bishop of *The Wall Street Journal*, as well as many others who have reported on hot reacting and stress.

Now, with the completion of the first major phase in the development of our program, I look forward to and gratefully acknowledge the personal and professional support offered by our new friends and colleagues in Arizona. These include William Baker, Dr. Gordon Ewy, Dr. Jerry Hansbro and Kay Hansbro, Leonard Huck, Janet Johnson, Dr. Merlin Kampfer and Paulina Kampfer, John Lamb, Richard W. and Colleen LeGrand, Brian and Carol Lockwood, Dr. David Long and Sandy Long, Robert Matthews, Paul Milus, Andy and Chris Rinde, Dr. Charles Rucker, Dr. Ralph Wicks and Bunny Wicks, and Jerry J. Wisotsky.

Finally, behind those who attempt to find a better way there is often a critical person who offers early support and continuing inspiration. That person for me has been Phyllis Eliot, my wife of twenty-seven years. She is a remarkable, lovely, dynamic, spirited, gracious, and capable woman. Fortunately, she chose to share her life and challenges with me while she developed her own complementary professional interests in nutrition, stress, medicine, and administration. For example, she has worked with me by administering eleven programs for the American College of Cardiology. And along with this she also raised two great children, Bill and Susan. As a family we have learned from the stresses of our lives, met challenges together, and developed a supportive understanding, respect, and deepening love. If this book is effective in helping others today, it is because my life partner has supported and shared my goals and commitment. Finally, I will always remember that when my heart attack hit, Phyllis was not only my best physician but my best medicine as well.

Foreword

For more than a half century, stress has been a subject of interest to medical investigators. In the 1920s Walter Cannon, one of the most distinguished American physiologists, first called attention to stress as the "fight or flight" response, and Wilhelm Raab subsequently demonstrated the risk effects of excess adrenaline and cortisol. It was Hans Selye, however, whose lifetime of research gave new meaning to the term *stress* and who proved, in his animal investigations, that it contributed significantly to the development of disease. This disease, he discovered, could be fatal and could occur in man.

Although others subsequently studied stress in human beings, much of this research was concerned with behavioral and psychological issues. These studies often lacked good scientific methods of measuring in a uniform manner the effects of stress on the body; a stressful environment for one person may be an exhilarating experience for another. The consequence of these approaches was scientific controversy.

Dr. Eliot, however, approached the problem by using well-established scientific methods to measure the physiologic, biochemical, and clinical responses to stress. These measurements could be standardized and thus provide a uniform and scientifically valid basis for determining the response of any person's body to a stress test.

In this book, Dr. Eliot has synthesized his extensive research in this important field and describes, for the general public, as well as for the medical profession, the important effects of stress on the cardiovascular system. Of equal or even greater interest are the detailed and extensive descriptions of methods for coping with stressful situations and the preventive measures that can encourage salutary responses to stress. I am confident that those who are concerned about the consequences of stress will benefit from the information in *Is It Worth Dying For?*

MICHAEL E. DEBAKEY, M.D.
Baylor College of Medicine
Houston, Texas 77030

"Every affection of the mind that is attended with either pain or pleasure, hope or fear, is the cause of an agitation whose influence extends to the heart."

—William Harvey, Physician, 1623

Introduction

My body cried out for rest, but my brain wasn't listening. I was behind schedule. My timetable read that by the age of forty I should be the chief of cardiology at a major university. I was forty-three when I left the University of Florida at Gainesville and accepted the position of chief of cardiology at the University of Nebraska in 1972. All I had to do was run a little faster and I'd be back on track.

Years of preparation had led to this opportunity, starting with medical school and cardiology residency at the University of Colorado. Then came five years of practicing academic and private cardiology at the University of Minnesota, where I trained and worked with giants like cardiovascular pathologist Jesse Edwards and open-heart surgeons C. Walton Lillehei, Richard Lillehei, Aldo Casteneda, Norman Shumway, and Christiaan Barnard. Then it was on to the University of Florida for five years as a professor and as chief of cardiology at the Gainesville Veterans Administration Hospital.

It was time to find out if I could build something myself, a cardiovascular center that would do innovative research. Nebraska needed such a center. I saw the university as a place of opportunity and promise.

What I didn't see was how hard it is to start an expensive new project in an established institution. I thought we'd worked out the essential issues in advance, but when I arrived the frustrations started to pile up. I would argue for autonomy, facilities, and funds, and would run into ever-growing problems of bureaucracy, budget, manpower, and timing. I came to feel that the walls were closing in on me and I would never break free to make my dream a reality.

Desperately, I did what I had been doing all my life. I picked up the pace. I tried to force things through. I criss-crossed the state to provide on-the-spot cardiology education to rural Nebraska physicians and build support among them for the university's cardiovascular program. I scheduled academic lectures across the country, continually flying in and out at a moment's notice. I remember that on one trip on which my wife Phyllis helped with the business arrangements, a seminar went superbly, and on the plane ride home Phyllis wanted to savor the memory. Not me. I was rushing through the evaluation forms, worrying about how to make the next seminar better.

I had no time for family and friends, relaxation and diversion. When Phyllis bought me an exercise bike for Christmas, I was offended. How could I possibly find time to sit down and pedal a bicycle?

I was often overtired, but I put that out of my mind. I wasn't concerned about my health. What did I have to worry about? I was an expert in diseases of the heart, and I knew I didn't have any of the risk factors. My father had lived to be seventy-eight and my mother, at eighty-five, showed no sign of heart disease. I didn't smoke. I wasn't overweight. I didn't have high blood pressure. I didn't have high cholesterol. I didn't have diabetes. I thought I was immune to heart disease.

But I was running a big risk for other reasons. I had been pushing too hard for too long. Now all my efforts seemed futile, and I carried an extra burden, knowing I had brought promising associates to what looked like a losing situation. A feeling of disillusionment descended on me, a sense of *invisible entrapment*.

I didn't know it then, but my body was continuously reacting to this inner turmoil. For nine months I was softened for the blow. It came two weeks after my forty-fourth birthday.

*   *   *

It was a Friday afternoon, the first day of spring, and my adrenaline was pumping. I had been lecturing in New Orleans and had had little sleep before flying back to Omaha and heading straight into a confrontation with administrators over support for the planned cardiovascular center. I ran into a brick wall: again, problems with bureaucracy, budget, manpower, timing. Suddenly I snapped, exploding with anger. I thought my life's work and that of my colleagues was being torpedoed. Leaving the office, I was still enraged, and could not calm down as I started a two-hundred-mile drive west for a weekend cardiology conference at a community hospital—a trip on which my family was coming along so the kids could finally have a weekend with Daddy.

I was too angry to drive, so Phyllis did. I was bone-tired, past the point of exhaustion, and as we pushed on through miserable weather—a rainstorm that beat down on the car for hours—I realized that my resources were all but gone. Yet that night I could not sleep; the events of the day left my mind no rest.

The next morning I lectured on heart attacks and sudden death. After a heavy lunch, I began to discuss some heart attack cases. One of the faculty members from my department showed some slides. I tried to provide the commentary.

I couldn't think straight.

Normally I could have diagnosed the cases being shown on the slides in a second. Today, the faculty member had to gently lead me into making the correct diagnoses. I could not concentrate, could not assemble any thoughts. I felt exhausted. My voice was hoarse. My eyes were blurry. Vaguely aware of my fuzziness, I continued to talk and somehow made it through the hour.

The next speaker was our youngest faculty member. I had known him since he was a medical student, had watched him develop over the years, and was very proud of him. But, sitting in the back of the room, I was still having trouble concentrating. He was young and energetic, and I felt old and weary. I sat watching him, anxious for him to do well.

Suddenly it hit: an elephant sat on my chest.

The pressure was intense and went from my breastbone up into my shoulders and neck and jaws, and down both arms. I had trouble breathing. Two minutes of pain seemed to last an eternity. I changed my breathing; I changed my seating position. The pain persisted.

Indigestion? Incredibly, I thought it must be the fatty, spicy cold cuts I had eaten for lunch.

I started to sweat. The room must be too warm, I thought. I walked outside, but the discomfort continued. Could I have a hiatal hernia—was my stomach pushing up into my chest? I got on the elevator and made it to the coronary care unit, where only that morning I had conducted grand rounds.

I asked the head nurse for nitroglycerin. She gave me a funny look but brought two tablets. I went outside and put one under my tongue. I had never taken nitroglycerin before.

The pain didn't go away. I took a second tablet. No relief. I began getting bowel cramps. Nausea. It must be gallbladder trouble, I told myself. I went to the bathroom. The pain got worse. The game was over.

I diagnosed myself: myocardial infarction of the inferior wall.

I went back to the head nurse and asked to be taken to a vacant bed. As I stretched out, I said, "I've just had a heart attack."

I was lucky. I had the kind of heart attack everyone should have—mild and in a hospital. From the time the elephant sat on my chest until the time I was strapped up to an electrocardiograph to have my heartbeat checked, only twenty minutes passed. Had the trouble started before we reached the hospital, I probably would have died.

As I looked up from the wrong side of the sheets in the coronary care unit, I realized that this insult to my heart was providing me with a new insight into my life:

I had brought on my own heart attack. I knew this because, when I asked myself if I could have avoided it, the answer was, "Yes, I really believe I could have." The way I reacted emotionally to work stress had made me vulnerable. For years, I had pushed myself. Jobs during high school and college. Completing a four-year pre-med course in three. And after that, my constant drive for achievement as a resident, teacher, public speaker, and consultant. I had won recognition, but at what price? Worse, I was a prime candidate for a second heart attack if I didn't change my ways.

It took several hours for tests to confirm the diagnosis. Finally there came a burst of rapid heartbeats, proof of the heart attack. The doctor injected Xylocaine, a local anesthetic, into a vein, and the danger was over. I could go to sleep now. As I drifted off, I came to a second conclusion:

Life was not a matter of victory or defeat. Ever since childhood I had been told, and had believed, that success was worth any demand, any sacrifice. But now I had to ask myself: Is it worth dying for?

During my recovery, I began to piece together my past and to construct a new future. My life had been a blur of overachievement to gain rewards, but I had never asked what I really wanted for myself. The only child of a Lebanese immigrant and a British blueblood, I had been told from birth that if you worked hard you would be treated as an equal in America, but it was best to be your own boss. My mother, Ruth Buffington, was a delightful, optimistic Victorian lady. My father, Salim Elia, was a wise, complex, brilliant, and scholarly research chemist who worked for thirty-five years for a pharmaceutical firm, and felt that his best ideas had been pirated by others who were higher up in the company and politically more shrewd. He was bitter to the day of his death.

We lived on what some considered the wrong side of the tracks in Wilmette, Illinois, an affluent suburb north of Chicago that borders some of the wealthiest communities in the nation. I grew up knowing that the only way for the son of an immigrant to belong on the North Shore was to become a lawyer or an executive—maybe a professor, definitely a doctor. My father had always admired doctors because they were compassionate scientists who had independence. When I won a scholarship and was accepted to medical school in Colorado, it was the happiest day of his life. The next month, he died.

After my father's death, I changed my name to Eliot, though retaining his first name, Salim, as my middle name. It was my father's wish: "Son, there's no sense handicapping yourself by going through life with a name that people don't understand."

Other changes came with those years. As a junior in medical school, when I finally got to put on the white coat and look at people instead of cadavers and frogs, I began to feel for the first time that I might amount to something. That year was also when Phyllis Allman, a dietitian from Wisconsin, came into my life. After a stormy three-and-a-half year courtship, we settled down to a long, stable marriage. But I was always busy taking care of business. We never had enough time to be with each other—until my heart attack.

It sounds strange, but the heart attack was the best thing in the world for me. With a week in the hospital, an additional week of bedrest at a vacation cabin, and three months at home, I had a lot of time to think, with a loving wife to help me sort it all out. I realized how much Phyllis really loved me. She protected me like a mother grizzly bear. I realized that my children, Bill and Susan, were surprisingly sensitive and loving. I also realized that my blind pursuit of academic medicine would have left my family in a terrible financial predicament if I had died. Money had never been a motivating force for me, but it was frightening to realize that the ones I loved were financially so vulnerable.

I took time to rediscover my wife. We spent many hours renewing memories and making plans for our future life together. I rediscovered an old romance with model railroading and turned a room of our basement into an elaborate railroad complete with whistles, steam, and brakemen. I took time to rediscover my body. After years of treating it like a sack of potatoes, I began to listen to it. I took walks. I made time to sleep. I learned how to say "no" to things when I was tired. I watched my diet. I was again becoming a human being instead of a robot.

During three months of recuperation, I rethought my life and clarified my values. As Nietzsche has observed, "If you stare long enough into the abyss, it begins to stare back." I had stared into the abyss of death and it made me a believer in life. I would face up to stress and make it friend, not foe.

Years later my wife testified to the difference it made after I decided to confront stress and do something about it. "You know, Bob," she said, "if you had died from your heart attack, I don't think the kids and I would have missed you. We never really knew you. If you were to die now, we would miss you very much."

I was my own first stress patient. Before my heart attack, I had already begun to look into stress as a cause of sudden cardiac death. But there's nothing like coming close to death yourself to make you realize that something terribly important is happening to people under stress—and that we don't know nearly enough about the response to stress.

After my heart attack, I felt a new urgency about bringing the study and management of stress into mainstream medicine. As a cardiologist, I was trained to be one of the high priests of medical technology. Now I wanted to use that technology to help link behavior and medicine—to show the physical effects of behavior on the body. I wanted medical information that could be measured in objective terms and reproduced by physicians at my clinic and elsewhere.

Today, I have that information, provided by the hundreds of patients and research subjects who have gone through our Life Stress Simulation Laboratory at the University of Nebraska Medical Center's Department of Preventive and Stress Medicine and through a similar program at St. Luke's Hospital in Phoenix, Arizona. Recently we have screened 6,000 people with a portable version of the lab as well.

The lab originated with an idea by my colleague and fellow cardiologist James Buell. I was seeking an objective way of measuring the impact of stress on the body, and a break-through came about when I was joined in that effort by Jim Buell, who in 1977 wrote a proposal to measure physiological reactions to mental stress testing. Over the next year we worked out the ways and means of making this painless, computerized system practical and effective, and the result was the Life Stress Lab. In the lab we fit patients with electrodes and seat them in a soundproof room. We challenge them with tasks like mental arithmetic and video games. And we record on computers many critical functions, including what their heart rates and blood pressures are doing.

The computer printouts demonstrate beyond doubt that different individuals pay dramatically different physiological prices for these simple mental tasks. I call the people with the most extreme and dramatic heart and blood pressure responses to stress "hot reactors." There is increasing evidence that they are the ones most at risk of developing stress-related heart trouble. In the Life Stress Lab, we can pinpoint who these hot reactors are. We have a tool that allows us to establish a crucial link between health and stress.

We use this information in our comprehensive Stress Clinic, where we not only do research on "hot reacting," but also spend one and a half days with patients in stress diagnosis and treatment planning. We consider the patients' sources of stress and their own particular styles of coping with it in their emotional life, behavior, and cardiovascular responses. Evaluations by a psychologist, dietitian, and exercise therapist supplement the Stress Lab tests and a medical evaluation. Then the entire staff develops a complete program of health promotion and stress management for each person based on his or her individual circumstances. Finally, the physician and patient together thoroughly review the overall evaluation and plan for treatment.

Now we have brought together our methods of diagnosis and treatment and adapted them for you. This book brings our Stress Lab and Clinic into your living room. You will be able to measure the effects of stress in your life. You will see for yourself whether you are a "hot" or "cold" reactor and judge for yourself how vulnerable you are to stress-related heart disease. And you will be able to develop your own custom-tailored course of treatment, which can range from simply taking regular three-day vacations to relaxation therapy, changing the way you talk to yourself, and medical management to be prescribed by your physician. Indeed, there are many ways you can learn to change your lifestyle and behavior to control the stress in your life so you can *be productive without being self-destructive*.

In the eleven years since my heart attack, I have learned that if the mind-body interaction can make you ill, it can also make you well and keep you well. I have learned to change my self-destructive behavior and habits and to get the job done without killing myself. I know now that it's not what you do but how you do it that counts. I have learned to make stress work for me, not against me, and these eleven years have been the best of my life.

Your future can open up for you, too, if you act on the information provided in this book—and don't wait, as I did, for a heart attack to prove you need it. Best of all, you don't have to be sick to feel better. You can increase your enjoyment of all the things you do now by learning to make stress a friend that can help you live a healthy, productive, creative life.

Part One:

Stress and the Hot Reactor

1
Stress:
The Modern
Epidemic

We all have colds. We all have stress. Colds, however, go away. Stress can be with us for months, years, decades. It can cause tension and illness. And, over long periods, stress can kill.

You are not alone if you think you are under too much stress. More than 80 percent of those responding to a recent national poll said that they "need less stress" in their lives. And my colleagues in family medicine have consistently told me that the majority of their patients' visits are related to unrelieved stress.

Modern stress is due, in part, to modern lifestyles. Our circuits are overloaded. Alvin Toffler called it "future shock." Technology has radically altered our everyday lives—what we need to know, the problems we have to solve, and the threats we have to meet. We are bombarded with constantly changing mental challenges. The mass media, the jet plane, the knowledge explosion, and the computer have all expanded our personal worlds enormously. Researchers estimate that we encounter a thousand times more events per year than our great-grandparents did, but the time available for decision-making remains the same or even less. And personal relationships, which might help us find our place in a huge, impersonal world, are themselves complex, fragile, and ever-changing.

Our society offers few buffers against all this uncertainty

and mental overload. Instead, we feel we must manage it all, keep on going, and come out on top. But sometimes it's tough to keep going, and our bodies protest against the struggle. Consider:

- Painkillers are the leading over-the-counter drugs in this country.
- The tranquilizer Valium is the leading brand name drug prescribed in America.
- In addition to alcohol, perennially America's most abused drug, the current recreational drug of choice is cocaine, a stimulant that relieves stress by artificially causing the kind of high someone gets right after doing something great in life. Unfortunately, this high only lasts for ten minutes or so and then leaves the user flat.
- 13 million Americans are problem drinkers.
- One out of every four American adults has high blood pressure, potentially a very serious disease that can be caused or aggravated by stress.
- America's number one killer, heart disease, can be caused or aggravated by stress.
- According to the American Medical Association, half of this nation's annual $250 billion tab for medical services is due to unhealthy lifestyles.

Stress—Cause and Effect

Until recently, stress management has been largely the concern of psychologists and other mental health professionals. But many physical complaints are caused or aggravated by stress—in fact, *stress may be the greatest single contributor to illness in the industrialized world.* The mind and body are astonishingly interrelated, and explaining or treating stress-related conditions in terms of one or the other alone just doesn't work. This is certainly true in the special area of cardiovascular (heart and blood vessel) disease.

The major traditional risk factors—high blood pressure, high cholesterol, diabetes, obesity, and smoking—fail to explain approximately half of the world-wide cases of coronary heart disease. There is good reason to believe that stress is a major missing piece in this puzzle. Moreover, researchers are increasingly recognizing not only that stress is an independent contributor to heart disease, but also that it is closely interwoven with the five traditional risk factors. *Controlling unnecessary stress may therefore be the single most important key to preventing heart attacks.* Realizing this has led medical researchers to look beyond the heart and blood vessels to the brain.

The Russians have a proverb, "The brain is capable of holding a conversation with the body that ends in death." I began to understand the wisdom of this saying when I went to Cape Canaveral in 1967 as a cardiovascular consultant to the U.S. government. Young aerospace workers, some as young as twenty-nine, were dropping dead of heart attacks at an alarming rate.

The problem, I found, was not the firing of rockets but the firing of people. The government had started making the space race a lower national priority, and each time there was a successful launch, 15 percent of the workers who made it happen were fired. From 1965 to 1973, the work force at the Cape was cut in half, from 65,000 to 32,000. One month these highly trained young professionals were putting in sixteen-hour days in critical, highly paid jobs. The next month they were out of work. Worse, they had no transferable skills. I found them repairing TV sets, sacking groceries, and working as ticket-takers at Disney World.

Physical and laboratory exams of engineers at the Cape showed no unusual levels of the standard coronary risk factors. What I found instead were anxiety and depression and a universal, pervasive feeling of hopelessness and helplessness. Cape Canaveral families led the nation in drinking, drug-taking, divorce, and sudden heart attack deaths. The space workers were a whole population suffering from the acute stress of knowing that at any moment they could lose their work, income, status, and identity as skilled professionals.

At the lab, I analyzed autopsies of workers who had dropped dead without warning. What I found suggested that adrenaline and other stress chemicals had spewed into their bodies with such strength that they had literally ruptured the muscle fibers of their hearts. It appeared that the brain had the power to trigger heart-stopping emotional reactions to stress.

What I had found fell right in with the trail of animal-research evidence linking stress to disease:

Mice flown from Boston to Seattle took three days to recover from dangerously high levels of adrenaline, cortisol, and other body chemicals that the stress of the flight had activated.

White rabbits which were alternately housed alone and then in densely crowded quarters—but never long enough in either to allow for adjustment—dropped dead within six months of their introduction to the stressful environment.

Squirrel monkeys restrained as an experiment displayed a familiar pattern. Six pairs of the animals were kept in chairs for eight hours a day, and once a minute one of each pair had to push a lever to turn off a light or both animals would receive a tail shock. The "executive" monkeys assigned to push the lever every minute developed high blood pressure and heart disease. That's bad enough. But of the six "helpless" partners who could neither control the situation nor cope with it, four collapsed and died of heart-rhythm disturbances.

In a series of experiments with adult male tree shrews, a submissive animal was introduced to an experienced fighter shrew. The dominant animal attacked but was removed before harm could be done. Separated, but still within view, the two shrews were left to stare at each other. What happened next shows the high price paid for the stress of chronic vigilance. The subordinate shrew lay absolutely still and for 90 percent of its waking time did nothing but anxiously watch the dominant animal. Within 2 to 16 days—an agonizing period for the scared subordinate animal—the threatened shrew fell into a coma and died. During the death watch, its tail hair stayed erect, indicating sustained stress.

One of the most compelling cases for the adverse effect of

long-term stress is what I call the "fourteen-foot risk factor" for heart disease. The Hamadryas baboon forms a strong lifelong attachment to its mate. Russian researchers removed male baboons from their mates and placed them some distance away—perhaps 14 feet—in a separate cage and in full view of the mate. A new male was placed in the female's cage. The displaced baboon was forced to observe his long-term mate with a new lover. He was helpless to change the situation, yet had to endure it. With no alteration in diet or any other factor, within six months the baboons experienced the whole spectrum of heart disease in the modern industrial world: some developed high blood pressure, some had heart attacks, and some died of sudden cardiac death.

They're Playing Our Song

Animals are not humans, of course, but it now seems very likely that in humans, too, a sense of helplessness and hopelessness can fire off stress chemicals that overpower the body's resistance. That's what happened to the Cape Canaveral aerospace engineers.

If you've ever heard Peggy Lee's mournful song, "Is That All There Is?" you know that it is a dirge about a modern malaise—the sense of invisible entrapment that haunts many people, the feeling that life is a joyless struggle, the lingering sense of loss and anger turned inward. This kind of chronic stress can lead to disillusionment, despair, and disease.

My patients who have the "Is That All There Is?" syndrome feel they are not winning the game of life on their own terms. For many, the sense of loss stems from uncertainty about what they really want or realistically can achieve. Often they have struggled to gain what society values instead of developing their own personal values. Gradually, life begins to seem empty, the future hollow.

These people are anxious and angry about losing control of their lives. They often avoid turning their anger outward, for fear of losing even more. Instead, they turn it inward on the only "safe" target—themselves. And, like the tree shrews in the experiment, they are always vigilant against perceived further loss.

Sufferers from chronic stress pay a high price for losing a sense of control over their lives—they often feel a loss of identity and self-esteem as well. It is in trying to regain this crucial sense of control that many cross the line from productive into self-destructive behaviors. The irony is that their feelings of stress result not from chance, but from choice.

It took a heart attack for me to make some new choices, to get out of the trap of joyless struggle. Now after eighteen years of research on stress and the heart, I am convinced that the question "Is that all there is?" is the best clue to the cause of harmful, long-term stress: the sense of being trapped, hopeless, and helpless to get what you really want out of life.

How about you? Check yourself out with this simple question. Don't stop and think about it. Answer immediately with your first gut response:

Are you winning?

If you answered "Yes," without thinking of what you "ought" to say, chances are that you feel you can rise to the challenges in your life and look forward to new ones. "Winning" in this sense means feeling able to learn from your mistakes, being open to new options, and having a sense of control over your life.

If you answered "No," chances are that you see yourself in a losing situation, without enough control over your life. You are a high-stress risk.

If you didn't answer immediately because you couldn't decide, or if you qualified your answer ("Well, it depends. . . ."), you also may be vulnerable to stress. Perhaps you have reservations about the direction your life is taking. Is something missing? Are you giving up too much? Are you stuck? What would it take to win your own goals? Whatever the answer, everyone can benefit from learning to deal better with stress.

You've just taken the very simplest stress test. Over the years I have found that this question makes true feelings rise to the surface. As you think about your own response, consider the following signs of stress that you may recognize in yourself or the people in your life.

Early Warning Signs of Stress

Are you under too much stress? Are your friends and co-workers? Air Force psychologist Capt. Neil S. Hibler has developed a list of early warning signs:

Emotional signs
- Apathy—the "blahs," feelings of sadness, recreation that is no longer pleasurable.
- Anxiety—feelings of restlessness, agitation, insecurity, sense of worthlessness.
- Irritability—feeling hypersensitive, defensive, arrogant or argumentative, rebellious or angry.
- Mental fatigue—feeling preoccupied, having difficulty concentrating, trouble in thinking flexibly.
- Overcompensation or denial—grandiosity (exaggerating the importance of your activities to yourself and others), working too hard, denying that you have problems, ignoring symptoms, feeling suspicious.

Behavioral signs
- Avoiding things—keeping to yourself, avoiding work, having trouble accepting responsibility, neglecting responsibility.
- Doing things to extremes—alcoholism, gambling, spending sprees, sexual promiscuity.
- Administrative problems—being late to work, poor appearance, poor personal hygiene, being accident-prone.
- Legal problems—indebtedness, shoplifting, traffic tickets, inability to control violent impulses.

Physical signs
- Excessive worrying about, or denial of, illness.
- Frequent illness.
- Physical exhaustion.
- Reliance on self-medication, including overuse of drug-store remedies like aspirin.

• Ailments—headache, insomnia, appetite changes, weight gain or loss, indigestion, nausea, nervous diarrhea, constipation, sexual problems.

No set number of these symptoms indicates difficulty in coping with stress. If you have a combination of these warning signs and have had them often over a long period of time, you should read this book carefully and talk with your doctor and/or a counselor about what is bothering you.

Managing Stress

Whether you feel you are winning, losing, or just hanging on has a lot to do with how you feel about the challenges in your life. "Stress" isn't just a negative word. In fact, stress can be defined as "challenge." Too little challenge leaves you bored and stagnant; too much, overloaded and out of control. But the right amount of challenge spurs you to develop your talents and gain a sense of accomplishment and purpose.

As psychologist Donald Tubesing puts it, finding the right amount of stress is like adjusting the strings of a violin; too loose and you won't like the music; too tight and they might break.

No one can escape stress, because we all have to meet challenges in our daily lives. But you can manage stress if you know when and how your personal circuits get overloaded. This is a very individual question, because events affect people differently. Folk wisdom is full of sayings that recognize this truth: "One man's meat is another man's poison"; "Beauty is in the eye of the beholder"; "What is work for one is play for another." Where stress is concerned, what feels like pressure to one person is stimulation to someone else. Everyone has an individual definition of too much, too little, or just enough stress. That's why there is no objective definition of what a stressful event is or how many events add up to "too much" stress.

Stress is only a burden when you respond to it with the feeling that you have lost control. Most of the time, this happens when there is a mismatch between your expectations and your environment. In other words, what you hope will happen doesn't, and you begin to think it never will. In the face of this mismatch, you may withdraw and resign yourself to losing control, or you may struggle to make things happen in order to regain control. Either way, if the event is not resolved as you want it to be, you will usually feel stressed. But there are alternatives.

You can regain your sense of balance and control by changing your environment (the conditions under which you work and live), and by changing your expectations (which are often overreactions to your environment and events in it). Usually a combination works best. But it is crucial to realize that you can never make *everything* in the environment go your way. If you focus only on the environment, you cannot succeed in controlling stress. Your own reactions—and overreactions—are the key.

Managing stress actually means managing the anger and anxiety you feel in stressful situations so that you can move on to solving problems creatively. As you become more flexible and resilient, you learn to see and develop options for yourself. That doesn't mean you won't suffer at times. Rather, it means you will not be overwhelmed, and will learn to see your situation as a challenge you can meet. And the more you find you can rise to the challenge, the more you will feel a sense of self-mastery and accomplishment.

Stress can be the spice of life as well as the kiss of death. It only becomes a trap if you allow it to be—if you believe you are helpless in the face of life's forces. But that is a belief, not a fact. Your inner resources make the difference, and you can strengthen these resources. You can recognize the signs of stress in your own life and learn techniques to cope with them. You can make stress work for you.

2
Stress in Action: How Your Body Responds

The signs of stress are familiar and troubling: anger, anxiety, sleeplessness. Along with these come headaches, muscle tension, maybe an ulcer. But more dangerous are the reactions you can't feel: the body's outpouring of chemicals, the rise in blood pressure and heart rate, the preparation for "fight or flight."

The body responds to emotional stress as it would to a physical crisis. A sense of danger heightens activity by the heart and other organs in case you have to attack or run for your life. Your body produces chemicals for extra strength and energy. This chemical reaction to stress is a physiological process that has evolved over millions of years. We have been three million years in the forest, three thousand years on the farm, but only three hundred years in the factory. *The life we are living today, the life of modern technology, has only existed for about fifty years.*

In the twentieth century, the fight-or-flight response is physiologically neurotic. That is, people are reacting to today's problems with yesterday's primitive responses. When stress was primarily physical—when cavemen fought saber-toothed tigers—people really did have to fight or flee. Sometimes we still need to do that, but for the most part modern stress is of a different nature. Rather than battle tigers, for example, you must be subtly attuned to the nuances of office politics. As a result, you end up pumping high-energy chemicals (those needed for fighting or fleeing) for low-energy needs. The price is high; over the long haul you turn the energy inward and burn out, physically as well as mentally.

You do not have three million years to evolve a suitable response to modern stress. But you can train your mechanisms to respond more appropriately. If you can cool down your reactions to stress, your body will be less vulnerable to a wide range of physical breakdowns, from headaches to heart attacks.

The Miracle Muscle and How It Works

Over time, strong reactions to stress can contribute significantly to high blood pressure and hardening of the arteries. These conditions set the stage for a variety of diseases, including heart attack.

To understand how stress can damage your heart, it helps to know how your cardiovascular (heart and circulatory) system works.

The editors of the magazine *Your Health and Fitness,* in a rather poetic metaphor, compare the blood circulated through the body to a "personal Red Sea" of life-sustaining fluid that delivers oxygen and nutrients to the body's cells and removes waste material, just as the ocean did for the first animal, the single-celled amoeba. In place of waves, the continuous bathing of each cell in refreshed fluid is accomplished by an internal pumping system—the heart and blood vessels—that keeps the fluid recirculating and maintains the pressure.

The cardiovascular system maintains blood pressure by pumping blood from the heart through thick-walled *arteries* to networks of smaller *arterioles* that empty into tiny blood vessels called *capillaries*. The capillaries deliver blood directly to the organ tissues. The blood then picks up carbon dioxide and tissue wastes and returns through the veins to the right side of the heart, which pumps it through the lungs. There the blood discharges its carbon dioxide and picks up a fresh supply of oxygen. Other wastes are removed as blood circulates through the kidneys, and then the blood

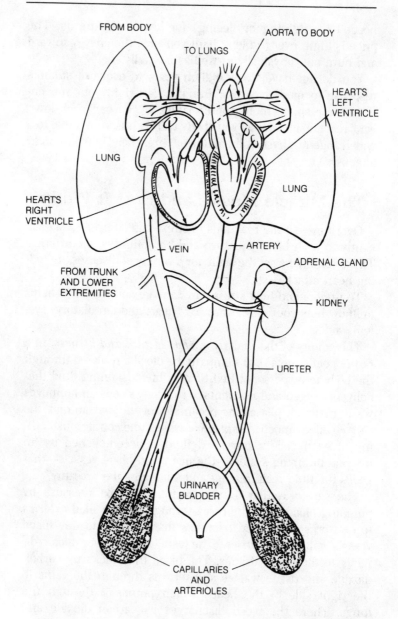

returns to the left side of the heart, ready for another journey through the body.

The heart is basically a large, hollow muscle, weighing 11 to 16 ounces and spanning the size of two clenched fists together. It has three major elements: the muscle, consisting of two pumping chambers; the arteries that supply the heart muscle with blood (the coronary arteries); and the electrical system that regulates the heartbeat. The pumping is managed by a rhythmic contraction and relaxation of the muscle. To keep the contractions going at a proper rate, electrical signals are routed from a "pacemaker" node in the heart through bundles of specialized heart fibers.

What Your Blood "Pressure" Means

Blood pressure is the force with which blood pushes against the walls of the blood vessels. When the heart beats and pumps blood into the arteries, the pressure rises to a peak. That's the *systolic* pressure. When the heart relaxes between beats, the pressure falls to its lowest point. That's the *diastolic* pressure.

YOUR MIRACLE MUSCLE AND HOW IT WORKS

Blood begins its journey through the body in the largest vessel, the *aorta*, and then moves through smaller branching arteries until it eventually reaches the smallest vessels, the *arterioles*. The arterioles distribute the blood directly to the *capillaries*, which are tiny, delicate structures that make possible the free passage of fluids and gases into the vital organs of the body. The capillaries not only deliver nutrients to the organs, they also pick up carbon dioxide and waste products. The capillaries then return the blood and tissue wastes to the *veins*, which are the other side of the circulation system. The veins return the blood and wastes to the heart's *right ventricle*, which then pumps them to the *lungs*. The lungs eliminate the carbon dioxide and add oxygen to the depleted blood. Special arteries branching off the aorta transport the wastes to the *kidneys*, where they are converted to urine. Meanwhile, the oxygen-enriched blood moves to the heart's main pumping chamber, the *left ventricle*. Under four to five times the pumping pressure of the right side, the left ventricle pushes the blood out, full and fresh, to supply the entire body.

Your blood pressure can rise for three reasons:

(1) The heart increases its output of blood by beating faster and/or harder.

(2) The arteries constrict and allow less room for the blood to flow.

(3) Both of the above.

To understand the effect of constriction on blood pressure, think of a garden hose. Water from the same spigot will push harder and exert more pressure on the insides of a narrow hose than it will on the insides of a wide hose. In the same way, if your arteriolar blood vessels constrict into narrow tubes, the blood trying to get through will have to push harder and your blood pressure will rise.

In measuring your blood pressure, the physician wraps a cuff around your upper arm. The cuff is attached to a barometer that contains a column of mercury, or its equivalent. The physician gently inflates the cuff, squeezing the main artery in your arm until the flow of blood stops. Then the physician slowly deflates the cuff, reducing pressure on the artery. He or she places a stethoscope over the artery and notes the barometer reading when the pulse sound starts again. This gives the *systolic* pressure (maximum pressure in the artery when the heart is beating). The reading when the pulse sound disappears gives the *diastolic* pressure (minimum pressure in the artery between heart beats).

The physician records the numbers as, let's say, 120/80, or "120 over 80," meaning a reading of 120 mm Hg (millimeters of mercury) systolic and 80 mm Hg diastolic. These numbers are based on a universally recognized measurement of the force required to move a column of mercury to a specified height. On the continuum of possible readings, 120/80 is considered average for adults, and 140/90 is considered the beginning, or borderline, of high blood pressure. As with all human measurements, there is variability within the range of normal. However, readings above 140/90 are abnormally high and carry increased risk of future cardiovascular disorder. Except in rare cases of shock, low readings (low blood pressure) are not harmful and often mean a longer life. Healthy adults and teenagers may have normal readings as low as 95/55.

The level of your blood pressure is one important way of measuring the efficiency of your cardiovascular system. Normal blood pressure suggests that the heart is working properly; high blood pressure is a sign that the heart is working extra hard to keep the blood moving.

Two Stress Responses: Alarm and Vigilance

Despite its amazing endurance, your heart is not fail-safe. After years of stress and strain, improper care, and dietary abuses, hearts have a way of quitting. *Heart and circulatory diseases kill more people in the industrialized world than all other causes of death combined.*

What role does stress play in promoting these diseases? It stimulates two stress responses in the body—an "acute alarm" reaction (preparing the body for fight or flight) and a "chronic vigilance" reaction (preparing the body for long-term endurance). One of the organs most affected by these stress responses is the heart.

Alarm and vigilance are both stimulated in the adrenal glands located above the kidneys ("renal" means kidney). To picture how these glands work, think of them as golf balls. The inside of the ball is the *adrenal medulla*, which produces adrenaline, the hormone stimulating the alarm reaction. The shell of the ball is the *adrenal cortex,* which produces cortisol, the hormone stimulating the vigilance reaction.

Both stress responses make sense when extra strength and endurance are necessary to meet some unusual physical demand. But they can be highly self-destructive when they are stimulated repeatedly in response to everyday stress. Let's look at alarm and vigilance more closely.

The Short-Term Alarm Reaction

This is the *emergency* system that prepares the body instantly for fight or flight. Think of the fireman charging

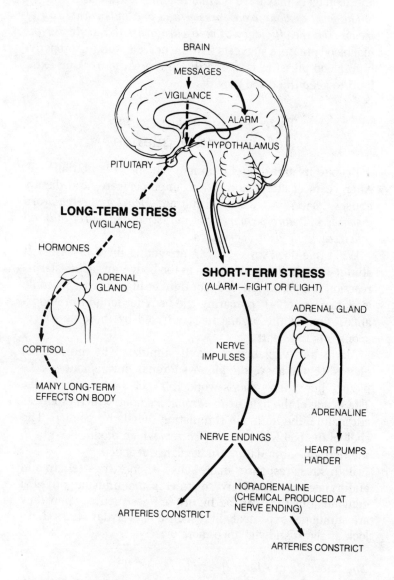

BRAIN

MESSAGES

VIGILANCE

ALARM

HYPOTHALAMUS

PITUITARY

LONG-TERM STRESS
(VIGILANCE)

HORMONES

ADRENAL GLAND

CORTISOL

MANY LONG-TERM EFFECTS ON BODY

SHORT-TERM STRESS
(ALARM – FIGHT OR FLIGHT)

ADRENAL GLAND

NERVE IMPULSES

ADRENALINE

NERVE ENDINGS

HEART PUMPS HARDER

ARTERIES CONSTRICT

NORADRENALINE
(CHEMICAL PRODUCED AT NERVE ENDING)

ARTERIES CONSTRICT

down the pole, the child fighting in the schoolyard, the mother rushing to pull her toddler from oncoming traffic. The alarm reaction is the *acute* response to stress. Adrenaline races through the body, commanding a series of physical changes: the heart beats faster and stronger so blood pressure rises abruptly; automatically, blood is shunted away from the stomach and skin, where it is not needed, to the muscles, where it is; high-energy fats are rushed into the bloodstream for energy; chemicals are released to make the blood clot more quickly in case of injury. The nerves command a series of rapid changes: the pupils of the eyes dilate, the facial muscles tense, blood vessels in the skin open up and the face flushes, the breathing quickens, and blood sugar increases. You're ready for physical action.

The Long-Term Vigilance Reaction

This is the body's conservation-withdrawal system that prepares you for long-term survival in the face of scarce nutritional resources. It is the body getting ready for cold and storms and for going days without food, water, and salt, conserving vital resources when there is no control over a

HOW YOUR BRAIN PREPARES YOUR BODY FOR STRESS

In times of crisis, the stress chemicals cortisol, adrenaline, and noradrenaline alert the body to respond to danger. They are stimulated by the hypothalamus, a thumb-tip-sized portion of the brain that acts as the body's field general. In the long-term stress of vigilance, the hypothalamus signals the pituitary gland to produce hormones that travel through the blood to the adrenal glands. The outer layer of each adrenal gland then produces cortisol. In the short-term stress of alarm, the hypothalamus stimulates nerve impulses to produce noradrenaline and to pass into the core of the adrenal gland to produce adrenaline. The stress chemicals then rush into the blood and through the cross-talk of millions of specialized nerve fibers spread the word throughout the body to prepare for either long-term vigilance or short-term alarm. The body responds with raised blood pressure, increased strength, conservation of necessary chemicals, and other functions that increase endurance or the power needed for fight or flight.

hostile environment. Vigilance is the *chronic* response to loss of control. When you are in a state of vigilance, cortisol moves slowly throughout the body, commanding a series of physical changes: blood pressure rises slowly; body tissues retain vital chemicals like sodium; high-energy fats and clotting agents are released into the blood; production of sex hormones like testosterone is repressed (sex hormones direct energy away from vigilance, competing with the effects of cortisol). The cortisol increases gastric acid to maximize digestion. It also lowers the immune system's defenses against disease. The body's alertness is chronically aroused. You're ready to survive over the long haul.

The twentieth century maladaptation to everyday stress can be described in one word: *uncoupling.* Your cardiovascular system, nudged by the chemicals the brain releases in response to stress, may be all set for physical combat. But the office memo that prompted the alarm reaction doesn't call for a physical fight. A miserable job or a marriage that's going on the rocks may be sounding a chronic "all stations alert," but you are pushing toward a string of hopeless tomorrows, not the western frontier, and nobody tells your rising blood pressure that it's not needed to help you survive.

In short, your cardiovascular system is "uncoupled" from your muscles and joints—you cannot spring into action and use the stress responses in the complete way nature intended. There's nothing for your body to do but stew in the juices you've produced.

How Alarm and Vigilance Can Hurt Your Heart

In brief, the alarm and vigilance reactions have many similar effects on the heart and arteries. Both adrenaline and cortisol *raise blood pressure* during stress; in time these reactions may contribute to fixed high blood pressure, a serious health risk. Adrenaline and cortisol also increase the stickiness of platelets (blood-clotting fragments), causing them to adhere to artery walls and create a nest where blood fats can collect. When these fats harden, they narrow the arteries.

Furthermore, excess adrenaline and cortisol may bombard the artery walls, damaging them and leaving places for the blood fats and other elements to lodge. Thus, repeated unleashing of the alarm and vigilance reactions can pave the way to *hardening of the arteries (atherosclerosis)*. In extreme cases, they may even help produce a *blood clot* (or thrombus) in an artery at the rough edge of a hardened, fatty projection

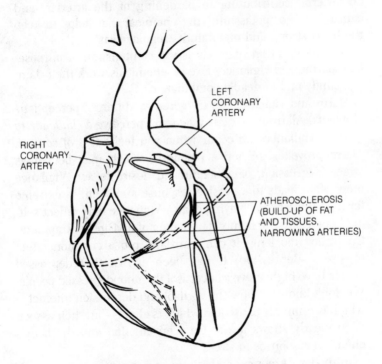

LEFT
CORONARY
ARTERY

RIGHT
CORONARY
ARTERY

ATHEROSCLEROSIS
(BUILD-UP OF FAT
AND TISSUES,
NARROWING ARTERIES)

YOUR HEART'S VITAL ARTERIES

The heart is living tissue and needs a constant supply of oxygen to function. The coronary arteries supply oxygen to the heart. In atherosclerosis, a build-up of fats and tissues obstructs and narrows the arteries so much that the flow of oxygen is stopped, heart tissue dies, and the person experiences a heart attack. The heart's two major arteries, the right and left coronary arteries, have many branches. Dotted lines show artery branches on the other side of the heart.

(plaque). In addition, a signal from the brain and a sudden rush of adrenaline can bring about the *spasm* of a relatively normal blood vessel. Either a clot or a spasm can block the flow of blood, oxygen, and nutrients to the heart.

Excess adrenaline can also overcontract and rupture heart muscle fibers, making the heart vulnerable to an electrical short circuit and weakening it. Excess cortisol can also raise cholesterol, contributing to hardening of the arteries, and cause a loss of potassium (the chemical that helps to keep the heart strong and maintain its regular beat).

Hardest of all on the body is the combination of purpose-less alarms and vigilance. Excess chemicals work their damage singly and in deadly combination.

Alarm and vigilance are triggered by different perceptions of events. Alarm can occur when you perceive a *challenge to control*; vigilance can occur when you feel a *loss of control*. Alarm provokes an active response, which may be felt as anger, aggression, or a heightened desire to act. Vigilance more often leads to a passive response and even, in extreme form in animals, to "playing dead." Vigilance may reflect self-doubt or a sense of failure or a feeling of invisible entrapment. Continued too long, it can translate into a common effect of stress—depression. It has been shown that depressed people have higher levels of cortisol than nondepressed people. We don't know yet how the cortisol and depression interact— which is primarily cause and which is effect—but their association clearly shows a link between emotion and the body's chemical responses to stress.

In modern America, both alarm and vigilance are common responses to everyday stress. Alarm can occur from two or three to forty times a day. People may have the alarm reaction by remote control over the phone. They may have it in confrontations on freeways and with red lights. They may have it eight times in a single block if they're driving cross-town through Manhattan at high noon on a hot summer day. They may be infuriated by something on TV and not be able to fight back. The body is getting ready to fight, but no external blows are ever struck. Instead, the blows are internalized, steadily bombarding vulnerable and delicate inner structures.

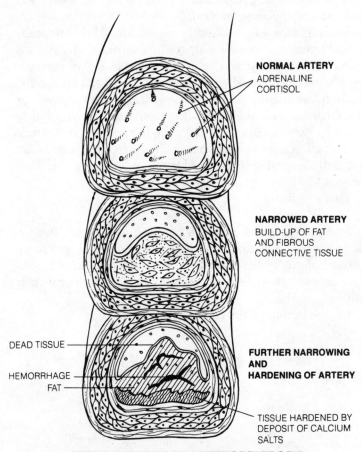

NORMAL ARTERY
ADRENALINE
CORTISOL

NARROWED ARTERY
BUILD-UP OF FAT
AND FIBROUS
CONNECTIVE TISSUE

DEAD TISSUE

**FURTHER NARROWING
AND
HARDENING OF ARTERY**

HEMORRHAGE

FAT

TISSUE HARDENED BY
DEPOSIT OF CALCIUM
SALTS

**WHAT HAPPENS IN ATHEROSCLEROSIS
(NARROWING AND HARDENING OF THE ARTERIES)**

Cortisol and adrenaline can contribute to atherosclerosis by damaging artery walls, increasing the stickiness of platelets that attract blood fats to artery walls, and raising blood cholesterol levels, making it easier for fats and connective tissue to build up inside the arteries and obstruct the flow of blood and oxygen to the heart.

Vigilance can occur on a limited basis if you need to stay up all week to pass your final exams or you are trying to write a novel while holding down a full-time job. If you are an accountant working night and day during the tax season, you will use the vigilance reaction.

But vigilance can also be a way of life. The chronically vigilant person may be an air traffic controller who has too many planes in the air. Or a mother who always agonizes over her teenage daughter's whereabouts and sits up into the small hours waiting for the phone to ring with bad news. Or the engineer who, on a diesel locomotive that's going ninety miles an hour pulling a hundred freight cars and takes a mile and a half to stop, worries continually about a truck or cyclist suddenly appearing in front of him at an unguarded highway crossing.

That's vigilance.

Stress in action is a blessing as well as a curse. But too often the body's alarm and vigilance reactions wear you down instead of strengthening you. This is especially true of certain people whose internal reactions to stress are unusually strong.

Let me introduce you to the hot reactors.

3
The Hot Reactors

Hans Selye popularized the word "stress" and brought it to the attention of a wide public in 1956 in his book *The Stress of Life.* He was not the first to use this concept, however. In the 1920s Walter Cannon described the "fight or flight" response, and beginning in the 1930s, Wilhelm Raab, one of the most advanced medical thinkers in stress research, demonstrated the risks of excess adrenaline and cortisol. Then Selye proved that stress contributed to illness and death in animals and proposed that the same effects occurred in humans. Selye's main contribution was demonstrating that the body pays a price for the way it responds to stress.

After Selye's seminal work, the next crucial step was taken by Drs. Meyer Friedman and Ray Rosenman. In trailblazing research begun over twenty-five years ago, and described for the public in 1974 in *Type A Behavior and Your Heart,* they established that behavior is linked specifically to coronary heart disease in humans. Previously, scientists had known that traditional risk factors like smoking and obesity involved behavior—people chose to smoke and eat too much. But Friedman and Rosenman defined a new risk factor that did not involve consuming something affecting the body's organs. Their risk factor was more general: a way of responding to life. They called it "Type A" behavior.

Type A behavior, as Friedman and Rosenman defined it, is a designation given to a whole set of specific behaviors observed in a structured interview conducted by a trained researcher. The researcher looks for verbal and nonverbal signs of impatience and hostility, including fidgeting, eye-blinking, grimaces, rapid or explosive speech, sitting on the edge of the seat, interrupting others, and filling in incomplete sentences during a pause. People who do a number of these things in the interview are described as showing Type A behavior.

The person who shows Type B behavior, on the other hand, acts very differently, appearing more relaxed, sitting back in the chair, rarely if ever interrupting, and listening much more.

Type A behavior occurs with or without stress. Under stress, however, the Type A person has more opportunities to act in a typically impatient, irritable, and competitive fashion.

Friedman and Rosenman found that 15 percent of Type A's had heart attacks, compared to 7 percent of Type B's. This research has since been borne out by others. In 1980, a panel convened by the National Institutes of Health published its conclusions that Type A behavior is a risk factor equal to or greater than other risk factors in coronary heart disease.

Like all risk factors, the Type A designation describes a risk, but it can't tell us whether a specific individual will or will not get cardiovascular disease. In America, depending on how it's figured, about 70 percent of men and 50 percent of women are said to be Type A's. When more than half the population is at risk but a much smaller fraction becomes ill, it is hard to predict what will happen for any one Type A person, especially since some Type B individuals will also have heart trouble. Plenty of old and crabby Type A's have seen their younger Type B friends and colleagues die of heart attacks. However, statistically the risk is greater for Type A's.

Are You a Type A?

If you have many of the following common Type A characteristics, you may be among those who run a higher risk of developing a narrowing of the heart's arteries that can lead to heart attack. Here is a run-down of the Friedman-Rosenman criteria by *New York Times* health columnist Jane Brody:

- Scheduling more and more activities into less and less time.
- Failing to notice or be interested in your environment or things of beauty.
- Hurrying the speech of others.
- Becoming unduly irritated when forced to wait in line or when driving behind a car you think is moving too slowly.
- Gesticulating when you talk.
- Frequent knee-jiggling or rapid tapping of your fingers.
- Explosive speech patterns or frequent use of obscenities.
- Making a fetish of always being on time.
- Having difficulty sitting and doing nothing.
- Playing nearly every game to win, even when playing with children.
- Measuring your own and others' success in terms of numbers (e.g., number of patients seen, articles written, etc.).
- Lip-clicking, head-nodding, fist-clenching, table-pounding, and sucking in air when speaking.
- Becoming impatient when watching others do things you can do better or faster.
- Rapid eye-blinking or ticlike eyebrow-lifting.

The Type A designation has been invaluable in establishing a statistical link between behavior and coronary heart disease. Friedman, Rosenman, and other researchers have further contributed in identifying anger, impatience, and competitiveness as the Type A characteristics that appear to be most closely linked with the risk of heart attack. Current research is focusing on how this behavior gets translated into physical illness.

In our clinic we also are interested in the links between feelings, behavior, and heart disease, but we have concentrated on looking at the stress profile from *inside* the body. As a cardiologist whose behavior under stress was almost fatal, I wanted to determine specifically which of my patients were most at risk, so I could help them before they had heart attacks, or keep them from having second ones. That required an objective diagnostic tool more selective and specific than Type A behavior. In developing a system to measure the body's responses to the stress of standard mental tasks, our clinic developed the concept of the "hot reactor."

What Is a Hot Reactor?

Our basic hypothesis is that "hot reacting"—extreme cardiovascular reactions to standardized stress tests—indicates how people handle stress physiologically in everyday life. It's only logical to suppose that those whose cardiovascular systems react most strongly are at the greatest risk of developing stress-related cardiovascular disease.

It will take years to establish all the dimensions of this new concept. Preliminary studies, however, already show a greater risk of cardiovascular disease for those with extreme reactions to standardized stress tests. Right now we're dealing with risk statistically, in terms of groups, but we have a tool—the measurement of "hot reacting"—that shows promise of detecting and predicting *individual* risk much more precisely.

You'll recall the alarm and vigilance reactions described in the last chapter. Some people experience alarm and vigilance so strongly that when they are under stress their bodies produce large amounts of stress chemicals, which in turn cause great changes in the cardiovascular system, including remarkable rises in blood pressure. These people are the "hot reactors." Their blood pressure may be normal when they are not under stress—say, in a doctor's office, where blood pressure is usually taken. What is unusual about them is that their blood pressure rises like mad when they respond to everyday stresses.

For our research we have approximated such stresses in the Stress Lab by having healthy men, aged 25 to 65, do quick mental arithmetic and then try for a high score on a video game. Electrodes taped to their bodies measured cardiovascular performance, and computers processed hundreds of thousands of pieces of information about each man to produce a printout showing how his cardiovascular system responded.

We found that fully 17 percent of the men in this study reacted to the stress with a sudden, dramatic rise in blood pressure. In each case, the reading was in excess of 160/95—without question, a hypertensive level. Furthermore, among our patients at the Stress Clinic, 20 percent (mostly men) are hot reactors whose blood pressures soar under stress.

Most people, of course, come to our clinic precisely because they are concerned about stress and their health. And to some extent, our cut-off point of 160/95 is an arbitrary one—blood pressure is a continuum, and there's no set point at which it becomes a problem for everyone. At 160/95, however, concern is definitely warranted.

Judging from the evidence our testing has produced, we can estimate that *approximately one out of every five healthy persons who feels under stress is a hot reactor*. And what's worse, these people *do not suspect* that their bodies are paying a high price for overreacting to stress.

Are Hot Reactors Always Type A's?

No. Sometimes they are and sometimes they're not. Among the people we've studied, and with the tests we use, Type A behavior occurs in cold reactors as often as it does in hot reactors.

Type A behavior and hot reacting are two very different things. To put it simply, hot reacting is an extreme cardiovascular response to stressful tasks, while Type A behavior is a particular style of interacting with an interviewer. We identify Type A behavior by watching verbal and physical reactions when an interviewer acts in a provoking or challenging way. On the other hand, we identify hot reacting by measuring the level of cardiovascular response to a set of mildly challenging mental and physical tasks that simulate daily life experience (the type of test I've just described).

Type A behavior and hot reacting both reflect feelings, but

one shows up in external behavior, while the other operates at the hidden (but scientifically observable) level of physiology and metabolism. Some people may react at one level, others at the other level, and some at both. At the moment, the reason why the body selects either or both remains a mystery for research to solve.

Who Are the Hot Reactors?

These are people who overreact to stress with extreme blood pressure and chemical changes. Such people endanger themselves by expending enormous energy. They burn a dollar's worth of energy for a dime's worth of stress. They overwork their cardiovascular systems until, ultimately, their hearts may give out.

It's like drag racing with the family car. With years of that kind of treatment, the standard engine wears out. In fact, the three ways that hot reactors raise their blood pressure can be compared to three styles of dangerous driving.

Output hot reactors work their hearts hard by increasing their output of blood when they're under stress. Either they pump blood faster than normal or they pump more blood per beat. They're like drivers who speed without knowing it. When you're going eighty miles an hour and think you're doing fifty-five, your chances of hitting something—hard— are pretty high.

Output hot reactors are usually young men or women who are otherwise perfectly healthy. Often, only their blood pressure under stress identifies them as people with a potential health problem. Usually the blood pressure of output hot reactors jumps because they are burning far more energy than is required for simple mental tasks. Fortunately, young people usually have healthy hearts and their cardiovascular systems can—for a while—handle the intensified demands.

Combined hot reactors not only pump more blood, but do it against more resistance, because their blood vessels constrict in response to stress. They're like drag racers who speed at eighty miles an hour—but with the brakes on.

Combined hot reactors are often middle-aged people who

started out as output reactors. Their blood pressure jumps mainly because their blood vessels are tightening up under mental stress and resisting the blood flow. Fortunately, though, their hearts can—usually—still pump harder to meet the increased resistance.

Vasoconstrictive (vessel-constricting) hot reactors raise their blood pressure mainly because their blood vessels severely constrict under stress. Most dangerously, their weakened hearts are no longer able to pump extra hard. These people are like drag racers who have been speeding with the brakes on for a long time, and the engine is beginning to sputter and give out.

Vasoconstrictive hot reactors are at highest risk. Their vessels are always constricted, and the heart is beginning to wear out. These people may have started as youthful output reactors and progressed through combined reacting. Now their hearts are having trouble working against the constant high resistance. If a sudden stress clamps the small vessels tight, their hearts may be unable to pump harder to keep up, and they may suffer a sudden heart attack.

Let me share some case histories with you.

Scott—an Output Hot Reactor

It was Christmas vacation and Scott was on his first trip home from an out-of-state college where he was taking pre-med courses. He wanted to become a doctor and his friends knew him as a "straight arrow." He had just made the dean's list for high grades. He loved sports and in his high school he was a local star basketball player. Walking through the Omaha airport, he appeared the picture of good health—tall, blond and slim. On impulse, he stopped at a blood-pressure machine, strapped the cuff on his arm, and put in the coins. The electronic figures were unblinking, but Scott did a double-take:

170 over 110. That was the reading, although the chart on the machine said that "normal" was 120 over 80.

It must be the machine, he figured. You can't trust these things. He was only nineteen years old. There was no way he could have high blood pressure.

Scott was the son of a colleague of mine. That night I got a call from his father, and minutes later, Scott was in my doorway. In ski jacket and winter boots, he looked more like a member of the U.S. Olympic team than someone with a health problem.

We went into the den where I keep a blood pressure cuff and stethoscope. I placed the stethoscope on his arm and inflated the cuff. His blood pressure was 180 over 110. Since Scott was worried, it had jumped a little higher than the reading at the airport. We were sitting in the den having a simple conversation and his heart was laboring at a level that would take most people his age about thirty minutes of hard running to reach.

"Scott, what's wrong? What's going on in your life?"

He started slowly, but the words soon tumbled out. He was determined to become a doctor, but the effort was taking a toll. He was having trouble adjusting from high school to life in a college dorm in another state. He never seemed to have time for sports or relaxation or friends. He was determined to help pay his way through college, and he was working several odd jobs. He was taking a correspondence course at night to help him with his daytime classes. He was highly motivated and intelligent, but medical school is extremely difficult to get into. He had made the dean's list, but some had done better. He was doing well, but he didn't feel good about himself.

He had high blood pressure, the "silent killer." People as young as Scott can have it and not have the slightest idea that they do. They do not feel ill. Meanwhile, the disease quietly works its damage throughout the body.

My hunch was that he had high blood pressure because he was a hot reactor. When a person's blood pressure shoots up to 180/110 while he's carrying on a conversation—as Scott's did in my home—he's displaying a powerful cardiovascular response to a mild stress.

I asked Scott to come down to my office at the medical center the next morning. Our team gave him a thorough medical examination, including having him walk on a treadmill.

There was no organic cause for his high blood pressure. He appeared to be in perfect condition. He had adjusted to a number of life changes recently, but a healthy 19-year-old should have been able to handle them. Furthermore, Scott was not a Type A personality who acted intensely competitive, impatient, and hostile. He was a well-mannered, soft-spoken young man.

Our laboratory stress tests showed that Scott's blood pressure was high because his heart rate and output of blood increased dramatically under stress. His total systemic resistance—the constriction of his blood vessels—was normal. His problem was due to constantly being in the combat state—the stress reactions of alarm and vigilance—for simple mental tasks.

Scott was an output hot reactor. He was typical of many highly motivated young people who burn high-energy chemicals for low-energy needs and who are undetected early hypertensives. At Scott's age, adrenaline and cortisol have not been bombarding the arteries long enough to do serious damage; it is the heart's intensified pumping that causes the blood pressure to rise. One purpose of our laboratory evaluation is to provide an early warning system that can catch this condition before there are fixed body changes and the high blood pressure becomes chronic.

Hot Reacting Versus Hypertension

Doctors refer to fixed high blood pressure as hypertension and to people who have this chronic high blood pressure as hypertensives. Hot reacting—showing a strong increase in blood pressure under stress—is a separate phenomenon from having fixed high blood pressure at rest.

Many people develop high blood pressure for reasons unrelated to hot reacting—old age, too much weight, too much salt in the diet, and genetic predisposition, to name a few. And some hot reactors, due to compensating factors in the body, never develop fixed high blood pressure. However, hot reacting to daily stress may well precede fixed high blood pressure, because after repeated rises the body tends to adjust upward and tolerate a higher resting blood pressure.

This is a serious matter. Fixed high blood pressure can lead to a stroke or heart failure. The problem is especially serious for people who are both hot reactors and hypertensives at rest. Hot reactors may raise their blood pressure 30 to 40 times a day in response to stress—it's as though, without knowing it, they're fighting saber-toothed tigers internally over and over. The effect is to push their blood pressure higher for a longer time; and the higher the pressure is and the longer it remains high, the greater the risk of chronic hypertension and heart disease. Moreover, sudden blood pressure changes in people with weakened cardiovascular systems can set off a heart attack.

In Scott's case, the problem probably started out as occasional hot reacting to stress, alternating with periods when his blood pressure remained normal. After two or three years of hot reacting, Scott had developed established high blood pressure. But there was still time to reverse it.

Therapy for Scott involved not only medication but motivation. That meant talk, a lot of talk.

At first, Scott took medicines to reduce his high blood pressure. Then, over a period of months, he learned to recognize the stress cues that set off his blood pressure. He learned how to "feel" when his blood pressure was rising and to avoid hot reacting. Three years after starting our program, Scott was accepted to medical school. He is now a cool reactor who controls his own blood pressure without medication.

Bill—a Combined Hot Reactor

Bill is middle-aged and at risk of heart failure. Already he has had surgery to bypass clogged coronary arteries.

Most days he runs a blue-chip corporation. Today he'll just operate a simple electronic television game, the kind you might find in a bar or amusement arcade. But this game is programmed according to house rules. Our hard-driving exec must really be a pro to beat the machine. The game will get tougher as Bill gets closer to winning.

In the Stress Lab, Bill enters a soundproof room. His bare chest is festooned with sophisticated electrodes that monitor every heartbeat. From outside the room, we observe him on closed-circuit television.

As he sits down, Bill's baseline blood pressure is 134/89—the high end of the normal range. He keeps it from going higher by medication.

The game begins. The first three battles with the video game are easy, and Bill is winning.

But the computer printout shows that Bill's body is reacting with changes similar to those a long-distance runner might go through. His systolic blood pressure jumps to 207, his diastolic pressure falls to 66, his heart rate jumps 30 beats a minute, his heart's output of blood doubles, and the total resistance (constriction) of his blood vessels drops in half. In other words, his heart is pumping harder and his blood vessels are widening to accommodate the increased blood. Remarkably, after only a few seconds of playing a video game, Bill's cardiovascular system is working at a rate that took him several minutes to reach while walking uphill on a treadmill. Though Bill's heart and blood vessel reactions are following a normal pattern for a person who is excited and involved in what he is doing, the degree of this response to mental stress is nevertheless extreme.

I call for a rest period and step in to chat. Bill is eager for more.

"I'm going to lick this game yet, if it's the death of me."

"Well, pay attention. Things are going to get more difficult."

The game resumes. Suddenly the little blips on the screen are getting smaller and moving faster. Bill is losing.

And not just the game. His blood pressure has abruptly started to reverse direction—displaying a potentially fatal pattern. Within minutes, the vessels constrict, causing their resistance to the blood flow to triple, while the heart's pumping pressure drops. The heart is overtaxed and starts to falter against the dramatically increased resistance. Quickly, we stop the game.

I go into the testing room and sit down to talk to him. Bill is very angry that we have stopped. He has no idea of the price his body is paying in his effort to win at all costs.

"I'm just starting to get the hang of it. Give me a few more minutes and I'll beat this machine."

"You'll probably never beat the computer. And even if you did, would it be worth dying for?"

Bill sighs. He still wants to win the game.

Bill is a "combined" hot reactor. His blood pressure rises because both his heart's output and his blood vessels' resistance increase under mild mental stress. After years of hot reacting, Bill still burns as much energy in a business meeting as another man might while playing basketball.

Chances are that decades ago Bill was a lot like Scott, an output hot reactor with the beginnings of high blood pressure. A lifetime of headstrong competitive living has put Bill in the second stage of the hot reacting spectrum. Unfortunately, he didn't take an airport blood pressure test early enough. His arteries are resisting pretty hard fairly regularly now. His heart is still able to meet the added stress, but if he keeps the brakes on long enough, the engine is bound to fail.

For Bill, I prescribe medicines to relax the muscles of his arterial walls (opening the vessels to increased blood flow), to reduce the extreme swings in contraction and relaxation of the arteries, and to moderate his heart's extreme reaction to stress.

I also try some common sense. "Bill, don't you think it's time you learned to take things a little less seriously? Why do you give everything in your life the same high priority and attack it with an all-out effort?"

I wish I could say that he listened. But Bill has a mind of his own. It has catapulted him to the top of a Fortune 500 firm.

And if it catapults his heart into failure? "I'll take the risk," he says. "And the medication, thank you."

Believe it or not, there are a lot of people like Bill. To them, the exhilaration of winning seems worth dying for. Of course, they don't really believe it will happen. But it does.

Henry—a Vasoconstrictive Hot Reactor

Henry was tall and shuffling, with sandy hair and blue eyes. He always had something nice to say about everybody. His friends thought nothing bad would ever happen to him. Of course, they knew he had high blood pressure, but it was controlled by medication. And he had a bit of a paunch—in fact, he was clearly overweight—but then, Henry had always been "hefty." A cigarette was always drooping from the corner of his mouth, and he liked his martinis, but how could you object when these were about the only pleasures he had in life?

Henry was a public relations executive for a major East Coast insurance firm, and he knew his best days were behind him. At fifty-five, he had stayed on too long. His friend and mentor had died, and the new boss was contemptuous of Henry. The boss gave him less and less real work to do and more and more insults to swallow. After a while, Henry found himself in a smaller office without a window. When the staff went to Hawaii for a convention, Henry was left behind to tend the phones. At raise time, he was given the minimum. The boss always executed the putdowns with a big smile and a gracious, "I wish it didn't have to be this way, but. . . ."

Henry was made to feel he was lucky to have a job. And he did need the job. He was still putting four sons through college. He had two years to go to earn the pension he thought he needed to assure his happy retirement. So he took the boss's smiles and lies and tongue-lashings and tried to hang on. But there was little or no real work left for him to do. He felt purposeless.

What he ended up doing was a lot of scut-work. The boss had him editing letters, making hotel reservations, ordering coffee and Danish for staff meetings, and writing long memos about things nobody cared about and nobody would read.

Henry would start his mornings by shaving and cussing

out "that tyrant who runs our office." Every night he'd down a couple of martinis to blur the memory of the day's humiliations. At work, though, he seemed calm, almost phlegmatic. The younger members of the staff thought he must like his "soft" job.

A stress specialist might have guessed that Henry was constantly in a state of vigilance. While Scott and Bill responded to stress with the alarm reaction, the arousal to performance brought on by the challenge to control, Henry's feeling that he had lost control of his life and his fear of expressing his true feelings openly made him try to survive by stifling himself, by deadening his emotions. But vigilance raised his blood pressure as much as alarm raised Scott's and Bill's.

Came a hot Monday in June: Henry was one year away from being vested in his company's pension plan. Three sons had graduated from college and the fourth was a junior. Henry had been interviewing for another job with a related organization, a job he could begin after earning his pension. It was much less money, but his wife was begging him to take it. Then the boss called Henry from a nearby hotel: a convention was in session and he insisted that Henry carry over two boxes of newspapers containing an article the boss had written.

It was only a two-block walk from the company to the hotel; the boxes were not all that heavy. So it came as a shock to everybody when Henry, riding up the hotel escalator, abruptly collapsed face-downward onto the cardboard boxes and died—the victim of a sudden heart attack.

Henry was killed by one of the leading causes of death in this country. Sudden cardiac death strikes up to 450,000 Americans a year. But as with Henry, these deaths are not really "sudden." They are the end of a long process of weakening. Henry's blood vessels had constricted so often as part of his alarm and vigilance reactions that eventually the pattern became fixed. His heart fought against this increased resistance, but after years of being overtaxed—including heavy drinking that weakened the heart muscle and plenty of nicotine and carbon monoxide from cigarettes to tighten his blood vessels even more—the heart gradually lost its ability to pump as hard as it once did. Henry's output of blood fell. When the sudden mental stress—his outrage at still another insult—hit, his cardiovascular system just couldn't adjust to the increased demand for blood. He collapsed and died.

What might have saved Henry? Drugs would have helped, but behavioral management would have been the name of the game. A crucial question someone might have asked him was, "Why do you feel such intense stress at this point in your life?"

Almost certainly he would have described a life of joyless struggle. His answer would have been, "I'm in a losing situation. I hate this job, but I can't afford to say what I think and lose this job."

In fact, Henry could not afford *not* to say what he was feeling. I would have recommended that he accept immediate intensive help, both medical and behavioral. If he would not do that, I would have suggested that he leave his job. I would have told him:

"Quit, immediately. Transfer elsewhere in the company, if you feel you must have the pension. If that is not possible, leave anyway. I know it's important and you've got years of your life invested. But is it worth dying for?"

Scott, Bill, and Henry were all hot reactors. But as you probably surmised, they were not all Type A's. Bill's behavior tested out as Type A on questionnaires and in interviews. Scott and Henry, however, looked like models of calm and tested out as Type B's, despite their being hot reactors internally.

Then there was Jeff, a classic Type A. He traveled on the fast track and wanted to stay there. If he had to break a few rules and upset a few people along the way, he was willing to do it. Yet Jeff wasn't what you might think. Let me introduce you to a cold reactor.

Jeff—Hot Head, Cool Heart

Jeff was a thirty-five-year-old reporter for a major national publication.

Intensely driven, he hurried all over the country and occasionally the world to report breaking stories. He liked the adrenaline rush, the obstacles swept away. He loved getting the story, writing it, basking in the byline, framing the photos of celebrities he had written about, displaying the writing awards he had won. His office was a shrine to his travels and his stories.

But he worried about stress. There were a lot of deadlines. His job provided more glamour than money, and he wasn't getting any younger. He spent a great deal of time rushing for planes and drinking when the flights were delayed. Booze, in fact, was a constant companion. Someday, he wanted to find a woman he could marry—again. The first one left when he started traveling—at least he thought that was why she left. And he worked for a highly political organization. He was a hero on the road, but he would often return to find that his situation had been undercut by people in the home office.

No one ever said he couldn't write, but he had a lot of battles—over expense accounts, foreign travel, the accusations that he was a mercenary out for himself and cooperation be damned. He had to fight his own editors for photo and story placement. Sometimes he would even argue over the headlines they chose.

Could all this be harming his health? he asked.

Jeff came to Omaha for our SHAPE (Stress, Health, and Physical Evaluation) program. I found that he was in normal health. He had an unremarkable family history, and he had no trouble on the treadmill. Although he had long ago abandoned tennis and most of the other sports he enjoyed in order to stalk his stories, Jeff was in excellent physical condition.

On our psychologist's questionnaire, however, Jeff revealed that he was subject to a heart disease risk factor: he was a flaming Type A.

He got even hotter in the personal interview. Would he run a yellow light?—Always. If the car in front of him was going too slow, would he honk?—He would either get around that car or lean on the horn all day. If a person were speaking too slowly, would he hurry them along?—He would yank the words out of their throats. Jeff fidgeted in his chair, burned energy as he sat, constantly interrupted, and talked loudly and explosively. He had a number of grimaces, scowls, bursting smiles, and other facial expressions that came and went in the blinking of an eye, and he blinked more than normal, too. His voice rose and fell and he shifted back and forth in the chair, occasionally rising to pace about the room. His behavior was both frantic and hostile.

The conversation with the psychologist was taped and analyzed for what are called stylistics of speech. In loudness, explosiveness, and interrupting, Jeff was off the high end of the Type A behavior chart.

Yet, astonishingly, in the stress lab Jeff's baseline blood pressure was 105/63, or ideal. Under repeated and continuous stress testing—mental arithmetic, American history quiz, video games, plunging the hand in ice water up to the wrist—it rose no higher than 110/70. Jeff was a cold reactor. His surface behavior might be manic—he said he often appeared to be "an organism in distress"—but his heart's reactions were rock stable and cold.

On a hunch, I sent in a female interviewer to engage Jeff in a question-and-answer game. Jeff's psychological profile stamped him not only as a Type A but as a man who viewed career women as "interlopers." I thought he might rise to the competitive ploy, since the woman was supposed to win this game. But it was not to be. In checking the blood pressure of both parties playing this game, we discovered that Jeff, a trained interviewer himself, had managed to shoot the female interviewer's blood pressure up to 188/110.

During our final appraisal interview, Jeff expressed satisfaction in learning that his hectic lifestyle was not affecting his heart. But he admitted that the quality of his life was not exactly wonderful, despite his physiological calm in response to stress.

I advised him to take some time and try to even out the bumps in his roller-coaster way of life. His heart was good, but the effect of stress on the body is much like the effect of piling a load of bricks on a wooden platform. The weakest board breaks first. Jeff's cardiovascular system was healthy, but he did have a lot of headaches. Lately, he was getting a little fatigued, losing some of the joy in his work. He was drinking too much and wasting a lot of time worrying about things he couldn't change. He would do his work in manic bursts of energy and then throw away vast amounts of time. He was not well organized and, in fact, resisted organization as being "beneath a creative mind." He had exaggerated fears about his health—in fact, he was an Olympic-class hypochondriac—and he ruined a lot of personal relationships, particularly with women, by psychologically (not physiologically) overreacting to stress. Beneath the bluster, Jeff was extraordinarily sensitive, and all the turmoil was hurting him. His body was paying a price somewhere, though not in his heart and blood vessels.

I advised Jeff to establish different patterns of thinking about his life. His central problem was that his feelings were wildly exaggerated. Every time Jeff had a headache, he thought a blood vessel was going to pop in his head; every time his chest tightened, he checked his pulse to make sure his heart was still beating; every time he entered a dark bar and couldn't immediately adjust to the lack of light, he began to wonder if he were blacking out from too much booze.

A lot of people are like Jeff. They're insecure. They're sure they're going to call down something terrible on themselves and they want to be prepared, so they anticipate the worst. (I call this "horribilizing.") I convinced Jeff that he didn't need self-destructive thinking to remain creative and productive. That he could lead a balanced life. That he was better off shooting for results, not perfection.

I also taught him the most lifesaving word in the English

language: No. Jeff had been taking on writing assignments without regard to his overall work load. His ego overrode his common sense. A free-lance article here, a book there, another article elsewhere. And, then, out of guilt, he would redouble his efforts on his salaried job "to make sure they know I'm still around."

We taught Jeff to accept his accomplishments and his success, to stop trying to conquer the world continually, and to cool his reactions in those situations where he could neither control nor change things.

Sometimes it's better to yield gracefully than to bang your head against a brick wall. Give yourself a break, I told Jeff. Skip a few fights. Stay home a few nights. Miss a few stories. Take time for yourself and to be with others.

Years later, Jeff is happily married and still traveling about the country. He doesn't worry as much, is less of a workaholic, and enjoys his life more.

Jeff is a cool reactor and a reformed Type A.

Jeff was a living demonstration of the difference between Type A behavior and hot reacting. He was *psychologically intense* most of the time, but he was not *physiologically intense*. His blood pressure rose a little under mental stress, as everyone's does, but it did not rise very much.

Jeff was like a person driving without a muffler—the car may make plenty of noise, but that has nothing to do with how the engine is working. It could be in great shape or it could be burning up; you can't tell from the revved-up sound. At the same time, driving without a muffler isn't a good idea—the noise is a strain on everybody else, if not on the engine. Extreme Type A behavior is worth modifying for that reason alone. Jeff's psychological overreactions kept him in enough hot water to harm the overall quality of his life.

The ideal way to go through life is to maintain both physiological and emotional balance. People who take life in stride instead of struggling against it can respond to a true crisis with reserves that are—to use the Rolls-Royce understatement about horsepower—adequate. And, as I will explain more fully in the next chapter, they can protect themselves from the hazards of hot reacting, notably high blood pressure and heart attack.

4
Hot Reacting, High Blood Pressure, and Heart Attack

A lifetime of hot reacting to stress may well be a significantly shortened lifetime. The two major risks to your health are high blood pressure and heart attacks.

High Blood Pressure—the "Silent Killer"

High blood pressure (hypertension) is one of the more neglected health problems in America. It is both common and serious, and only a fraction of all hypertensives have their illness under control.

If you assume that borderline high blood pressure begins at 140/90 millimeters of mercury and established high blood pressure at 160/95, then over 35 million Americans have established high blood pressure and another 25 million have either fluctuating or borderline high blood pressure. In other words, about one of every three American adults has established or borderline high blood pressure.

Although this illness is very easy to diagnose and treat, one-third of all people with established high blood pressure—some *12 million* people—do not even know they have it! Millions more know it but are not doing enough about it. And untreated, high blood pressure can be a killer.

What High Blood Pressure Can Do to Your Body

If you're concerned about the stress in your life, you may

already have heard a good deal about the major health risks of high blood pressure—heart failure, stroke, and kidney failure. Even mild high blood pressure can reduce life expectancy, and in combination with other risk factors it is even more dangerous. By itself, high blood pressure doubles your risk of heart attack. If, in addition, you smoke *or* have high cholesterol, your risk is 8 times higher. If you have high blood pressure and you smoke *and* have high cholesterol, your risk is up to 12 times higher, and your life expectancy is markedly lower.

The fact is that uncontrolled high blood pressure will harm your vital organs. And there are generally no warning signs or symptoms, so organ failure can begin without your knowing it.

Sound alarming? Here's the story on what untreated hypertension can do to your body.

Your heart and arteries: The organ most commonly damaged by high blood pressure is the heart. It pumps harder, and over time this extra work causes the heart muscle to increase in size. This condition, called *hypertensive heart disease,* can lead to *congestive heart failure* if the enlarged heart cannot continue to pump hard enough. High blood pressure also contributes to *atherosclerosis,* or narrowing and hardening of the arteries due to a build-up of fatty deposits in artery walls. Atherosclerosis diminishes the supply of blood to the heart, causing chest pain (angina) during exercise or even serious injury to part of the heart muscle (heart attack). And high blood pressure can damage and narrow the large arteries that bring blood to the rest of the body, reducing their capacity to carry blood, with its oxygen and nutrients, to the body's tissues.

Your brain: A stroke may happen when continued high blood pressure critically narrows an artery in the brain, or weakens an artery so a blood clot occurs, or an artery ruptures and there is a brain hemorrhage.

Your kidneys: When high blood pressure damages the arterioles delivering blood to the kidneys, it becomes harder for the kidneys to rid the body of waste products, and eventually kidney failure can occur.

Furthermore, unchecked high blood pressure damages blood vessels in the eyes, which can lead to blindness. In fact, physicians can estimate the degree of vessel damage throughout your body simply by checking the blood vessels in the eyes.

If all this doesn't sound alarming enough, here's more. Uncontrolled fixed high blood pressure follows this grim course:

The time from the onset of untreated established high blood pressure to death is about twenty years. No warning signs other than a high blood pressure reading are likely to appear for about fourteen years. Then failure of one or more organs occurs. At this point, if the high blood pressure continues to go untreated, the average survival time is only about six years.

And the terrible irony of all this is that "the silent killer" is easy to detect and relatively simple to treat. Even *after* organ failure begins, effective treatment can add years to your life.

The Causes of High Blood Pressure

High blood pressure is usually detected during a routine physical examination. In 5 to 10 percent of the cases, the condition can be traced to an underlying disorder, such as disease of the kidneys, a benign tumor of the adrenal glands, localized narrowing of the aorta (the body's largest artery), narrowing in other arteries, and disorders of the central nervous system, including infections of the brain (encephalitis) and brain tumors. If these disorders are corrected, the blood pressure usually returns to normal.

The other 90 to 95 percent of people with established high blood pressure are said to have "essential hypertension." For these people the key contributors to the disease are stress, heredity, obesity, and excessive salt intake.

How Dangerous Is Stress for High Blood Pressure?

Very. The alarm and vigilance reactions raise blood pressure under stress, aggravating already established high blood pressure and increasing the likelihood of its becoming more firmly fixed and harder to treat. Stimulating alarm and vigilance strongly and frequently by hot reacting to stress increases the risk of these problems.

Stress can also be the straw that breaks the patient with high blood pressure. At a moment of peak stress, the person with high blood pressure can suffer a blow where the body is weakest. Perhaps the new assault hits a weakness in the heart's left ventricle, with a consequent heart attack. Or disease of the small blood vessels permits a stroke, or heart failure and sudden death.

Who Gets High Blood Pressure?

Clearly, high blood pressure discriminates—by genes, age, sex, and race. It is most likely to occur in these people:

• In the relatives of hypertensives. If one of your parents has essential hypertension, there is a 50 percent chance that one child in the family will develop it also (usually between the ages of 40 and 50). If both parents have it, the chance that you or one of your brothers or sisters will develop it rises to 90 percent; furthermore, it usually begins earlier.

• In men—more often, and with more severe consequences, than in women, though women develop it increasingly in later life.

• Under the age of 50, high blood pressure is more common in men than in women. After 55 or 60, it is more common in women than in men. However, overall, more men than women die from high blood pressure and its complications.

• In pregnant women and women who are taking birth control pills.

• In blacks, especially black men, more often and in a more severe form than among whites. Among women, high blood pressure is more than twice as frequent for blacks than whites. Statistics show that blacks in industrialized nations (as opposed to the rural areas of Africa) get high blood pressure earlier in life than whites, at higher levels, and twice as often. High blood pressure is a leading cause of death in the black population, with hypertension-related diseases *killing*

*up to one hundred times more black people than does sic
anemia.*

- In short, heavy people and overweight people in general.
- In people whose blood pressure fluctuates from normal to
high.

Although high blood pressure can begin as early as infancy,
the earliest that it usually appears is about age 30. It becomes
increasingly common at older ages. Half of all Americans
over 65 have high blood pressure. However, the illness can
hit anyone at almost any time.

How Is Stress-related High Blood Pressure Treated?

If at all possible, and if the high blood pressure is new and
mild, I strongly favor trying to change self-destructive living
habits rather than taking drugs. Often, though, both drugs
and behavioral changes are required for the patient with high
blood pressure, especially at first.

Obviously, you can't be your own doctor. But if you have
high blood pressure or suspect that you might have it, you
are the key to your own survival. Only you can take the first
step of seeking the advice of your physician. And you are the
one who must decide to accept the guidance of your physician and follow his or her prescription for medication or
behavior change, or both. If lifestyle changes are recommended—losing weight, cutting back on salt, stopping
smoking, exercising, and resting—only you can bring them
about. If medicines are prescribed, only you can take them.
And only you can decide to stop overreacting to life's stresses.

Heart Attacks and Sudden Death

In the time it takes you to read this page, at least one
American will die suddenly from heart trouble. If sudden
death is considered to be within 24 hours of an attack, that
adds up to 1200 deaths a day and 450,000 a year. Sudden
cardiac death (SCD) is America's leading cause of death. One
of every three such deaths occurs with absolutely no warning
symptoms. Heart attack, a form of heart disease in which

part of the heart muscle dies, can lead to SCD, though it may not. However, those who survive a first heart attack have more than five times the risk of dying from another attack within five years. Altogether, heart and circulatory diseases account for nearly 50 percent of all deaths in this country, making them by far the top killers in America. The annual cost to the American economy is at least $65 billion, and the human death toll is almost a million people every year.

Stress increases the risk of heart attack by striking at the three main targets in the cardiovascular system: the arteries feeding the heart, the heart muscle, and the heart's electrical system. Let's take a closer look at how behavior, a stressful lifestyle, and hot reacting can damage these three crucial systems and set you up for a heart attack.

The coronary arteries. Not only can purposeless alarm and vigilance raise blood pressure and damage the arteries, but vigilance also raises cholesterol, a blood fat that in excessive amounts can dangerously block the arteries. Unrelieved stress can signal cholesterol production, and dieting does not totally stop the process. Follow an accountant during tax season or a medical student the night before an exam and you will find that cholesterol increases dramatically, by as much as 100 milligrams.

The heart muscle. Excessive drinking, which may be aggravated by stress, weakens the heart's muscle fibers.

Chronic vigilance causes the body to retain salt, or sodium, and lose potassium. Potassium preserves muscle soundness and function. Without potassium, the heart muscle becomes weak and oversensitive to stimuli. The heart also becomes bigger (hypertrophy) and has to work harder to supply itself with blood.

Excess stress chemicals can weaken the heart over time by rupturing the muscle fibers and replacing them with tiny patches of scar tissue. In the susceptible hot reactor, minute parts of the heart may be literally destroyed with every rage and combat reaction.

The heart's electrical system. Every heart fiber is connected to the electrical system that maintains a consistent heartbeat. When purposeless alarms repeatedly destroy fibers in a heart muscle, especially a heart weakened by a loss of potassium, a potentially chaotic electrical imbalance can occur in the heart. If thousands of these damaged fibers, representing thousands of hot reactions, become scattered throughout the heart, islands of short circuits and power failures create the risk of an outburst of chaotic electrical impulses. An electrical storm can erupt in the heart, making it impossible for the heart to maintain its normal coordinated beat. Instead, it begins to quiver crazily, its fibers acting more like a bag of frenzied worms than a synchronized pump.

Hot reactions assault all three parts of the cardiovascular system in a long softening-up process that can weaken the heart for a fatal blow, which may be triggered when stress causes sudden, intense emotion. It's like watching two boxers. For round after round, one is beating the living daylights out of the other, softening him up with blow after blow. All of a sudden, the loser is hit with a punch that doesn't look like much—but he's out cold. It would be hard to say which punch actually delivered the knockout, but it's obvious that the earlier blows set up the KO.

Catecholamines—Responsible for the Knockout Punch?

Catecholamines are the adrenalinelike chemicals that power the fight-or-flight alarm reaction. The surge of these strong chemicals can destroy thousands of heart muscle cells in laboratory animals within minutes. They also cause a dramatic influx of calcium and a sharp reduction in the major energy stores of the heart. At the same time, catecholamines increase the chance that chaotic heart rhythms can occur.

It is this combination of effects that can trigger sudden cardiac death. While it has not been proven conclusively that catecholamines cause sudden cardiac death, their footprints have been found in three-quarters of all cases examined by autopsy.

For example, microscopic slides taken from two human victims of sudden cardiac death—one from a woman who was mugged and threatened but not physically harmed, the other from a Cape Canaveral engineer who died immediately after being told he was fired—showed that their damaged heart muscle tissue was identical to the damaged heart tissue of laboratory animals that died after being injected with stress chemicals. Each showed the same muscle-fiber changes, or lesions, that catecholamines produce.

Since these lesions are found in 72 percent of autopsies following sudden cardiac deaths, there seems to be good reason to think that the brain—via the medium of cate-cholamines—is a powerful participant in the cardiac-knockout. What's more, some of these deaths occur even when the cardiovascular system is in apparently excellent shape—this was precisely the case with many of the Cape Canaveral victims.

On the other hand, some people escape heart attack even when their systems are in pretty bad shape. What could have made the difference for the woman who was mugged, the engineer who was fired, and so many others?

Their reactions to stress.

Knockout: Sudden Death on the Job

At age fifty-five, Joe became employed as a mobile home inspector for a government agency. His supervisors described the job as "high-pressure, highly stressful, time-consuming, emotionally draining, and physically exhausting." Joe kept it up for fourteen months. Then he was given additional responsibilities. He tried valiantly to meet them, but the load was too great. His colleagues, friends, and family noticed that his vitality, which was remarkable when he started the job, now appeared to be sapped a few hours after the workday began. But even though he was sleeping poorly and often appeared to be *pathologically fatigued,* Joe kept working long after his vitality dropped.

About this time, Joe experienced a powerful shock. He had to investigate a fire in a mobile home in which seven people burned to death. The horror and stench were such that Joe developed the symptoms of a heart attack: pain down both arms, a strange sensation of pressure in the chest, nausea, vomiting, profuse sweating, trembling, heart palpitations, and emotional and physical weariness. Joe asked for a few days' annual leave. He was exhausted.

While resting, Joe faced up to the truth: he had experienced a heart attack. Five days after the fire, he went to the hospital and was treated for the aftermath of his attack. A few months later, a treadmill test showed frequent irregular heartbeats, but no evidence that the heart was not functioning effectively. Joe was considered fit and fully recovered. It was time to go back to work.

On the job, Joe soon developed persistent angina—intermittent pain that felt as if a knife were being stabbed into his chest. He was now in a fearsome double bind. He hated the job, but felt he couldn't quit because he needed the pension. He didn't want disability or workmen's compensation insurance because they contradicted his self-image as a vigorous worker.

But a year later, Joe's terrible chest pains forced him to stop working. X-rays showed that one of his coronary arteries was completely blocked. Another was 50 percent blocked. There was also a slight elevation of his systolic blood pressure.

Yet, Joe was told, even at this point his clinical outlook for a long life was still relatively good if he would leave his job. He gave in and filed a claim for workmen's compensation. A month after filing the claim, Joe learned from the government that he was not entitled to compensation. His company told him that if he didn't return to work, he would be replaced. There seemed no way out. He went back to work.

Less than a month after his claim for workmen's compensation was denied, Joe died of a heart attack. He was fifty-nine, three years short of retirement. The last things he had shared with his family were his feelings of failure, disillusionment, abandonment, and loss.

The government recorded Joe as a sudden cardiac death. But only the end was sudden.

What had been going on inside Joe's body—probably for

many years—is pretty clear. Step by step, stress killed Joe. Most likely, he went through his adult life as a hot reactor, until fixed high blood pressure and powerful stress chemicals had done their irreversible damage to his cardiovascular system. Eventually, his job situation delivered the final blow.

Doctors can put patients like Joe on exercise treadmills and test for damage brought on by hot reacting to mental stress. Unfortunately, not much can be done about such end-stage physical changes in the heart.

But if hot reactors to stress can be persuaded to become cool (or at least cooler) reactors in time, *there is a good chance that their heart disease can be prevented or delayed.* That's a goal worth working for. And fortunately, the methods for cooling down are now available.

5
Are You
a Hot Reactor?

Are you under too much stress? Are your reactions to stress likely to harm your health and heart? Some simple tests will give you an idea of how you are responding to stress in your life, in your emotions, in your behavior, and ultimately in your cardiovascular system.

For the first test, read each sentence and circle the number under the answer that most applies to you.

Test 1: Simple Stress and Tension Test

	Often	A few times a week	Rarely
(1) I feel tense, anxious, or have nervous indigestion.	2	1	0
(2) People at work/home arouse my tension.	2	1	0
(3) I eat/drink/smoke in response to tension.	2	1	0
(4) I have tension or migraine headaches, pain in the neck or shoulders, or insomnia.	2	1	0
(5) I can't turn off my thoughts at night or on			

	Often	A few times a week	Rarely
weekends long enough to feel relaxed and refreshed the next day.	2	1	0
(6) I find it difficult to concentrate on what I'm doing because of worrying about other things.	2	1	0
(7) I take tranquilizers (or other drugs) to relax.	2	1	0
(8) I have a difficult time finding enough time to relax.	2	1	0
(9) Once I find the time, it's hard for me to relax.	Yes	(1)	No (0)
(10) My workday is made up of too many deadlines.	Yes	(1)	No (0)

Total score: _____

Source: John W. Farquhar, M.D., *The American Way of Life Need Not Be Hazardous to Your Health* (New York: W.W. Norton Co., Inc., 1979). Reprinted by permission of the publisher. Copyright 1978 by John W. Farquhar, M.D.

—A score of 12 or higher indicates a high tension level and difficulty coping with the stress in your life.

We can also explore the stress in your life by finding out how many changes you've faced recently. Below is a list of some events that commonly occur in life. Check the left-hand column if the event has happened to you during the last twelve months.

Test 2: The Life-Event Test

Life Event	Points
_____ Death of spouse	100
_____ Divorce	73
_____ Marital separation	65
_____ Jail term	63
_____ Death of close family member	63
_____ Personal injury or illness	53
_____ Marriage	50
_____ Fired at work	47
_____ Marital reconciliation	45
_____ Retirement	45
_____ Change in family member's health	44
_____ Pregnancy	40
_____ Sex difficulties	39
_____ Addition to family	39
_____ Business readjustment	39
_____ Change in financial state	38
_____ Death of close friend	37
_____ Change to different line of work	36
_____ Change in number of marital arguments	35
_____ Mortgage or loan for major purchase (home, etc.)	31
_____ Foreclosure of mortgage or loan	30
_____ Change in work responsibilities	29

Life Event	Points
_____ Son or daughter leaving home	29
_____ Trouble with in-laws	29
_____ Outstanding personal achievement	28
_____ Spouse begins or stops work	26
_____ Starting or finishing school	26
_____ Change in living conditions	25
_____ Revision of personal habits	24
_____ Trouble with boss	23
_____ Change in work hours, conditions	20
_____ Change in residence	20
_____ Change in schools	20
_____ Change in recreational habits	19
_____ Change in church activities	19
_____ Change in social activities	18
_____ Mortgage or loan for lesser purchase (car, TV, etc.)	17
_____ Change in sleeping habits	16
_____ Change in number of family gatherings	15
_____ Change in eating habits	15
_____ Vacation	13
_____ Christmas season	12
_____ Minor violations of the law	11
Total score _____	

Now, add up the point values of all the items checked. If your score is 300 or more, statistically you stand an almost 80 percent chance of getting sick in the near future. If your score is 150 to 299, the chances are about 50 percent. At less than 150, about 30 percent.

This scale seems to suggest that change in one's life requires an effort to adapt and then an effort to regain stability. Probably this process saps energy that the body would ordinarily use in maintaining itself, so reserves of energy are depleted, and susceptibility to illness increases.

In our clinic, we help patients maintain their energy by helping them change their self-destructive *perceptions* of events. The event itself is really less important in the stress equation than how you react to it.

This next test helps assess how you are living. The questions are not weighted for relative importance; they are meant to give you a general idea of how you are doing and to alert you to some signs and sources of stress in your life.

Test 3: Life-Assessment Test

Physical and Environmental Factors

1. Number of business or social dinners spent out per week:	0	1	2	3	4 or more
2. Number of caffeinated beverages drunk per day:	0	1	2	3	4 or more
3. Business lunches per week:	0	1	2	3	4 or more
4. Overnight business trips per month:	0	1	2	3	4 or more
5. Number of years since last medical check-up:	0	1	2	3	4 or more
6. Number of tranquilizers per month:	0	1	2	3	4 or more
7. Smoking:	0 (don't smoke)	1 (pipe)	2 (cigars)	3 (cigarettes, 1 pack a day or less)	4 (cigarettes, more than 1 pack a day)
8. Overweight:	0 (5 lbs. or less)	1 (6–15 lbs.)	2 (16–25 lbs.)	3 (26–35 lbs.)	4 (36 lbs. or more)

	0	1	2	3	4
9. Number of business phone calls per day:	(none)	(1–5)	(6–10)	(11–25)	(26 or more)
10. Blood pressure:	(less than 120/90)	(120/90)	(130/100)	(140/110)	(150/115)
11. Cholesterol:	(160–180)	(180–200)	(200–225)	(225–250)	(250 or more)
12. Drinks per week: —Hard liquor (1 ounce each)	(0–3)	(4–6)	(7–10)	(11–14)	(15 or more)
—Wine (6 ounces each)	(0–3)	(4–6)	(7–10)	(11–14)	(15 or more)
—Beer (12 ounces each)	(0–3)	(4–6)	(7–10)	(11–14)	(15 or more)
13. Subordinates (directly responsible for):	(0)	(1–3)	(4–6)	(7)	(8 or more)
14. Superiors (directly responsible to):	(0)	(1–2)	(3–4)	(5)	(6 or more)

	0	1	2	3	4
15. Retired, with no hobbies or other activity:	(not retired)	(¼-time)	(½-time)	(¾-time)	(full-time)
16. Drive on freeways or in a city to work (number of minutes):	(0–10)	(10–20)	(20–30)	(30–40)	(more than 40)
17. Occupational position:	(independent professional)	(employee)	(supervisor)	(top management)	(foreman, middle-management, self-employment)
18. I take work home:	(not at all)	(occasionally)	(once a week)	(twice a week)	(more)
19. Moving traffic violations within the past year:	0	1	2	3	4 or more

Score yourself: 19 or less—low stress; 20–38—mild stress; 39–57—moderate stress; 58–76—high stress.

Here's a test that assesses *how you are feeling about your life*. Study the following statements and circle the answer that best applies to you.

Test 4: Stressful Attitudes

Attitude or Feeling	How Often Feeling Occurs			
	Almost never	Occa- sionally	Fre- quently	Almost always
(1) Things must be perfect.	1	2	3	4
(2) I must do it myself.	1	2	3	4
(3) I feel more isolated from my family or close friends.	1	2	3	4
(4) I feel that people should listen better.	1	2	3	4
(5) My life is running me.	1	2	3	4
(6) I must not fail.	1	2	3	4
(7) When overworked, I cannot say "no" to new demands without feeling guilt.	1	2	3	4
(8) I need to generate excitement again and again to avoid boredom.	1	2	3	4
(9) I feel a lack of intimacy with people around me.	1	2	3	4
(10) I am unable to relax.	1	2	3	4
(11) I feel increasingly cynical and disenchanted.	1	2	3	4

Attitude or Feeling	How Often Feeling Occurs			
	Almost never	Occa- sionally	Fre- quently	Almost always
(12) I am unable to laugh at a joke about myself.	1	2	3	4
(13) I avoid speaking my mind.	1	2	3	4
(14) I feel under pressure to succeed all the time.	1	2	3	4
(15) I automatically express negative attitudes.	1	2	3	4
(16) I seem further behind at the end of the day than when I started.	1	2	3	4
(17) I forget deadlines, appointments, and personal possessions.	1	2	3	4
(18) I am irritable, short-tempered, disappointed in the people around me.	1	2	3	4
(19) Sex seems like more trouble than it's worth.	1	2	3	4
(20) I consider myself exploited.	1	2	3	4
(21) I wake up earlier and cannot sleep.	1	2	3	4
(22) I feel unrested.	1	2	3	4
(23) I feel dissatisfied with my work life.	1	2	3	4
(24) I feel dissatisfied with my personal life.	1	2	3	4

Attitude or Feeling	How Often Feeling Occurs			
	Almost never	Occasionally	Frequently	Almost always
(25) I'm not where I want to be in my life.	1	2	3	4
(26) I avoid being alone.	1	2	3	4
(27) I have trouble getting to sleep.	1	2	3	4
(28) I have trouble waking up.	1	2	3	4
(29) I can't seem to get out of bed.	1	2	3	4

Score yourself: 29—low stress; 30–58—mild stress; 59–87—moderate stress; 88–116—high stress.

The next questionnaire alerts you to physical, emotional, and behavioral overreactions you may be having to stress. View them as clues, not tests. In many cases none of the answers will fit you exactly, but check all those that most clearly apply to you.

Test 5: How Are You Reacting to Stress?

1. When you go to bed at night, do you usually—
   (a) Watch television before falling asleep?
   (b) Read before falling asleep?
   (c) Organize your next day's activities?
   (d) Ruminate over this day's events?
   (e) Fall asleep immediately?
   (f) Meditate, relax, or otherwise quiet yourself?

2. How often do you waken during the night?
   (a) Very seldom.
   (b) Some, but I always go right back to sleep.

   (c) Some, and I have trouble getting back to sleep.
   (d) Fairly often.
   (e) Quite often.

3. Have you ever had an illness that kept you from completing an important job, course, or assignment?
   (a) Yes, once or twice.
   (b) Yes, upon several occasions.
   (c) No.

4. Has your appetite or weight decreased drastically during the past few months?
   (a) Yes.
   (b) No.

5. Have your attitudes toward sexual behavior changed recently?
   (a) Yes, I find it more attractive and engage in more sexual behavior.
   (b) Yes, I find it less attractive and engage in less sexual behavior.
   (c) No, but I engage in sex less frequently than before.
   (d) No, my attitudes toward sexual behavior are the same.

6. If you made an appointment with someone to meet with you at work and he or she were 20 minutes late, which of the following best describes the response you would probably have?
   (a) You'd check your watch or clock frequently, but not start any other activity in case he/she showed up.
   (b) You'd utilize the time to get some work done.
   (c) You'd call his/her office or home to remind him/her of the appointment.
   (d) You'd leave the office—after all, if someone can't be on time, he/she doesn't deserve the appointment.
   (e) You'd have a cup of coffee and visit with the other office personnel, since it's "free" time, basically.

7. What might you think while waiting for this person?
   (a) "I'm always punctual and everyone else should be, too."

(b) "Time is money; don't people know that?"
(c) "I wish she/he would get here."
(d) "She/he should be here by now."
(e) "I wonder if she/he forgot about the appointment."
(f) "I wonder if she/he was detained unavoidably."
(g) "I may have to make alternate plans because of this delay."

8. Suppose you are having dinner with your family or friends at a restaurant. The waiter arrives to serve you, and accidentally drops a plate of food in your lap. Would you—
    (a) Grimace with disgust, but not say anything?
    (b) Make some comment to the waiter?
    (c) Yell or scream at the waiter?
    (d) Make an apology to the waiter for getting in his way?
    (e) Ask for a towel to clean up and leave the table?
    (f) Make a joke of the incident?

9. When the prior incident occurred, what would you most likely think?
    (a) "Clumsy fool!"
    (b) "That's the last time I come here to eat!"
    (c) "Waiters should never drop food."
    (d) "I look like an idiot, and everyone is watching me."
    (e) "I am so unlucky; this had to happen to me."
    (f) "How can this mess be cleaned up easily?"

10. Which of the following best describes your attitudes?
    (a) Rules are made to be broken.
    (b) Stretching the rules of an organization is sometimes a good idea.
    (c) Rules are made for a reason, and we should follow them.
    (d) Rules work best when they are flexible.
    (e) If you don't stick to the rules, things get out of hand.

11. Which is most often true?
    (a) I often don't know what's going to happen to me until it does.

(b) I can often see what's going to happen to me, but I can't do much to change it.

(c) I can generally influence events and the way things turn out in my life.

12. Do you often feel that time is passing much too quickly for you to get everything done you need to do?
   (a) Yes, and it makes me feel tremendously frustrated.
   (b) Yes, but I can live with it pretty well.
   (c) No.

13. Which of the following adjectives would often apply to your state of mind? (Circle all that apply.)

(a) Anxious	(h) Healthy	(o) Powerful
(b) Amused	(i) Hostile	(p) Safe
(c) Sad	(j) Impatient	(q) Suffering
(d) Cooperative	(k) Lucky	(r) Unhappy
(e) Displeased	(l) Nervous	(s) Unsociable
(f) Enthusiastic	(m) Outraged	(t) Whole
(g) Happy	(n) Peaceful	

You'll find comments on your answers below.

Question	Your Answer	Comments
1	(a),(b),(e), or (f)	You have probably developed one or more ways of relaxing in the evening. This usually helps you sleep well.
	(c)	If you don't sleep well, it is important to realize that your body needs to shut off the input from your brain. If your organizing is obsessive, it may reflect a tendency to engage in exaggerated ruminating as well.

Question	Your Answer	Comments
	(d)	You should probably have relaxation training to help you eliminate a constant source of arousal, your own thoughts.
2	(a) or (b)	You are fairly average.
	(d) or (e)	Do you awaken because of a physical problem such as postural pain, muscle spasm, shortness of breath, or need for urination? If so, consider consulting your family physician about this problem.
	(c)	Your thoughts may be keeping you overaroused. People who have trouble falling asleep often wake up thinking about work, school, finances, or other problems and cannot get back to sleep. This interference with the proper sleep cycle can lead to an abnormal level of general fatigue and can make you less able to cope with actual stress situations during the day.
3	(a) or (c)	Continue to Question 4.
	(b)	Consider two possible explanations: First, you may be taking on these demanding tasks without being properly

Question	Your Answer	Comments
		prepared (your energy levels are low because of the chronic stress from your own thoughts). Then, when your body has to perform at high-output levels, it "runs out of gas" and breaks down. The result is physical illness.
		Secondly, you may not see yourself in a very positive light, and these tasks give you an opportunity to reinforce this negative self-image. If you don't believe you can cope, then you probably won't. Instead, you will carry out a self-fulfilling prophecy. Because you think you are not capable of handling stress, you don't. Physical illness often allows us to fail gracefully. Of course, this may or may not apply to you. But if you answered (b), you should consider each possibility.
4	(b)	Go to Question 5.
	(a)	Psychologists and psychiatrists have identified a behavior pattern associated with depression. This is called the "SAWS diagnosis." Sex, Appetite, Weight, Sleep.

Question	Your Answer	Comments
		A person who shows marked decreases or disturbances in these four areas may be suffering from acute depression.
5	(a) or (d)	Go to Question 6.
	(c)	Many things can alter the frequency of your sexual behavior, including time of year and age. It is not unusual to experience fluctuations in your sexual behavior. As long as your interest level remains *fairly* constant, you should not be alarmed.
	(b)	If you have lost a significant amount of interest in sex and you are also getting less sleep, and your appetite and weight have decreased, you may be showing signs of depression.
6	(b) or (e)	You probably are not particularly "time-urgent," or at least you have a good perspective on how important your time is. Whether you picked (b) or (e) should depend upon your specific job situation. Remember, relaxation breaks often help you to be more productive generally.

Question	Your Answer	Comments
	(c)	Examine your reason. If the appointment was tentative, or made quite a few days in advance, this might be a reasonable thing to do. If, however, you are doing this just to emphasize your punctuality, you may be engaging in an irrational desire to impose your rules on the rest of the world.
	(a) or (d)	You have allowed this situation to upset your work routine and make you feel impatient and angry. You may also be allowing your body to overreact, just as if a true threatening event had occurred instead of a simple missed appointment. You feel under stress.
7	(a), (b), or (d)	"Should" and its first cousins "must" and "ought" do a lot to make you feel under stress, including the stress of impatience. Reality, however, may not let you impose your wishes on the rest of the world. You'll feel less under stress if you realize that rule-making like this tends to be both unrealistic and stress-producing.

Question	Your Answer	Comments
	(c), (e), or (f)	These are rather neutral thoughts simply designed to play mental "I-wonder" or "what-if" games. They keep you mentally engaged. However, excessive rumination may lead you into unproductive behavior and thought patterns.
	(g)	This seems a reasonable response—after all, you need not let this incident alter your routine dramatically.
8	(b), (e), or (f)	You are probably acting rationally, depending on what comment you make to the waiter.
	(c)	Open anger like this probably produces as much stress in you as in the waiter.
	(a) or (d)	Blaming yourself or bottling up your feelings completely may produce as much stress as yelling and screaming.
9	(a) through (e)	Encouraging this kind of thinking in yourself produces a lot of stress. The first two are aggressive, while (c) imposes an unreasonable rule, and (d) and (e) reflect a low level of self-esteem.

Question	Your Answer	Comments
	(f)	This is a rational thought that is likely to keep you out of a self-destructive cycle of unrealistic thoughts, stressful feelings, and unproductive behavior.
10	(c) or (e)	The more rule-bound and inflexible you are, the harder it is to avoid the stress of having to conform to your own rigid inner rules. These answers reflect rule-bound points of view.
	(a)	This attitude probably produces stress for you if it keeps you from getting along in groups.
	(b) or (d)	These seem the least stress-producing choices.
11	(a) or (b)	The first reflects a greater and the second a lesser degree of hopelessness and helplessness, feelings which can lead to depression. The key to alleviating stress is gaining control of yourself and your life.
	(c)	This is a healthy, resilient attitude.
12	(a)	This suggests an extreme and compulsive attitude to time, and may be generat- ing a lot of unnecessary

Question	Your Answer	Comments
		stress. Time-impatience and the need to "push" time aggressively may only result in your placing unrealistic demands on yourself.
	(b) and (c)	The first sounds like a realistic response to actual circumstances; the second is also unlikely to produce unnecessary stress.
13	(a), (c), (e), (i), (j), (l), (m), (q), (r), or (s)	These are emotional symptoms of stress. You need to decide what thoughts and/or behaviors are creating these feelings.
	(o)	A nonstressful response if it comes from a feeling of power (control) over your own life. Stressful if it means you are driven to hold sway over other people.
	(b), (d), (f), (g), (h), (k), (n), (p), or (t)	These are feelings you can achieve by becoming a more optimistic, self-confident person who copes well with stress.

Do You Have the High-Tension Habit?

Hot reactors to stress may be especially subject to anger, anxiety, or depression. Caroline Bedell Thomas, M.D., of the Johns Hopkins University School of Medicine, has identified the nervous habits associated with these three states of mind:

open anger, griping, and irritability; anxious feelings, general tension, difficulty sleeping, loss of appetite, tremulousness, and the urge to confide; and exhaustion, sad feelings, decreased activity, the urge to sleep, concern about one's health, and the urge to be alone. This last group is always a sign of depression, a malady that afflicts millions of Americans. (Since depression, like the symptoms of irritability and anxiety, can be a valuable and important warning signal for other disturbances, you should talk to your physician about getting special help for this problem if any of these symptoms lasts for some time.)

The other nine habits in Dr. Thomas's description of the twenty-five most common signs of nervous tension are also indicators of stress. These are the physical signs of *nausea, vomiting, diarrhea, constipation,* and *urinary frequency,* and the psychological reactions of *exhilaration, increased activity, compulsion to check and recheck work,* and *philosophic effort.*

If you look at these nervous symptoms and find that quite a few describe you, the chances are high that you have far too much stress in your life. Remember, *a habit never rests,* and in many cases these tension habits and your reaction to stress can become locked in a vicious cycle that leaves you continually angry, anxious, and depressed. But since habits and reactions are learned behaviors, you can also unlearn them.

Taking Your Stress Temperature

It is now time to measure your physical reactivity to stress in an area where it really counts—your blood pressure. You'll recall that in our Life Stress Simulation Laboratory we put people under psychological stress by asking them to do mental arithmetic and play a competitive video game. Our computer system measures whether that person is reacting more strongly to mental tasks than to physical ones, such as walking on the treadmill or plunging a hand into a bucket of ice water.

The treadmill test has decades of reliability as a predictor of potential coronary heart disease, depending on how it is used and with what kinds of patients. We have found both the treadmill and cold pressor (ice-water) tests to be useful in testing healthy people. If during the cold pressor test a patient's blood pressure goes up beyond 164/106 mm Hg, we know that the patient is paying a high physiological price for a moderate physical demand.

What we are finding is that some people pay a much higher price for mental challenges than they do for physical ones. For example, during a simple video game like Atari's "Breakout," some people will run their blood pressures from 130/80 at rest to 220/130. This happens within minutes. In the real world, most of us confront mental, not physical challenges. We have evidence that people who overreact to mental challenges in the lab are overreacting to a similar degree in real life.

Most people whose blood pressure jumps from 130/80 to 220/130 while playing a video game have *absolutely no awareness of what is happening to them.* Approximately one out of five Americans overreacts physiologically to psychological stress, and it is this *unsuspected* overreactivity that puts our hearts at the mercy of stress.

You can find out if you are a hot reactor simply by taking your blood pressure at rest and then under mild stress. To do this, you must accurately take your own blood pressure. It's not difficult. As part of the fitness revolution, blood pressure kits are readily available. Most drugstores and medical supply houses sell them or can direct you to a supplier. The devices are common enough to rate a recent evaluation in *Consumer Reports*, and the instructions are easy to follow. The important thing is to get a reliable kit. You can buy a blood pressure cuff and a stethoscope for about $35. For optimal ease and reliability, I recommend an electronic kit or a digital readout kit. They are more expensive, retailing for $60–175, but they are a valuable investment in your health. With this type of kit, testing is a matter of three easy steps: attach the pressure cuff, pump the bulb, and the machine will tell you the readings you need.

If you have heart trouble or any concern about your heart's ability to tolerate any type of stress testing, check with your physician before taking these tests. And if during the testing you develop symptoms of any kind (chest pains, palpitations, lightheadedness, or other symptoms), stop immediately and check with your physician.

For the following tests, you will start by measuring your *resting* blood pressure. For about ten minutes, do whatever relaxes you most. Dim the lights and listen to soothing music. Or close your eyes and imagine you are digging your toes into the white sand of a Caribbean beach. Or close your eyes and breathe deeply with your abdomen. Then, take your blood pressure, wait a few minutes, and take it again. The first set of readings tends not to be a reliable measurement, so use the second set as your resting blood pressure. Do not talk while taking your blood pressure, or you will get falsely high readings.

Here are three tests adapted from our lab that you can try. When we do these procedures in the lab, we take blood pressure during the test. You can do this too if a friend is available to take your blood pressure. Otherwise, take readings yourself immediately *after* each test. They will be somewhat lower than they would be in the lab, but they will still give you a good idea of how you react to the tests.

The Cold Pressor Test

This test requires only a blood pressure cuff and a basin or bucket of ice water. First, measure your resting blood pressure. Next, place your hand up to the wrist in the water for 70 seconds. For valid results, approach the test in a gentle and nonchallenging fashion. Give yourself an instruction that goes like this: "I'm going to put my hand into this ice water and hold it there for the next 70 seconds. I know that the water will be extremely cold, but it's important that my hand remain there for the full 70 seconds. If it becomes too uncomfortable, though, I'll remove my hand before the 70 seconds are up."

When you are finished with the cold pressor test, immediately record your systolic and diastolic pressure. Remember: "Normal" is around 120/80, while borderline high blood pressure begins at 140/90.

The Mental Arithmetic Test

First, measure your resting blood pressure. Next, give yourself these instructions: "I am going to subtract mentally by sevens continuously, starting with the number 777. It is important to do this as accurately and rapidly as possible. I have three minutes. I will begin immediately." (Use a timer, if possible.)

When the three minutes are up, immediately take your blood pressure.

We use both the cold pressor and mental arithmetic tests because they give us different information about blood pressure. The cold pressor tends to make blood vessels constrict, increasing the resistance to blood flow. The mental arithmetic tends to make the heart pump harder. Both effects of stress can raise blood pressure—the cold pressor by putting on the brakes and the mental arithmetic by revving up the engine in the cardiovascular system.

Video Games

If you have a video game computer, you can test yourself on that as well (we use Atari's "Breakout" in the lab). Do this test with a home-TV set. Simply measure your resting blood pressure, then play the video game for three to five minutes, and then immediately check your blood pressure again. (Like mental arithmetic, video games tend to make the heart pump harder.)

Daily Life Stress Test

Finally, you can test how you react to the actual stress in your daily life. First, you'll want to take your resting blood pressure (at several different times, if possible, to verify the readings). Then you'll need to be prepared to check your blood pressure immediately after a stressful event in your daily life. You are the best judge of what stresses you. Pick a time when you have had a worrisome phone conversation or an argument with your spouse or your boss (take your blood pressure kit to work too). Maybe you get upset after getting traffic tickets or after a prolonged wait for someone who fails to show up, or any time you can't get something you really want. The provocation doesn't matter as long as you choose an occasion when you are truly upset. That is the time to take and record your daily life stress blood pressure.

Interpreting Your Scores

Blood pressure reactions to stress range along a continuum. There is no one point where cold reacting stops and hot reacting starts; instead, there are infinite shadings between cold, cool, warm, and hot reacting. The problem builds as you move further toward the hot end of the continuum.

Measuring how hot a reactor you are works the same way as the continuum of resting blood pressure. Your resting blood pressure may fall within a wide range and still be considered normal, but there is a gray zone toward the high end of the continuum where a physician's concern begins to build. Your doctor will probably begin to worry about your blood pressure at a reading of 140/90. At that point you have crossed into a gray zone of high blood pressure.

The hot reacting diagnosis is arrived at by the same reasoning; that is, at a certain point you cross over into the gray zone where hot reacting begins. The further the readings go beyond that point, the hotter your reactions are and the greater the probable cause for concern. We believe that the hotter you are the more important it is that you begin to do something for yourself under your doctor's guidance.

We have identified points where gray zones of concern begin for the hot reacting tests in this chapter. If your *systolic* blood pressure rises to about 160 mm Hg on the mental arithmetic, video game, cold pressor, or daily life stress test, you are probably living in the hot reactor zone. If your *diastolic* blood pressure increases to 95 mm Hg after the mental arithmetic, video game, or daily life stress test or to 105 mm Hg after the cold pressor test, you are also likely to be a hot reactor, and you should see a physician. Most people whose diastolic pressure reacts this way are middle-aged hypertensives who may already be taking medication. If your diastolic pressure rises to 90 mm Hg or more, you may want to check again periodically to see if you go higher at a later time.

Two quick caveats about these tests for hot reacting:

First, you must take accurate readings, during or *immediately* after the test, to make the exercise useful.

Secondly, you should take the readings over a period of two weeks and then average the results. Just as you cannot judge your golf game on the basis of one or two shots, you cannot judge your stress level on the basis of one or two readings.

If you take the time to accurately record your blood pressure when you are truly at rest and truly under stress, you will have an invaluable thermometer that shows whether you are hot reacting to stress, including the everyday stress that you actually experience in your own life. You will know your stress temperature and can learn how to keep it cool.

Stress: What You Can Do about It

Now that you know more about how stress is working in your own life, you are ready to plan your strategy for living with it creatively.

If you are among the many people who suffer from too much stress, you know what it's like to feel out of control, with a decreasing sense of who you are and what you have to offer. People in this spot try to make up for their perceived loss of identity and self-esteem by struggling for some form of control. Many paths seem to lead toward that goal, but some are really detours, and others are dead ends. The key to making a friend of stress is knowing *how* to gain that sense of control. And the first step is recognizing the difference between rigid or artificial control and truly taking your life into your own hands.

When you feel in control, stress becomes the spice of life, a challenge instead of a threat. You aren't worried about being pushed off balance—you know you'll land on your feet.

More than that, you know you can work with whatever comes and create some good from it. And you can do that because you are in charge of your health, your feelings, and your behavior.

Taking responsibility for how you feel and what you do brings a sense of self-mastery that puts you in charge of stress. Paradoxically, this sense of personal mastery often comes not from an effort of will but from letting go. When you let go of trying to control an inflexible environment and all the people in it—when you realize that your feelings, behavior, sense of self-worth, and identity do not depend continually on outside influences—you stop struggling with fantasy and the pain of unrealistic expectations. You let go of stress.

The rest of this book is designed to help you find in yourself the means to enjoy your life. You will learn how to control your responses to stress and how to strengthen your sense of self-direction in four areas of your life: your feelings, your body, your work, and your relations with others.

Keep in mind that these areas overlap. That is why stress has such important consequences: it touches so many aspects of life. That is also why no single technique for managing health or stress is sufficient. You need to choose, from many possible approaches, the ones that fit your own lifestyle, behavior, and stresses—not those of your next-door neighbor, or even your identical twin.

Some ways of approaching stress are basic for everyone: talking to yourself constructively; clarifying your values; understanding that your mind and body are powerfully affecting each other; connecting with other people; putting balance into your life; above all, recognizing your own role in what happens in your life. Then there are the many applications of these techniques to your own situation. Only you can choose the ones that work for you. So custom-tailor your stress-management program to your personal needs.

Make stress your friend and you will be productive without being self-destructive. Here's how to begin.

Part Two:

Learning to Manage Stress

6
Changing Your Self-Talks

Much of our stress is due to conversations we have with ourselves. Psychologists call the thoughts that are always running through our minds "self-talks." Unfortunately, we often talk ourselves into the ground. Our mental tapes are always running, and if they are programmed with negative messages, they become a prime cause of stress.

Some self-talks are merely distractions—for instance, as you read this chapter, you may be wondering if you can finish it before dinner, or whether your spouse will be home by the time the TV movie starts, or why that dog is barking across the street. Other self-talks are more useful and constructive, as when you think about your day and organize your priorities, or praise yourself for a job well done.

But there are also plenty of harmful self-talks, and some of us use them to run ourselves down all the time, or to create stress for ourselves without knowing it. Negative self-talks come in many different forms—attitudes, beliefs, evaluations, expectations, interpretations, or predictions—but they all tend to make us feel badly and act ineffectively. Some common examples:

—"Who does he think he is, telling me what to do?"

—"Oh no, I'm going to be late—can't this traffic move any faster?"

—"I can't tell her what I think—she'd just get angry and do something terrible."

You get the idea.

A great many people—Type B as well as Type A—devote an extraordinary amount of attention and energy to useless, unproductive self-talks. Often these messages impose unreasonably high standards on both the world and the self. Even more often, they convey the message, "I have no control over my life, my feelings, or my behavior—other people and other things control me." The result: feelings become heated up and exaggerated; energy that could be used elsewhere gets tied up in self-talks that make life seem hopelessly out of control; and behavior becomes counterproductive and self-defeating as stress carries the day.

I often say that stress contributes to diseases of choice, not chance. At our clinic, we believe that you can choose how stress will affect you. Replacing certain negative and irrational self-talks with more constructive, helpful ones lets you cultivate a "thick-skinned" reaction to stress. People who respond in thick-skinned ways pay the minimum psychological and physical price for stress.

Thin-skinned people are easily upset. They're at the mercy of everything and everybody who comes along; worse, they perceive themselves as being unable to change this situation. They're like china dolls—when hit with a hammer, they break. Thick-skinned people, on the other hand, are like rubber dolls—when stress comes along, they bounce back. But being thick-skinned in this case doesn't mean being insensitive—in fact, thick-skinned people can afford to be more open with others because they are not preoccupied with defending themselves from emotional hammer blows.

There's even clinical evidence that thick-skinned people whose self-talks are positive live longer than thin-skinned pessimists. For example, a study of over 3,000 elderly Canadians by Yale researcher Jana Mossey showed that those who maintained optimistic attitudes about their health had a smaller risk of dying over a seven-year period than those whose attitudes were pessimistic, regardless of how doctors rated their health objectively.

In our clinic, patients learn to change their self-talks through "cognitive restructuring." This is a commonsense method of altering the way you think about problems so you can put them in realistic perspective. Developing more constructive self-talks helps you spend your energy on problem-solving instead of on needless worrying and unnecessary stress.

The ABCs of Emotional Habits

Emotional behavior is like any other behavior. If we practice it long enough, it becomes a habit. To a great extent, we are a product of our own emotional habits. This view of behavior is an axiom of Rational Emotive Therapy, a type of therapy that owes much to the work of Albert Ellis, Maxie Maultsby, Jr., and others. Its basic premise is that your emotions are largely determined by how you think and talk to yourself. In other words, *you—not something or someone outside you—play the most important role in determining what you feel.* Therefore, if you can gain control over destructive self-talks that have come to be habits, you will also gain control over the feelings of stress that follow from these self-talks.

To change your self-talks, you need first to be aware of how they work. Rational Emotive Therapy holds that thinking influences feeling in a step-by-step, A-B-C fashion:

"A": This is the *Activating Event* that commands our attention. It may be something external (smelling a flower; seeing an accident) or internal (becoming aware of a headache; remembering a forgotten appointment). For example, you are waiting for a friend to pick you up for dinner; suddenly you look at your watch and notice that your friend is fifteen minutes late. Now you move to the next stage of the sequence, which is

"B": the *Belief* you have about the meaning of the event, your interpretation of its meaning. This takes the form of a self-talk. Any number of self-talks about your friend's lateness are possible. The self-talk might be neutral ("That's okay; I don't have any other plans for this evening anyway") or even positive ("Good; I'll use the time to finish another chapter of this novel"). Or it might be an appropriately negative response based on a rational appraisal of reality ("He/she is usually late, and then we enjoy ourselves less because we end up rushing through dinner, but I knew that when I agreed to go out").

The problem arises when "B" takes the form of an irrational, negative self-talk. Like most self-talks, the ones that get in our way are often based on habit. Many people add needlessly to their own stress by interpreting events according to long-standing habitual beliefs they have carried with them all their lives—but which often have little to do with actual reality, and which may, in fact, be self-defeating and destructive. These *irrational self-talks*, which are rooted in feelings and attitudes that began in childhood, may seem to make perfect sense to the speaker. But when they keep that person from objectively evaluating the reality of a situation, they are likely to create unnecessary stress. In this case, self-talks like "It's rude to make someone wait"; "People should always be punctual"; "Lateness shows that a person doesn't care about how you feel" mean there's trouble ahead, in the form of

"C": the *Consequence* of "A" and "B." This is your response to the thoughts at "B," and it can take three forms—feelings, physical reactions, and behaviors. Depending on how you talked to yourself when you realized that your friend was late, your response might be stress-free (indifference, if the self-talk was neutral; cheerfulness, if it was positive). Or it might be somewhat stressful if the self-talk was appropriate and rational but negative (for instance, you might be slightly annoyed at the prospect of having to rush through dinner). But if you respond according to an irrational negative thought, watch out, because the result is very likely to be a great deal of unnecessary stress ("He's always late for everything—he doesn't care about my feelings at all. We'll have a miserable evening, and it's all his fault. I feel a headache coming on. Am I going to give him a piece of my mind!").

What makes matters worse is that often we become aware of the event or situation ("A") and react with a reflex feeling, physical symptom, or behavior ("C") without being truly conscious of the evaluative thought, or self-talk ("B"). Thus we have no opportunity to become aware of the irrational nature of certain negative self-talks, or even that they are going on, because they have been short-circuited by habit. To use a simple example, some people shudder with revulsion at the sight of a harmless garden spider without being aware of the evaluation ("B") that took place long ago when they learned that some spiders were poisonous and decided they wanted nothing to do with *any* spiders. "B" has been abbreviated and only "A" and "C" are left, with the result that they become upset at seeing any spider. Yet most people who are afraid of harmless spiders will tell you that their fear is a "natural" one.

In fact, there is nothing "natural" about anyone's emotional habits, except to the extent that it is "natural" to respond in a habitual fashion when you have always reacted that way in the past. If your emotional habits heat you up and cause you unnecessary, self-destructive stress (not to mention their influence on those around you), you would be wise to ignore the "naturalness" of old habits and learn new ones that are more useful to you. How to do this?

Start listening to your irrational self-talks.

Diane—a Self-Stress Superwoman

Diane was a middle-aged woman with stomach problems and a tendency to nervous headaches. After the second of her two children went off to college, she and her husband decided to get a divorce. Diane went to work as a receptionist in a large private medical clinic in her town. She enjoyed working in an office for the first time, and her obvious competence and perfectionism about details made her popular with the doctors there. Her boss, the director of the clinic, willingly promoted her to administrative assistant and office manager after only a few months. Another doctor began encouraging her to think about getting a graduate degree in health administration.

Yet despite the fact that she was making a good comeback from her divorce (which Diane regarded as "the worst failure that can happen to a woman"), her life was an ongoing battle with stress. "Things *always* upset me," she would say. "I was just devastated when Harold and I decided to separate."

The last person who had anything to say about her feelings, she seemed to think, was Diane. "Things" happened, and she felt helpless to control how strongly she felt about them or how long her "upset" would last. One of the "things" that had gone wrong in her marriage, in fact, was her refusal to allow any arguments about her opinions—she was afraid that if she felt too strongly about her point of view, her anger might get out of control, and she had no idea how long it might last.

Diane was convinced that her reaction to conflict and stress was inherited. "My mother was just like me," she would say with a sigh. "I guess it's genetic. I know I can't change the way I react to things."

Needless to say, Diane took these attitudes straight from her private life to the workplace. Although her abilities and an outgoing personality kept her on good terms with the doctors in the office, she felt continually discontented with the performance of people she had to work with. "I can't stand it," she would say, "when things aren't going right. If one of the nurses forgets to give me a patient's insurance form, or if we don't get the billing out on time, I get a stomach-ache and can't sleep that night. I can't help it. It's just the way I am."

Diane's special nemesis was a nervous young nurse named Frieda who often forgot where she put things. "I like Frieda," Diane would say, "but she's so irresponsible! Why can't she remember to put everything where it should go? She's been there as long as I have! If *I* were like her, the place would be a shambles." Diane felt that Frieda's forgetfulness was a danger to her own performance as office manager. Nevertheless, she hated herself whenever she gave Frieda a talking-to. "She drives me crazy, but I feel awful when I criticize her. The poor kid mopes around for the rest of the day, and I just know everyone thinks I'm an ogre. I can't seem to get along with people when I have to criticize them. Anyway, I'm sure everyone expects me to blow up, because they know that's one of my problems."

One day Diane's battle with job stress reached a crisis point when the nurse confessed that she had lost a patient's chart. Diane's temper snapped. In front of a patient and one of the doctors, she told Frieda sharply that she was "sick and tired of seeing things get mislaid around here." That afternoon, Diane's boss called her into his office and reprimanded her for scolding the nurse in public. He warned her that her intolerance was undermining office morale—and in this case, he pointed out, it had also put the office in a bad light in front of a patient.

Diane went home with stomach cramps. That evening, she called a friend. She was both outraged and shattered by her employer's criticisms. "I can't believe it," she fumed. "I just can't understand it! I'm only trying to do what I *should* do—it isn't fair." But her anger quickly gave way to self-reproach. "I feel horrible. I'm no good at relationships with other people. It's hopeless. Things will never get any better."

Diane is a classic example of how habitual destructive self-talks lead us down the thorny garden path of stress. While her negative, irrational self-talks alone may not have been responsible for all the stress, they eventually led to just the loss of control over her life that she feared—and to more unnecessary stress.

How did Diane's reactions after the discussion with her boss work against her? Let's go back to the three stages of an emotional event:

"A" (activating event): Her boss reprimands her for being tactless.

"B" (belief/self-talk): "I can't understand it—I'm only trying to do what I should do," followed by, "I'm a failure—it's hopeless—things will never get better."

"C" (consequence): Anger, stomach upset, an increased sense of loss of control—and more stress.

Obviously, Diane's reactions are a sure-fire guarantee that the stress in her life will, if anything, increase. When stress is excessive, we experience it as a loss of control. When we lose control, we feel under stress. The self-destructive cycle perpetuates itself.

Yet Diane did not have to respond as she did. The secret of effective stress management lies in realizing that each event acquires emotional significance through the particular meaning that each human being attaches to it. It is not the event, but how we view it, that determines our emotional and physiological responses. This means that if you rather than events or "things" are what's upsetting you, then you can learn *not* to upset yourself. You, not people or external "things," are in charge of your response.

The Ten Basic Irrational Self-Talks

In a practical stress-reduction workbook called *Becoming Thick-Skinned,* which he uses in his practice and in seminars conducted around the country, psychologist Hermann Witte of our medical team identifies ten basic irrational self-talks that he considers the most common factors in unnecessary stress. Some reflect basic misconceptions about our relationship to our own emotions; others trigger specific kinds of stress reactions. Recognizing these negative self-talks for the unhelpful, self-defeating, stress-producing thoughts they are is the first big step toward managing stress. By the same token, changing to more rational self-talks can put you in greater control of stress. Let's look at these negative self-talks—every one of which Diane uses regularly—and some possible antidotes in the form of "anti-stress self-talks."

1. *"Things upset me."* This self-talk represents a fundamental misconception about feelings. It implies that external events exclusively determine your emotional reactions. Even statements like "the fear of failure" or "the trauma of divorce" imply that the event automatically determines the feeling. If that were true, everyone would be a robot, a helpless pawn with no control over life. Yet Diane, far from being helpless,

made the decision—conscious or unconscious—that she was going to take charge of her life when she went to work and again when she decided to try to move up at her job. Her belief that she is the helpless victim of her feelings simply isn't true.

Anti-stress self-talk: "I *upset me.*" Only by accepting responsibility for your behavior can you begin to make changes that will help you feel better.

2. *"I have no control over the nature, intensity, and duration of my emotional responses."*

Another basic misconception. Responses to stress are not fixed. You can, in fact, temper the intensity of your reaction. This is especially true if you can anticipate a stressful experience and have a chance to talk to yourself about it. But even if it happens suddenly and you feel overwhelmed, you can still regain emotional balance by realistically reviewing the circumstances and holding constructive, rather than destructive, conversations with yourself.

On the other hand, controlling your response doesn't mean stifling it. It's important to experience emotional response, especially in reaction to a major event such as divorce, the loss of a job, or the loss of a loved one. Emotional reactions are part of a cycle of adaptation, a healing process, and they can motivate people to change and grow. People who cope well with stress and conflict do not cut off their (or others') feelings prematurely.

Neither do they get stuck in their distress. Diane's fear that "being upset" might last indefinitely is contradicted by common sense: we all know from experience that a response to the same event changes and is tempered by the passing of time.

Anti-stress self-talk: "I *may not be able to control getting upset, but I have significant control over the intensity and duration of my feelings.*"

3. *"My emotional and stress responses are inherited."*

Another misconception. You are not your parents; contrary

to Diane's belief, the resemblance of her way of handling stress to her mother's doesn't mean that it is fixed and unchangeable. As you grew from infancy to adulthood, your genetic makeup remained the same, but you made dramatic gains in controlling your emotions and dealing with frustration. So don't assume you're stuck because of your heredity. Stress is not an inherited response.

Anti-stress self-talk: *"My feelings and behaviors are learned, and if they're ineffective, they can be unlearned."*

4. *"I can't change the way I react."*

Another radical misconception. You *have* changed over the years, and you will continue to change. However, you will have more control over the process of change if you learn to talk to yourself realistically and constructively.

Anti-stress self-talk: *"I can change my emotional responses to stress through realistic, constructive self-talks."*

5. *"Things should and must go as I demand."*

If, like Diane, we make inflexible demands of ourselves as well as those around us, the results are hard on everyone. It's easy to imagine life in the office as Diane runs it: Deadlines are absolute. Choices are minimized. Judgment and self-judgment are everywhere. Anger and frustration—whether Diane's anger at her associates or theirs at her—accompany every demand that isn't met. Diane's expectations are a major source of unnecessary stress. The demands they imply come from two attitudes: perfectionism and the belief that human behavior is governed by rigid rules.

Perfectionists are hypersensitive to signs of imperfection. Most people gloss over them; perfectionists magnify them. Their demand for perfect functioning is really an attempt to suppress and compensate for the painful fear that they will fail in some way and attract criticism that "proves" they are inadequate. The more fearful they are, the more demanding they are that everything be done exactly right.

Perfectionists especially tend to believe they get upset because "things" go wrong. Like Diane, they do not realize that they upset themselves by their own habitual responses to the stresses of life. Instead, they think that the only way to be free of distress is to "make things" go right. Their vigilant watchfulness for any signs that they or others do not measure up leads to anxiety, tension, and muscular and psychological rigidity. "Things" usually go worse, not better.

The belief that human behavior must be governed by rigid rules—"shoulds" and "musts"—also produces and then escalates anger. "Shoulds" are a great producer of stress in oneself and in others. In Diane's running battle with Frieda, her view that Frieda was violating some universal moral rule ("She's so irresponsible! Why can't she remember to put everything in its place?") made the problem worse instead of solving it. And Diane's explosion at Frieda, who was not living up to Diane's "shoulds," produced nothing but more anger—in Frieda, in the doctor who reported Diane's behavior, in Diane's boss, and ultimately in Diane herself.

When we use the word "should," we are often demanding that reality be different than it is—"He *should* have been here ten minutes ago"; "You *should* have known better than to do it that way." Focusing attention and energy on the past will not get on with resolving the issue in the present. Denying reality is futile and only gets you mired down in distress. And the use of the self-righteous "should," while it may fill the speaker with satisfying anger, will probably also result in the listener becoming angry and self-defensive. Expending energy on pointless reproaches is far less useful than expressing irritation and disappointment in a way that leaves the door open for communication and change: "I wanted you here ten minutes ago"; "I wish you had done it differently."

Nor is there any reason to be less forbearing with ourselves than with others. We may not like the reality of a situation, but instead of using our energy to righteously deny it, creating anger and guilt in ourselves, we can use that energy creatively to influence change. Or, if change is not possible, to get on with something else. Where is it written, after all, that things have to go a certain way and no other?

Anti-stress self-talk: *"It would be great if things go the way I want, but I am prepared to deal with whatever happens."*

6. *"I can't believe it. I don't understand it."*

Diane may feel that she is being unfairly criticized by her boss, but telling herself that an upsetting situation has neither rhyme nor reason is just a way of getting stuck in her distress. If she doesn't give herself a chance to understand the problem, how can she deal with it? Insisting in her self-talks that she cannot figure things out plunges her into feeling more out of control, and escalates stress. A more constructive approach would be to acknowledge that there must be a reason—in this case, her boss's fear that her behavior is undermining morale and putting his clinic in a bad light.

If Diane would stop to analyze her boss's reasons for the reprimand, she could try to determine for herself the extent to which his fears were really justified. She might even be able to discuss the matter with him and develop appropriate strategies for change. This would do much to alleviate the cause of her unnecessary job stress.

Of course, sometimes there seems to be no explanation for someone else's behavior. There are a certain number of people around who invariably behave in ways we don't like and apparently without any reason. In this case, try the "brain tumor" analogy—a frequently humorous way of helping you see someone else's aggravating behavior in a new light.

Consider Diane and Frieda. Diane could say to herself, "Poor Frieda has an unusual kind of brain tumor that makes her put everything in the wrong place. She just can't help it!" Then she could get a chuckle out of a situation that she always took to be deadly serious, and that would relieve some tension for both of them. And she could go on to ask herself what else besides a brain tumor could have the same effect— what impulses might Frieda have that she felt no control over and that would produce this behavior? That would be the beginning of understanding what was really going on.

The brain tumor analogy alerts you to the thought that

some people are in the grip of impulses they feel no control over, and that's their problem, not yours. You may be able to help them figure out what's going on and change the situation, or you may decide just to make allowances, let it roll off your back, and get on with your life. Either way, when you realize it's one of those "brain tumor" situations, you're out of the trap of feeling helpless because you don't understand.

Anti-stress self-talk: *"I can understand my sources of stress if I put my mind to it."*

7. *"It's horrible. I can't stand it."*

This is what we call "horribilizing." Because the words are emotionally loaded, they heat Diane up and keep her stuck at the point of reacting, instead of moving on to solve the problem. If you exaggerate your feelings by horribilizing, you will get stuck in stress. Instead, describe the situation realistically and moderately, with more neutral words like "unfortunate," "sad," "painful," "uncomfortable," or "embarrassing." This defuses your reaction without preventing you from experiencing it.

Anti-stress self-talk: *"Things are never as bad as I can make them seem."*

8. *"My shortcomings make me a bad person; a loser; a failure."*

Diane is engaging here in another form of horribilizing. We all have shortcomings and are fallible, yet some of us manage to be basically satisfied with ourselves and to function well, while others whose imperfections are no worse become immobilized by their "failures." Instead of concentrating on the effects of a particular behavior, try thinking of your behavior as part of a mosaic. Each thing you do is one piece of an extremely complex design—you. You can behave in ways that reflect shortcomings but you can nevertheless be liked, respected, and loved despite your mistakes. Instead of deprecating yourself, concentrate on changing that particular piece of behavior in the future. And remember: your worth isn't at stake every time you make a move.

Anti-stress self-talk: *"I can accept what I am even if I have shortcomings in certain situations."*

9. *"Others think as little of me as I do of myself."*

Diane's belief that others constantly talk about her short-comings and the implication that they will always see her as she sees herself ("no good at relationships"; "hard to get along with") easily becomes a self-fulfilling prophecy. When she assumes that everyone thinks as poorly of her as she does, she then acts accordingly. The more we think nega-tively of ourselves, the more we assume that others think the same of us. But in fact, other people spend very little time thinking about us at all; most of the time they are thinking about themselves! Other people will almost always take us at our own value. If Diane can learn to stop horribilizing and start thinking of herself as someone others *can* get along with, she will probably start presenting herself that way.

Anti-stress self-talk: *"Others will accept me as I present myself—and I can present myself in the best possible light."*

10. *"It's hopeless. Things will never get any better."*

This is, in many ways, the worst of the irrational self-talks because it eliminates hope—the possibility that things (in-cluding feelings) can get better in the future. It also enables stress to do its greatest psychological and physiological damage. A feeling of hopelessness is the common thread that runs through the fabric of lives burdened by stress.

Yet things not only can, but very likely will, get better. As you know, you may be fatigued today or have the flu, but rest will help and you will feel refreshed after a time. You may be out of a job this month but working again in a month or a year. You may even have lost a husband or wife, but you can survive to love again. And even if your situation doesn't change, *you* can change so that you can live with it better. You don't have to make today's problem into a lifelong straitjacket. The simple passage of time really does make a difference. Things do get better.

Anti-stress self-talk: *"There is always hope, because in the long run things will look different—especially if I can learn how to cope better with them."*

Diane's exaggerated response to events might have perpetuated her stress indefinitely and gone on burdening her life and her health as well. Fortunately, she had a sympathetic boss who was able to persuade her to seek counseling. Diane began trying to change her ways of thinking and reacting to the normal stresses of office life. Gradually, she learned to recognize more easily when she was responding with an irrational attitude and unnecessarily stress-producing feelings and behavior. Slowly, she began to gain a sense of confidence in her ability to take control of stress.

She learned how to devise more constructive self-talks, which she used to replace her former self-destructive or ineffective ones. For example, in her mind the old phrase, "I was devastated by my divorce" eventually became, "I still have painful feelings about my divorce, but I am learning that I can put that event behind me more now and get on with my life in the present." If the billing doesn't get finished by the end of the month, or a chart is mislaid, she has learned to stop herself from demanding to know "why people are so irresponsible" (or make her look inadequate) and asks instead, "How can I solve the immediate problem and avoid its happening in the future?" And when an associate voices criticism, she tries to say to herself, "I can understand why he wants to tell me about this," or "I can show that I'm as good at giving her a fair hearing as anyone else in this office." The results are a far less stressful work climate for Diane and her associates, and a more confident, healthier woman who feels more in control of her life.

Changing your self-talks is a major step in the process of changing the old, stressful mental habits and becoming "thick-skinned." Like Diane, everyone has an individual version of the self-talks outlined above. I'm sure you've recognized at least a few of your own already. This is your first step: to gain *intellectual insight* and identify your own irrational self-talks. Then you can replace them with one or more anti-stress self-talks of your own.

The following chart contrasts the consequences of stress-producing self-talks and anti-stress self-talks.

A. Event
(work deadline; need for money; quarrel with spouse or associate, etc.)

B. Self-Talk

C. Consequence (poor, or "thin-skinned" coping)	C. Consequence (healthy, or "thick-skinned," coping)
• Rumination and worry	• Short-term preoccupation with problem; occasional reconsideration
• Shame, humiliation	• Embarrassment; uncomfortableness
• Hatred	• Dislike
• Feelings of inferiority, inadequacy, failure, worthlessness	• Disappointment with the way(s) I behaved or appeared to others
• Anxiety and panic	• Apprehension, nervous anticipation
• Outrage; hostility; aggression	• Disappointment; displeasure; frustration
• Depression	• Sadness
• Exhaustion—leaden heaviness, fatigue, feeling that everything is simply too much to deal with	• Feeling out-of-sorts; indisposition, tiredness; weariness

Intellectual insight, however, only leads to changes in behavior when you *practice*. It's like playing golf or tennis. The lesson only lasts an hour, yet you must hit thousands of balls for hundreds of hours if you are to achieve the "muscle memory" needed to play a good game. Controlling your emotional responses to everyday stress is the same. You need to learn to do it consistently, by practicing new thoughts.

Initially you may notice that you are practicing your new anti-stress self-talks but are still bogged down in old feelings. Stick it out. Habits die hard, and for a while your habitual responses will resist the new way of thinking. But if you persist, you will overcome this resistance.

The key to getting through this "dissonance stage" is simply to continue thinking your new self-talks. *Act as if you believe what you're thinking and ignore the old feelings.* If you practice your new thinking, responses, and "acting-as-if" long enough, your new thoughts will come to feel right and natural. You'll have learned a *healthy* reflex response to normal stress, and you'll no longer squander your emotional energy on overreacting to minor stress. Instead of spending a dollar's worth of energy on a ten-cent problem, you can now give major and minor problems the amount of energy each is worth. In doing so, you'll become like a good athlete, for whom economy of motion and energy is the mark of mature development. And you'll have energy left over to discover the things you really value in life.

7
Clarifying Your Values

Sorting out the things you really care about helps make a good match between you and your environment. When you know what you want, what you can do, and what your environment offers, you can be realistic about your expectations and your decisions for the future. Realistic understanding of your own feelings helps you live creatively with stress.

The Tombstone Test

I am so convinced that clarifying values is essential to managing stress that I make it part of my treatment plan. I start with the "tombstone test." I often ask patients, "What would you like to have written on your tombstone? How would you like to be remembered?"

This question has a way of crystallizing personal values. The answers of my patients often reflect, in their own words about their own lives, an idea that the late Hans Selye called "altruistic egoism." Most people want to feel that what they do in life has value for others. They want the personal reward of knowing they make a difference. For many, religion is a source of beliefs and values that can help in answering this question. The important thing is to answer it for yourself.

You begin to gain peace of mind when you clarify your values and talents in order to gain balance and perspective in your life. You need to find, in the French phrase, your *"raison* d'être," your reason for being. And you need to think about it periodically, because your *raison d'être* changes with time. Clarifying abilities, goals, needs, and values is a lifelong process.

One of my patients, Jeanne, was very moved by a film on prehistoric life called *Quest for Fire*. (In prehistoric times, of course, fire was a matter of life and death, since it meant food, warmth, and survival.)

"I never realized it before," Jeanne said, "but my work is my fire. Without it, I would never have discovered who I am, what I can do, and what I want to do. Without it, my life would be very cold."

Jeanne is a former teacher and the wife of a politician. In the first years of their marriage, she was her husband's "silent partner," always there to fulfill the public image of the happily married couple and to work hard for him behind the scenes. But though she knew she was important for her husband's success and that he valued her contribution, she was restless about her own lack of direction. She felt she was gradually losing a sense of her own identity as she became more and more dependent upon her husband and his world for money, stimulation, and approval.

Finally, she decided to take a big risk by opening a business of her own. Her social and teaching skills and outgoing personality enabled Jeanne to create a new career as the owner of an innovative children's book and toy store. As the operator of a new small business, she experienced some conflicts between her family and business roles, but she says she would never turn back.

"I figured out," she told me, "that what I was doing before had real rewards, but it's also very important to me to feel in charge, to take risks myself, to make decisions that really make a difference for my future. Starting the store gave me the chance to do that."

Jeanne took a hard look at her life, decided what she really wanted to do, and followed through. It was a process that required introspection, careful assessment of benefits and risks, commitment, and persistence. That's a lot of effort, but it helped Jeanne make some moves that were important for her happiness. Without them she would have felt increasingly under chronic stress.

Clarifying Values: Do-It-Yourself Tests

To help you in this process, here are some self-tests that give you a chance to reflect on what you want to do and what you actually do in your everyday life. The object here is to help you crystallize your goals and priorities, judge where you stand now in relation to them, and develop concrete plans to move toward the goals that are really important to you.

The Checkbook Test

Get out your checkbook and make a list of where you have chosen to spend your money in the past twelve months. You may be surprised. Some expenses are fixed—rent, mortgage, tuition—but take a close look at how you spend your discretionary income.

One man I know is concerned with how he will live in his old age, yet he never saves. Instead, he has a closet of new clothes. Another loves travel, restaurants, and theater, yet found that his wife was committing most of their money to buying antiques and wallpapering the bedrooms. There was never enough money for that trip to London or that special restaurant. After carefully recording how their money was being spent and discussing it together, they worked out a way to afford a vacation. Many people never find the money to buy what they really want because they spend it on things they want less. Concentrating on short-term rewards may keep you from reaching your major goals. So put your money where your values really are, and balance your short-term and long-term goals.

The Time Test

If you make a list of all the things you do in a normal month, plus what you do on special occasions or seasonally, you may be surprised again. The activities you give your time to might be your job, spouse or lover, or children. It might be your friends, community activities, finances, travel, education, recreation, health, retirement, home maintenance, fitness, personal appearance, personal reflection, sports, reading, commuting—whatever. In drawing up such a list, you might make some interesting discoveries about your use of time.

One patient made a list like this and discovered that commuting three hours a day on a crowded train to a city job was eating up years of his life that he would really rather spend differently. Whereas another person might have used this time to read the newspaper, prepare the day's agenda, or write a novel, this man found he couldn't develop much concentration on the train, and he hated sitting for that long. He decided to take charge of the situation and requested a transfer to a suburban division of his company. Making the list helped him realize that an activity he assumed was necessary had nothing to do with what he really wanted from life—and that he could change this.

The "Six-Months-to-Live" Test

Suppose you only had six months to live. What would you choose to do, and not do, in that time? It helps to group the activities you have been doing into three categories: (1) The things you have to do, (2) the things you like to do, and (3) the things you neither have to do nor like to do. Now, cross out Category 3—all the things you would neither have to do nor like to do if you had only six months to live.

For the rest of your life, try to forget about all those activities in Category 3. They are probably preventing you from doing what you want to do. You don't have forever, and there are only so many things in each day that deserve to get done.

Give yourself a break. First, do the things you feel you have to do. Then, spend the rest of the day doing what you want to do. Forget about the rest. You'll never miss it. What if the things you have to do take up the entire day? You're kidding yourself. Nobody has to be that busy. You can say "No" to the demands of your work and what others would like you to do for them. You not only need time for yourself, but time to do nothing. Nothing, that is, except stoke your fire.

Now take a hard look at the things you have listed under "have to do" and "like to do" and compare them with the list of things you have recorded on the checkbook test. Do they match up?

The Pride Test

What personal accomplishments give you the most pride?

Can the life you are living today provide more accomplishments like these?

The Change Test

What have you done in the past that you wish you could change?

Will the life you are living today ensure that those types of disappointment will never happen to you again?

The Adjective Test

What three qualities would you most like to see associated with your reputation? (In answering this question, it may help to ask yourself whom you admire most.)

Is the life you are living today distinguished by those qualities?

Great Expectations May Create Great Problems

Expectations are fragile things. They have to be high enough to keep you stimulated without being so high that attainment is impossible. It's hard for some stress-prone people to set ordinary, reachable goals—shooting for the moon is so much more exciting. Craving stimulation, they prefer to live their lives on a roller-coaster. But if you set impossible goals, you are sure to lose control of your life and retreat to surrogate pleasures like booze and fantasy.

Instead, lower your sights a little and raise your possibility of success. The "impossible dream" makes great theater, but in real life it often sets up a formula for stress and depression.

One of my patients, a liberal arts major, was a writer with

high literary ambitions. Secretly, he wanted to be a "cultural hero" to his generation, a modern Hemingway. Psychologists call this programming yourself for failure; a Hemingway only comes along once in a generation. After counseling, Alan finally decided to try using his writing talents in the service of an arts organization, and eventually he became public relations director of a major corporation, where his influence contributed to the company's support of the arts. Along the way, Alan discovered that he preferred making an art of living to pursuing his fantasy of living only for art. He transformed his fantasy into a way of life that he could succeed at and feel happy with.

Write down the five major sources of stress in your life that come from not getting what you expect out of life, and from not being what you expect yourself to be. Which of these sources are within your power to control and change? Which are not?

For those sources of stress that you can neither change nor control, keep in mind the advice in a well-known prayer adopted by Alcoholics Anonymous for just these circumstances:

"God, grant me the courage to change the things I can, the serenity to accept the things I cannot change, and the wisdom to know the difference."

For those sources of stress that you can change, make a list of exactly what you would like the changes to be and how you plan to go about making them happen. Draw up a timetable for the next day, the next month, the next year. And don't stop there. Where would you like to be five years from now? Ten? Even twenty? As you work toward your immediate goals, keep your eyes on the horizon as well. Make long-term plans and revise them regularly.

Taking Control of Your Environment

Write down the five major sources of stress that are related to your work, home, city, and other factors in your environment that determine your daily activities and movements. Which of these are within your power to control and change? Which are not?

For those situations you can neither change nor control, learn to yield gracefully and spend your energy elsewhere. For those stresses in your environment that you can change, make a list of exactly what you would like the changes to be and how you plan to go about making them happen. Draw up a timetable for action.

Maybe you would like permission to leave work early on a regular basis to be with your children when they come home from school. You might ask your boss if he or she will allow this in return for your starting work earlier. Do you travel too much on your job? Maybe your boss has been thinking for months that it would be better to get you off the road and back into the office where you can supervise others. You'll never know if you don't ask. Life is a big enough guessing game as it is; it helps to eliminate uncertainty where you can.

Here are some tips that will help you clarify your values and start to develop in new directions.

- Follow your feelings. If you are dissatisfied or want to improve your situation, recognizing that is the first step toward understanding what you do want and moving toward a new goal.
- Visualize the future. Dream a little; see yourself where you would like to be (but don't make it an impossible dream). Think about what you would like to have written on your tombstone. Define attainable goals, the kind that are achievable and realistic but still require you to stretch. As the poet Robert Browning said, "A man's reach should exceed his grasp." But be practical enough that you can take hold of something.
- Concentrate on the few key areas that are most important to you. Don't undermine your efforts by trying to be all things to all people at all times.
- Research what you want and what you have to offer. No one knows better than you what you do best. Take the next step and figure out what you will have to know to make your dream come true. Design your personal "research and development" plan.

- Look back to where you have been and figure out your strengths and weaknesses in various situations.
- Use your time wisely. Make a thorough study of how you spend your time and ruthlessly eliminate the things that you need not be doing. Remember, though, time spent doing "nothing" is often time well spent.
- Learn how to delegate. Consider the value of this motto: "Much can be accomplished if you don't care who gets the credit."
- Simplify, simplify, simplify. Thoreau said it, and it's probably even truer now than it was in his time that our lives are too often mired in detail. Less really *is* more.
- Be consistent in your behavior. People don't know how to relate to someone who is inconsistent. The more you know who you are and what you want and act accordingly, the more you promote trust and consistency in others.
- Take time to plan. Set aside one week a year to assess where you've been, where you'd like to go, and how you're going to get there.

  Understanding and planning are crucial in clarifying your values, assessing how you spend your money, time, and energies, and coming to grips with your expectations and environment.

It is a great burden trying to live out a script that someone else has written for you. The people who seem to be "luckiest" make the most of their opportunities because they know what they want, have thought about how to get it, and find ways to stick with the plans they develop. Realistically identifying and pursuing rewards that are meaningful to you is the first step in making your expectations and environment match. When you do that, you reduce inner conflict and begin to make stress work for you.

8
Relaxing Your Body

It's hard to be angry when you're smiling or to feel tense when you bow. These movements relax your muscles and uncouple anger from your body. When your body relaxes, your emotions follow suit. That's why smiling and bowing is such a pleasant custom in Japan. It's a beautiful form of body language that shows people you're relaxed and enjoying their company. When you're tensed up, you're sending the message, "I wish I weren't here." That's the type of body language the dentist gets all the time.

Relaxing your body sends a message to you as well as others. It tells you you're not in the grip of stress; you're in control, and you can determine how your body will respond. You can choose to use up less energy and feel less tense in responding to stress. You can even control your blood pressure by learning and regularly using relaxation techniques.

Is Relaxation Therapy for You?

The people who need relaxation therapy the most are, ironically, the very people who resist it the most—those who try to hold on to what control they feel they already have. Thinking that relaxation means loss of control is a mistake. Relaxation therapy does not mean making your mind blank; rather, it actually focuses your mind to rid your body of tension.

Ask yourself the following questions:

How many times a day do you use the words "should," "ought," and "must"? Do all your shirts have to be lined up just so in the closet? If you had to write a report and a friend said, "It's a beautiful day, let's go for a walk," would you allow yourself to go for a walk, or would you refuse to break your rule that "work comes first"? If you are inclined to be rigid in your behavior, you will probably benefit from relaxation therapy.

Relaxation Self-Assessment Test

To gauge your need for relaxation training, answer each of the following questions with one of these responses:

(a) Yes, frequently.
(b) Yes, sometimes.
(c) Occasionally.
(d) No, not very often.
(e) No, never.

Have you ever suffered from, or are you currently suffering from:

(1) *Insomnia* (the inability to fall asleep at night).
(2) *Breakthrough insomnia* (awakening in the middle of the night, with trouble getting back to sleep).
(3) *Headaches that begin at the back of your neck and work up over the scalp.*
(4) *Headaches that feel as if there is a throbbing pain on one side of your head.*
(5) *Upset stomach* (including constipation, cramps, diarrhea, feelings of nausea, or sharp pains).
(6) *Hypertension* (high blood pressure) or *angina* (chest pains from heart trouble).
(7) *Fatigue* without physical exertion.
(8) *Lack of concentration,* or the inability to focus on what you are doing.

(9) *Anxiety, tension, and feeling upset without apparent reason.*
(10) *Anxiety, tension, and feeling upset after you think you should have recovered* from an upsetting episode.
(11) *Feeling depressed* or sad.

Questions 1–6 measure physical expressions of your response to stress, including insomnia, headaches, upset stomachs, and the more serious conditions of high blood pressure and chest pain.

Questions 7–11 measure emotional responses to stress. If your body is chronically aroused but unable to go into action, you may become unable to concentrate, anxious without obvious reason, or depressed.

All of these questions touch on both physical and emotional responses to stress, and if you answered "frequently" or "sometimes" to several questions in either group, you are an excellent candidate for relaxation therapy.

Biofeedback

One of the first things learned in relaxation therapy is how to recognize your relaxation level through biofeedback—biological feedback you get from your body. Relaxation therapists have machines to measure skin temperature and electrical impulses in the muscles. There are also laboratory machines to measure signs of heart performance. However, you can get biofeedback in your office or living room simply by taking your pulse or your blood pressure.

The disappearance of the symptoms of stress is another form of biofeedback. If you notice that your headaches disappear, your stomach calms down, and you're able to sleep, you're reading your body's signals and using biofeedback. The same is true of noticing how and when your muscles relax.

Learning to read and change your body's signals through tension and relaxation of muscles is accomplished through practice. In the clinic, patients usually attend a dozen sessions over three months and do homework as well. The idea is to use these techniques over and over until you can summon them at will. This takes persistence, but it's not hard and it pays off measurably in your ability to manage daily tension.

Some basic relaxation techniques you can learn are abdominal breathing, progressive muscle relaxation, and visualization. The beauty of these exercises is that you can take them with you and use them anywhere at any time to cope with situational stress.

These techniques are not hard to learn. Even children, for example, can be taught at a very early age the difference between "fighting hands" (clenched fist and tightening of circulation) and "happy hands" (fingers spread and increased blood flow). For adults, one of the most popular parts of our stress seminars is abdominal breathing, a simple technique that you can put to use immediately.

Breathing—a Natural Therapy

There are three ways to breathe: raising the shoulders (shoulder breathing); expanding the rib cage (chest breathing); and expanding the chest cavity by moving the abdomen outward, pushing down the diaphragm muscle (abdominal breathing).

Chest breathing, the most common, tends to be rapid and shallow, especially under stress. Hyperventilation, an exaggerated form of rapid, shallow breathing, is a type of chest breathing associated with emotional upset and many physical symptoms, including heart palpitations, sweating, dizziness, anxiety, and fatigue. The slow, regular, and deep breaths characteristic of abdominal breathing, on the other hand, are associated with physical calm. There is a good deal of evidence that when people switch from chest to abdominal breathing, even temporarily, emotional and physical distress diminish significantly.

Properly trained singers, musicians who play wind instruments, and public speakers are usually abdominal breathers, but most people are chest breathers. What kind of breather are you? Ask a friend to watch you sometime when you're at

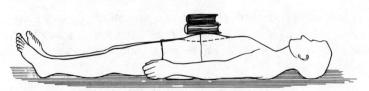

LEARNING ABDOMINAL BREATHING

rest and not aware of being observed, and have him or her note whether you're an abdominal breather or not. (If you are, your abdomen will push out as you inhale; as you exhale, it will pull in.) But regardless of how you breathe now or have breathed for most of your life, you can learn abdominal breathing by following these exercises.

Lie on your back and place a weight (two telephone books or the equivalent weight) over your navel, below the lower ribs. Relax. Now, simply breathe naturally and feel your stomach being pushed in when you breathe out and pushed up against the weight when you breathe in. At first, it is helpful to purposely exaggerate the inward and outward movements of your abdomen. When you know what abdominal breathing feels like, practice the exercise without the weight. Then, practice abdominal breathing while sitting, standing, and moving about.

The payoff will come the next time you feel stress gripping you and causing your body to tense up. Simply relax and take about twelve deep, slow abdominal breaths. You will feel some of your tension melt away.

Progressive Muscle Relaxation

The psychologists at the stress clinic use a cassette tape to guide patients through the steps of progressive muscle relaxation. The tape is reproduced below to give you an idea of what relaxation tapes are like and a chance to make one of your own, if you wish. (The tape works best if the voice is not yours—a friend's, perhaps—and is slow and soothing in tone.)

Progressive muscle relaxation, or PMR, means tensing and relaxing different groups of muscles in your body. This technique teaches you where your different muscles are and lets you know how they feel when you are tense and when you are relaxed. When you tense and relax a muscle, the relaxation is more profound than if you simply make a general, unfocused attempt to relax, at least in the beginning of your training.

Progressive Muscle Relaxation Exercise

Let's begin. First, find a comfortable spot in your home or office, preferably reclining or lying down. If you are sitting, find something to put your feet up on. Make sure the room is comfortable, that the lights are not bright, and the temperature is pleasant. Loosen your clothing if it is tight or uncomfortable. You may wish to remove your shoes also.

Now, close your eyes. Take a moment to examine the sensation. Can you hear my voice? Concentrate fully on my voice, and follow the instructions carefully.

Can you feel where you're touching the bed or chair? Are you comfortable? Doesn't it feel good? Yes. See yourself calm and peaceful and ready to relax.

Now, tense the muscles in your feet and legs by pulling your toes toward your head. Without moving your feet, tense your toes and pull them up as hard as you can. Hold it (five-second pause). Feel the spots where tension is present. Notice where any uncomfortable tenseness is present. Now, relax. Notice how good it feels to let all that tension go. Let your feet relax completely. Do you experience any unusual sensations in the muscles that you just tensed? Do they feel heavy? Do they feel warm or tingly? Does it feel hard to move your toes from their relaxed position? These are signs of profound relaxation. They are pleasant feelings which will continue as your muscles become more and more relaxed.

Now, push your toes away from your body. Push down as hard as you can. Again, notice where you feel tension. The tension is tight and painful. Really push down and hold that tension. Hold it (five-second pause). Notice where you are tense. Now relax completely. Let all of the tension run out of your feet, and let relaxation replace all the tightness. The feeling of relaxation is a good feeling, a quiet feeling. Enjoy this feeling now as your feet relax completely.

Now, move on to your legs. Tense your legs tightly. Notice where that tension is focused. Are your calves tight? Are your thighs tight and pulled together? Do your knees feel stiff and uncomfortable? Hold this tension (five-second pause). Feel where the tightness is. These large muscles are really tense and tight. Okay, let your legs relax. Let the tension drain away into the chair or bed, as your legs let go and relax deeply. Again, be aware of the accompanying feelings of relaxation. These are good feelings, peaceful feelings, quiet feelings in your legs and feet. It is so good to relax and let go.

Now, while keeping your legs and feet totally relaxed and quiet, tense your stomach and abdomen. Pull the muscles in your stomach taut. As you do this, you will feel yourself pushing down into the bed or chair. Push hard. Harder. Hold it (five-second pause). Feel the difference in the tightness of your stomach and the relaxation of your legs and feet. Now relax. Let wave after wave of gentle relaxation sweep over your stomach and abdomen. It feels good to let this area of your body relax and let go. Let your stomach melt and become relaxed and soft. It feels very good to relax your stomach.

Now, arch your back away from the sofa or chair. Pull yourself up tightly. Can you feel the tightness in your lower back? If not, pull up harder. Hold that tense, uncomfortable position. Remember to keep your legs and feet relaxed. Hold it (five-second pause). Let go and sink back into the chair or bed. Let your back collapse comfortably, and let all of the tension flow away. Let the bed or chair support you totally, as you surrender to gentle feelings of calm and relaxation in your back, your stomach, and your legs. These are good feelings. Again, notice the heaviness of your body as you become relaxed. Notice the feeling of immobility as the tension is drained out.

All right. While keeping your legs, feet, stomach, and back relaxed, I want you to tighten up your fists. Squeeze your hands into tight, tight fists. Tense your forearms and upper arms as well. Really squeeze your fists together tightly. Imagine you are pushing your fingers through the palms of your hands. Are your arms trembling? Notice the very uncomfortable feelings this causes. Hold it (five-second pause). Now let go. Open your hands and let your fingers dangle free. Let all of the stress pour out of your fingertips and let a warm, gentle, massaging relaxation sweep over your arms and hands. Let your arms relax totally, letting them collapse at your side. Can you feel the heaviness? If not, let your arms continue to relax. Let them join your legs, your feet, your stomach, and your back in being completely and profoundly relaxed. It feels so good to relax and let the tension disappear.

Now, shrug your shoulders. Pull your shoulders up as if you are trying to touch your ears with them. Pull tight! Feel the tension in your shoulder blades. Feel the tightness of the muscles on top of your shoulders and in your neck. Notice the discomfort, how it causes you pain. You may even feel pain in your back or in your head area. This is the side effect of tension. Okay, drop your shoulders and let them relax. Let them slide back down, relieving all the stress in the neck and shoulders. Let your shoulder blades snuggle back into the bed or chair comfortably. As before, the feelings of relaxation are much different from those of tension. Notice the difference. Notice how much better your body feels when it is relaxed rather than tense.

All right. Keep relaxing your arms, your body, and your legs. Let everything become loose and limp. Let the chair or bed do all the work in holding you up. While you are relaxing, tense up your facial muscles. Scrunch your face up. Really tighten up your forehead. Wrinkle it up! Also, clamp your jaw shut tight. Wrinkle up your eyes and nose. If you are not uncomfortable, you are not tensing enough. Redouble your efforts. Notice how unnatural and uncomfortable this feels. Notice the tightness beside your ears from clenching your jaws tight. Hold that tension (five-second pause). Okay, let go. Let your jaw drop slack. Let your eyelids gently smooth out. Let your forehead slide back into a relaxed and comfortable position. It feels terrific to let that tension subside, and to replace it with total relaxation. Check to see if your face is smooth and wrinkle-free. If not, stretch the skin slightly to make sure the relaxation can set in. Move your jaw slightly from side to side to clear any residual tension, and then let it hang loosely. Let your tongue lie passively in your mouth. It feels so good to relax completely.

You have now experienced tension and relaxation in the major muscles of your body. Now, while you are deeply relaxed, check your body to see if any tension or stress remains. Are your feet relaxed and heavy? If not, wiggle your toes gently, then let them relax. You might imagine a pair of invisible hands gently massaging your feet, to rid them of unwanted tension. Are your legs relaxed? Your stomach? Your back? Your arms? Your hands? Your neck and shoulders? Your jaw? Your eyes? Your forehead? If any of these areas are tense, gently tighten the area and then let it relax completely. Check your body now (30-second pause).

You have been examining the differences in tension and relaxation. Remember what it feels like when certain muscles are tense or tight. In this exercise, you consciously tightened each set of muscles in turn. However, during your actual working day, these muscles may tighten unconsciously, causing feelings of stress and/or fatigue. You should begin to become aware of when your muscles are tense, and attempt to relax them whenever possible. Remember, when you are relaxed, your body feels heavy—a safe, comfortable heaviness.

Now, for a few more minutes, enjoy your relaxation, and become aware of how good it feels. When you finish this exercise, open your eyes and stretch as you would when you wake up in the morning. You may feel a bit tired from tensing. If you do, simply sit and rest and relax for a few more minutes. Each time you practice this exercise, pay close attention to the accompanying feelings of tension and relaxation. By learning to spot tension easily and get rid of it, you can improve your health and sense of well-being. This will be a positive step toward a program of mental and physical wellness.

Visualization

Now that you have learned to identify tension, you are ready for a technique called visualization, in which you focus your mind on relaxing images. This technique works best after you have learned to recognize the difference between tension and relaxation through abdominal breathing and PMR. In the beginning, try doing these first to clear your mind of preoccupation with thoughts and symptoms. Then you can focus on the relaxing scenes you create in your imagination.

You can do this in many ways. As one example, sit back in

your easy chair again, put your feet up, and assume a comfortable position as you did to begin the PMR exercises. Close your eyes and focus on your breathing, slowly breathing in and out. Make sure that you're breathing abdominally. Now that you are sitting comfortably and are breathing deeply and rhythmically, become aware of your body and how it feels. Where do you feel tension and where do you feel relaxation? Do you feel limp and heavy? Is it hard to move? Allow your body to sink into the chair. Let the chair support you completely; just float on the chair.

Now you are ready to take a short trip in your imagination. Try to visualize a relaxing, pleasant scene. It can be as simple or elaborate as you like. Some people relax at the thought of lying on a beach on a warm summer day with the waves rolling in, breaking, and then receding; they like to picture the waves rolling in and out, in and out. Others like to picture themselves in a cool meadow with a brook flowing by. Still others find a mountain scene relaxing.

Find the scene that works for you and concentrate on it. Make this scene come alive in your mind and mentally transport yourself there. See the sights, smell the smells, feel the sensations. You may feel a warm sensation in your body and feel heavy, almost immobilized. Continue to visualize this scene for about 10 to 20 minutes. When you are through, slowly open your eyes, stretch, and yawn as you might in the morning when you wake up.

You will find that once you become proficient at this technique, you will be able to induce relaxation in a very short time and will feel relaxed and refreshed when you have completed the exercises.

Visualization is similar to self-hypnosis or meditation. In fact, it contains elements of both. Through your conscious will, you induce relaxation and control over your physical well-being.

How Relaxation Tamed a Hot Reactor
Relaxation is the most powerful proven behavioral therapy there is to reduce high blood pressure without drugs. People

with high blood pressure who regularly practice relaxation techniques have achieved dramatic drops in their blood pressure that were possible before only with medication.

It worked for Ray, a patient who came to us as an extreme hot reactor. Ray was controlled and rigid—a perfectionist. If he got mad, his jaws would clench, his face would turn beet red, his lips would twitch, his eyes would bulge, and the veins on his forehead would swell. But he wouldn't say a word. Or he would talk with a stilted rigidity and formality of manner that belied the churning emotions inside his body. To Ray, control was everything. Inside, he was full of corrosive stress chemicals from his hot reactions. He was on medication for high blood pressure, but his pressure would still climb when he was challenged by mental stress. When he came to the clinic, he would settle uneasily on the front part of his chair, every part of his body tense. He was afraid to relax. Relaxing felt alien and dangerous.

We taught Ray to take his own blood pressure and gave him some target numbers to shoot at—reducing his heart rate by a beat or two, reducing his blood pressure by 10 mm Hg. The biofeedback convinced Ray—it gave him evidence that he could get results. By the third week of the training, he would walk into the room, slide into a chair, relax his facial muscles, and begin to talk. When he relaxed, his whole face would open up and he would break into a smile.

Ray bought an easy chair for his office, took his blood pressure cuff to work, locked his door, and three times a day took stress breaks instead of coffee breaks. Ray stuck with it for a very compelling reason: every time he relaxed his muscles, his blood pressure dropped to normal levels. Every time he failed to take his relaxation breaks and let stress get the upper hand, his blood pressure broke through the medication barrier. After months of practicing, Ray learned to relax at will, even in the midst of a business meeting. The techniques he once practiced behind closed doors he now takes with him into the boardroom.

*   *   *

Like Ray, you can use abdominal breathing and muscle relaxation during your active day when you most need a break from stress. Here are two simple exercises that can significantly reduce the tension in your daily life. These exercises work best after you have already established awareness of how your body feels when it is tense or relaxed, and after you have practiced muscle relaxation techniques.

Relaxing to "Reminders"

Choose a "reminder stimulus"—a picture, a knickknack, any object in your daily environment that you enjoy seeing. You may choose more than one. My patients have chosen reminders like red stoplights, telephones, photographs, and stickers placed inconspicuously about the home and office.

Each time you see your reminder, sit down and get comfortable and take a deep abdominal breath. As you breathe in, your stomach should push out noticeably. Hold your breath. Then, exhale slowly, and as you exhale, imagine any tension you feel being blown out with the air from your lungs. As you breathe out, think gently to yourself, "I am relaxed. I am in control." Repeat the exercise. Then slowly stretch your arms and legs and go back to your normal activities. After you practice this exercise regularly for several weeks, you will find that relaxation becomes almost automatic every time you look at your reminder stimulus.

Relaxing on Breaks

This is a more intense form of relaxation. Take a five-minute relaxation break at least once a day to keep you in the relaxation habit. It will be most helpful if you take your relaxation break during the busiest part of your day.

Find a comfortable chair or sofa and make sure you will not be distracted. Make sure no bright lights or loud noises will bother you. Take a deep breath and hold it. Now exhale, and as you breathe out, think, "I am relaxed. I am peaceful." Gently push aside any intruding thoughts and focus clearly on the thought, "My muscles are relaxed and calm." Relax your jaw, then the rest of the muscles in your face. Keep your breathing slow and regular. Relax your shoulders and neck. If there is any tension in your chest or back, let yourself sink further and further into your chair or sofa. Relax your hands and arms. Then let your feet and legs relax. Take five minutes for this whole process. Then open your eyes, stretch, and resume your day, feeling invigorated and positive.

Recognizing Your Stress Cues

It is important to recognize when you are under stress and to try to reduce your stress at the first possible chance. Each person needs to identify his or her own stress cues. Some common cues are anxiety, anger, blushing, gritting your teeth, yelling, a feeling of frustration, or a physical sign such as shortness of breath, tightness in the chest or throat, clenched fists, or a feeling of fatigue. Any of these may be cues for you.

Make a list of things that happen to you when you are aroused by stress and pay particular attention to when they happen. Whenever you experience a stress cue, do one of two things:

If possible, immediately look at your reminder stimulus. Do some deep abdominal breathing. This will help you remind yourself that you are a relaxed and rational person.

If you cannot immediately do your breathing exercises, promise yourself that at the first opportunity you will take a relaxation break to practice abdominal breathing or muscle relaxation. This will clear the stress and tension from your body. It is important not to allow the cumulative effects of several stress episodes to wear you down.

Supervised Relaxation Therapy

Other kinds of relaxation therapy, such as meditation and hypnosis, are best done under professional supervision. If you would like the names of qualified relaxation therapists in your area, the Biofeedback Society of America, listed in the bibliography, may be able to help. The Society lists certified biofeedback practitioners, many of whom are also relaxation therapists. You may also have a state biofeedback society in your area.

A *final note:* Relaxation therapy is a very useful tool, but by itself it is not the sole answer. We use it in combination with other treatments, including medication and changing self-talks. Beware of claims that relaxation can cure everything from baldness to psoriasis. But you can count on relaxation techniques to make you more aware of how your body responds to stress. With enough practice, these techniques give you an excellent way of controlling your response to stress.

You will learn through relaxation that your mind can calm your body and your body can calm your mind.

9
Increasing Your Fitness

A kitten chasing a ball of yarn, a seal taking a morning plunge, a stallion romping in an open meadow—joyous physical expression is a fact of life for most animals. It is not, however, for most humans, who are often content to get by with the bare minimum of physical exertion. Americans pay more attention to their cars than to their bodies. We are a spectator nation: the majority of us prefer to enjoy the exploits of a minority of talented athletes who compete in the big-time sports.

Things are changing, however. In the past fifteen years tennis and then running have swept the nation. Millions of women have taken up physical conditioning and sports, once considered male preserves. Fitness has become fashionable, and exercise is now something most people want to do, even if they haven't gotten around to being systematic about it.

It is for the many who are still exercise hopefuls that this chapter is written.

How Fit Is Your Lifestyle?

To decide whether you need a fitness program, ask yourself a few questions about your everyday life: When was the last time you walked a mile? How about half a mile? Do you use your car to go to the corner grocery? Do you take an elevator to go up one or two floors? When was the last time you worked up a sweat? Do you exercise vigorously for at least 20 minutes, three times a week?

You can also find clues to your fitness level in the way you react physically to stress. Animals under stress show increased body movements, and so do humans. You may not be aware that you are under stress, but your body shows it if you become more physically agitated and your heart rate increases. Other nervous symptoms like insomnia and irritability may also be signs of poor physical conditioning. Once you have given your body a tune-up through exercise, you will find that you have fewer nervous mannerisms and unnecessary movements. It's like tuning up your car—the motor works better with fewer misses and sputters.

You may be drawn to exercise, but with the wrong expectations. Here are some common misunderstandings about fitness that I'd like to dispel:

- "Conditioning will lengthen your life." Unfortunately, there is no proof yet that this is true.
- "Exercise is ineffective without pain (no pain, no gain)." It is just the opposite—pain is not a desirable part of conditioning.
- "Fitness can be achieved by sweating off pounds with rubber suits, saunas, etc." No, these can produce shifts in body fluids and chemicals that can lead to dehydration, serious overwork of the heart, and all the complications you're trying to prevent.
- "You have to train like an athlete." No, just maintain a regular 20-minute program, three to five times a week.
- "Sports or recreational activities are fitness activities." Maybe; it depends on the activity.
- "You will be able to jog your whole lifetime." Not necessarily. Your joints may wear out before your heart does.
- "The best exercise is jogging." It depends on what you enjoy. Jogging is only one of many forms of conditioning. There are all kinds of ways to get fit, and you can combine

them with other things you enjoy, like being outdoors and being with people.

- "Walking around a lot and lifting things increases fitness." No. Fitness requires a regular, systematic program.
- "You have to be an athlete to enjoy exercise." Anyone can enjoy exercise if it fits his or her lifestyle and health.
- "Exercise helps lower blood pressure." It may if you lose weight in the process, but blood pressure is complex, and the relationship is not direct.
- "It reverses hardening of the arteries." No. It may slow or halt the progression of this disease, but there is no proof of that yet.
- "If a little is good, a lot is better." No. Our study of marathoners has shown they have the same incidence of high blood pressure and hot reacting as the nonconditioned, sedentary person. Indeed, too much exercise may raise the level of some stress chemicals, damage bones and joints, and undermine health.
- "Exercise improves collateral blood circulation (reserve circulation in the heart)." No, but it improves the efficiency of the heart's action.
- "Fitness can be accomplished with vigorous exercise once a week." Definitely not—this could even be dangerous. Three times a week is the minimum necessary for healthy conditioning.

If those are the myths, what is the reality? What can you expect to gain from a fitness program?

An appropriate exercise program moderates both your emotional and physical responses to stress. Emotionally, exercise is an effective treatment for depression. Physically, it conditions your heart to operate more efficiently, and it may dissipate excess stress chemicals.

Exercise may be particularly valuable for hot reactors, who regularly raise the level of stress chemicals circulating in their bloodstream. For three million years we have geared our heart and blood vessels to engage the muscles and skeleton in doing something physical. In stress situations, the chemicals triggered by the stress response can't be dissipated in physical activity and they end up bombarding the heart and blood vessels. Exercise appears to burn up excess stress chemicals by using them for energy expressed outwardly.

When you exercise, you don't lower your production of these chemicals. You actually produce more to meet the extra needs of your active body, but you also metabolize them more efficiently. One theory holds that in the process of exercising you metabolize excess stress chemicals that were already present as well. True, the level of these chemicals rises again in response to new stress, and it doesn't make sense to go out and exercise every time you feel under stress. But it does make sense to exercise regularly. That way you consistently burn up excess stress chemicals.

Aerobic exercise is the type that benefits your heart. In aerobic exercise you move your body continuously through space, as opposed to weight lifting or other isometric exercises where the body moves little and with interruptions, if at all. Aerobic conditioning requires continuing elevation of the heart rate for a given period of time.

Here's a list of the numerous benefits to be had from a simple routine of regular aerobic exercise for 20 minutes, three to five times a week:

- Lowers the heart rate necessary to sit, stand, walk, run and do the other physical activities so your heart doesn't have to work as hard as it otherwise would.
- Helps lower blood pressure.
- Raises HDL, a beneficial type of cholesterol that may protect against hardening of the arteries.
- Increases endurance.
- Delays loss of calcium from bones, which delays shortening of the spine in aging and makes people less susceptible to fractures.
- May delay deterioration of the heart and blood vessels.
- Lessens the need for insulin.
- Raises metabolism, decreases appetite, and burns up calories.

- Promotes a better muscle-to-fat ratio, which improves your body shape.
- Improves muscle tone.
- May reduce excessive stress chemicals currently present in your body.
- Relieves depression, tension, anxiety, and anger and increases your sense of self-control.

A word about exercise and weight: It is now universally recognized that exercising will help you lose weight, if you follow a regular aerobic fitness program over a period of months. Exercising helps because you use up extra calories when you are extra active and, according to one of the newer theories, you burn calories at a higher rate because exercise changes your metabolic rate. This theory runs as follows: everyone is born with a different "set point" for weight, and the body tries to maintain that weight range. Some people can eat everything in sight without gaining, because their metabolism causes them to burn calories at a high rate. Others find that as soon as they lose enough weight on a diet, their metabolism seems to slow down, and their body burns calories more slowly in order to maintain its former weight. But you can raise your metabolic rate if you maintain a regular program of aerobic exercise—so the theory goes—and your body will burn more calories, defeating the "set point" barrier to weight loss.

Regular exercise benefits the dieter in other ways. Researchers have found that exercise is nature's appetite depressant. Exercise decreases appetite by releasing chemicals that block hunger signals to the brain. And it helps you feel full, some experts think, because it increases the flow of blood to the stomach and also the level of fat in the blood (high blood-fat levels are associated with feeling full).

Which activities are aerobic? Any that are continuous and vigorous. Continuous very brisk walking, jogging, cross-country skiing, ice hockey, jumping rope, rowing, running in place, stationary cycling, bicycling, swimming, and aerobic dancing are examples. Sports like handball, racquetball, squash, basketball, and singles tennis can provide aerobic conditioning if they involve *continuous* vigorous activity. Note that other sports like golf, bowling, football, and baseball improve muscle tone and coordination but are not generally considered aerobic because they involve a lot of starting and stopping, so the heart rate doesn't stay up continuously.

Remember: It's *aerobic* exercise you need to benefit your heart and circulatory system, not calisthenics, weight lifting, or isometric exercise (flexing a muscle against an immovable force—for instance, flexing one muscle against another by pushing your palms together, or trying to push over a wall). Weight lifting and isometric exercises may develop muscles, but they're also like vasoconstrictive hot reacting—they cause the resistance of your blood vessels to rise and force the heart to work harder against it. Again, it's like driving your car with the brakes on. Using weights and isometrics to tone your muscles is fine if you combine them with a vigorous program of cardiovascular aerobic conditioning. Your goal is fitness, not Muscle Beach.

Getting Started

Frequently I hear, "I can't do it; I don't have the time to do it." Or, "I have to go away from my work to do it." Or, "It doesn't fit my lifestyle." Or, "I have to change too drastically to get into shape," or, "I travel too much," or "I'm afraid if I walk outside I'll be mugged," or "I'm too tired at the end of the day."

You may think you don't have time for an exercise program, but my guess is that once you begin you will find both the time and the way. Keep in mind that mental fatigue often dissolves with physical activity, because chemicals released during exercise activate you and can even have a mood-elevating effect. That's one reason physical conditioning is a therapeutic measure for people who are depressed and anxious. Exercise also helps some people require less sleep, so a good fitness program can actually open up more time. Even if you feel you don't have the time now, give it three weeks just as a trial. I'm betting you'll find the time to stick with it.

Before beginning any program of vigorous exercise, check with your physician. He may ask you to take a treadmill test before giving you the green light for an active fitness program.

You will become fit if you exercise aerobically for 20 to 30 minutes, three to five times a week, at 60 to 80 percent of your maximum predicted heart rate. (But remember: if you are a beginner and especially if you are 40 and/or sedentary, you must work up to this gradually.)

To figure that rate, subtract your age from 225. For example, if you are 45, your maximum predicted heart rate is 180 (225 minus 45). Your beginning target is 60 percent of 180, or 108 minimum training rate, provided you are healthy enough to attempt to reach it. Some people find that they can reach 60 percent without much effort and start at 70 percent. Do not attempt a training rate over 70 percent in the beginning and do not go beyond 75 percent at any time unless you have a careful evaluation by a physician. The important thing is to be aware of how your body is responding and to build up your training rate and time gradually.

To measure your heart rate, hold one hand in front of you with palm up. If you wear a watch, make this the hand *without* the watch. Then place three fingers from your other hand on the thumb side of the wrist of the first hand. You will find an artery with a pulse or beat. Using your watch or a clock as a timer, count the number of beats for 10 seconds, beginning with zero for the first beat, and multiply by six. This procedure gives you the heart's beats per minute—your heart rate. (In some exercise classes people are taught to use the artery in the neck, the so-called carotid artery. This is not always advisable. Pushing on the carotid artery may trigger nerves that can stop the heart in susceptible people.)

Our approach is to ask patients to start their program by walking as briskly as they can until they reach a heart rate that is 60 percent of their maximum predicted rate. You can do the same. At that point, listen to what your body is telling

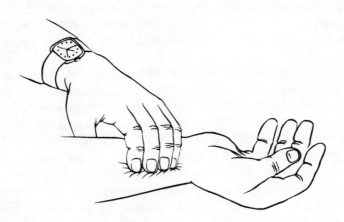

TAKING YOUR PULSE

you. Do you feel anything in your bones, joints, muscles, breathing, or chest that might suggest you are pushing too hard? If so, back off and get some professional advice from your physician before you go any further. On the other hand, if you can do this without any marked discomfort and you feel reasonably good, possibly even exhilarated, then continue at your minimum training rate for up to 10 minutes, or as long as you can without experiencing fatigue or discomfort. Cool down gradually for a few minutes by continuing the exercise more slowly.

Using the formula given here, a healthy person can achieve cardiovascular conditioning by exercising three to five times a week, gradually working up to an activity that keeps the heart at its minimum training rate for at least 20 minutes.

It is absolutely essential to build up your time and the vigor of your exercise gradually. Don't expect to maintain your minimum training rate even for as much as 10 minutes right at the start if you're a beginner or have been sedentary for a long time.

Be prepared to take at least six weeks, or even longer, to work up to 20 minutes at your minimum training rate. For some people, it may take six weeks to work up to 10 minutes. You're not in a big hurry—the point is for you to enjoy your new program of physical well-being, not to break a speed record.

Pay attention to your body rather than your watch each time you exercise. When the muscles you are using for the exercise start to feel heavy and tired, your body is signalling that, for the moment, you have reached a safe limit. At this point, you should cool down (see below) and then stop. To give your muscles a chance to recover, do not resume the same exercise for about 48 hours. (If you want to do aerobic exercise more often than every other day, alternate with an aerobic activity that uses a different set of muscles. For example, if you walk or run three days a week, you can swim or bicycle on other days if you wish—the optimum is between three and five times a week.)

You can tell if the intensity of your exercise is about right for you if you can carry on a conversation while you are exercising (which means *not* having to pant and puff); if while you exercise you find yourself occasionally taking deep, full breaths (this is called "sighing respiration" and means that you are exercising at your optimum training rate); and if you feel fully recovered without fatigue one hour after exercise.

The goal is to find the exercise intensity that feels right to you and then gradually get to the point where you can exercise continuously at that intensity for at least 20 minutes without fatigue or discomfort. Then, after a month at that level, you may want to increase the intensity, say from 60 to 70 percent or from 70 to 75 percent of your maximum heart rate—again, carefully checking to make sure your body is not sending you any worrisome signals and using the three indicators just mentioned to make sure you're not overdoing it. As time goes on and your endurance continues to build, you will have to work harder to push your heart to this point. You may have to walk in hilly areas or walk faster or begin to run.

If you get sick or for some other reason can't continue to exercise on a regular basis, you will need to start again at an earlier level in your program.

When you develop beyond the basics outlined here, you can get more details on how to exercise as well as a handy point system from Ken Cooper's books, including *The New Aerobics* and *The Aerobics Program for Total Well-Being.*

Fitness Goals

Four chief indicators of physical fitness are:

Body composition—the ratio between lean body weight (bone, muscle, and connective tissue) and fat weight (fatty tissue).

Cardiorespiratory fitness—the ability of the circulatory and respiratory systems to deliver oxygen and nutrients to the body's cells and carry away carbon dioxide and waste products.

Flexibility—the ability of the body or body parts to go through a full range of motion.

Muscular fitness—the ability of the muscles to exert force once (strength) or repeatedly (endurance).

A world-class athlete may be gifted in all of these areas, but most of us are good at some things and not so good at others.

Perhaps you are strong but have two left feet. You might want to emphasize balance and flexibility in your exercise program. Perhaps you are fast but run out of gas quickly. You need endurance.

If you are concerned about body composition, keep in mind that the average man who is past his early 20's has around 15 to 18 percent body fat and the average woman around 25 to 27 percent, but even people who are in excellent condition vary in their percentage of body fat, depending on their body type and the kind of activity they concentrate on. Among professional football players, defensive linemen average 18 percent body fat, offensive linemen 15 percent, and running backs only 9.6 percent. In general, women athletes carry higher percentages of fat than do men. For example, elite male distance runners average a superlean 3 percent, but elite female distance runners average 15 percent and show a much wider variation in percentage of body fat, including a few who are well under 10 percent.

Overall, in gauging your fitness what is a reasonable standard of comparison?

Yourself and absolutely nobody and nothing else. The only thing that counts is how much you personally improve. Set reasonable goals for yourself, goals that are attainable. When you reach them, you can always aim for higher goals. If you are going to use fitness as a tool to become competitive, hostile, and impatient, you are better off staying in your easy chair.

If You're over 40

The "great divide" occurs around age 40. Before that age, you will probably benefit from playing highly competitive sports like tennis, racquetball, competitive running (racing), and of course traditional games like football, basketball, baseball, and track and field. After the age of 40, however, the name of the game is endurance. Endurance creates reserves and resilience; it prepares you for the long haul. After 40 it is important to be cautious of activities that involve quick, sporadic movements and intense competition. Tennis singles, with its stops and starts, can be dangerous if you are not in condition. The candidate for disaster is "the weekend warrior"—the fortyish office worker who exercises only on the weekends but still goes all out to win.

For this reason, always warm up and cool down. Your muscles are attached to the bones and joints, and these need care when you exercise or they can cause trouble down the road.

Bones and joints seem to be designed for about forty years of durability, whereas the heart and blood vessel system is good for about seventy. Consequently, the person over the age of 40 who exercises without the proper techniques, without proper equipment, and with too much enthusiasm may attain not cardiovascular fitness but life in a wheel chair, traumatic arthritis, and a long list of orthopedic complications.

Warming Up, Cooling Down, and Stretching

Warming up is simple: just do your exercise or activity *slowly* for a few minutes before working up to your training rate. For instance, if you are going to take a brisk 20-minute walk as your aerobic activity, take an extra five minutes first and build up to the faster speed before the 20 minutes of fast walking. If you decide to pedal a bike, pedal it slowly for two or three minutes before you start to pedal harder. The same principle goes for cooling down: when you finish the activity, continue it at a slower rate for 3 to 5 minutes before stopping. You won't regret the additional few minutes at either end: warming up will do a lot to prevent injuries as well as long-term problems, and cooling down will help prevent muscle soreness.

Stretching exercises will aid greatly to your feeling of well-being and will keep you limber for your aerobic exercise. The following four stretches are suitable to accompany whatever exercise you choose. Moderation is the key, and speed is undesirable. Stay away from bouncing or quick, jerking movements. Move slowly until you feel a stretch; then briefly sustain the stretch. Do not strain. Breathe smoothly and regularly; do not hold your breath. Ten repetitions (five for each leg) are adequate to maintain flexibility *before* and *after* fitness activities.

Do the following exercises in any order.

FOUR WARM-UP STRETCHES

WARM-UP STRETCH #1

#1 Sitting with toes together: Sit with the soles of the feet together, heels about six to eight inches from the body, and let the knees fall apart. Place hands on knees and press down gently. Hold for a few seconds. Relax and repeat. (If your heels slide away from your body, bring them back between repetitions.) Your goal is to become flexible enough for the knees to rest naturally three inches from the floor.

WARM-UP STRETCH #2

#2 Sitting with leg extended: Sitting on the floor, bend one leg at the knee and extend the other one straight out with the toes pointed up. Reach both hands toward the toes, hold for six seconds, and relax. Do this five times with the same leg extended, trying each time to slowly reach the hands further, until eventually you can reach past the toes. Repeat five times with the other leg extended.

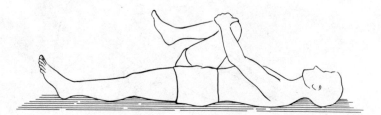

WARM-UP STRETCH #3

#3 Lying down with leg extended: Stretch out on the floor (a foam pad helps). Keep one leg flat and relaxed on the floor and pull the knee of the other leg to the chest with your hands. Hold for a few seconds. Relax and repeat with the other leg.

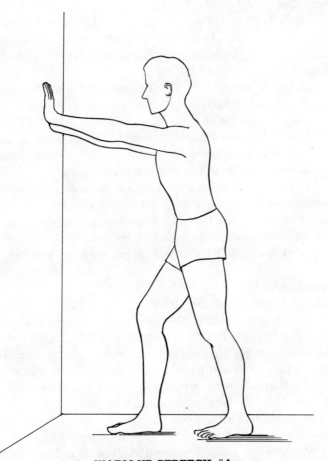

WARM-UP STRETCH #4

#4 Pushing the wall: Stand one to two feet from a wall with hands against the wall and one foot forward with the knee bent. Point toes straight forward. Keep both heels flat on the floor. Lean hips forward and hold for six seconds. Relax and repeat. You can do this five times with the same leg bent and then change legs, or you can alternate legs with each repetition.

Don't Overdo It!

Your body's signals are as real as the lights on the dashboard of your car. Don't talk yourself out of chest pain, lightheadedness, breathlessness, or bone and joint pain. They're trying to tell you something.

Exercise is a great way to take control of your life, but if you find yourself exercising for more than one hour a day and you're not training for the Olympics, you might ask yourself: "What am I running from?" If the amount of time you devote to exercise is disrupting your life—work, family, socializing—you are apt to lose, not gain control.

Furthermore, if you push yourself beyond a reasonably comfortable limit, you will gain injuries without increasing your fitness. In our study of marathon runners, we found that foot and joint problems were common.

So seek the middle path. More is not necessarily better.

Hard Work or Fun?

Some people think they have to huff and puff and sweat and strain to get results. What they usually get is stiff and sore. The flip side of this approach is that they miss out on the feeling of joy in exercise, the feeling of freedom. The single most important factor in becoming fit is to *choose an activity that you personally enjoy.* You're much more apt to stick with it. Weekend warriors usually overindulge once or twice and then forget about exercise for months at a time. Your exercise need be nothing more regimented than a brisk 20-minute walk. You will get results if you do it regularly and vigorously enough to reach your target heart rate three to five times a week.

You may even find that once you get started, the "high" feeling you get from a good workout is so pleasant that you want more and more. People who have been inactive and then become exercisers are often heard to say that they have grown "addicted" to their activity. Recently, scientists have uncovered some evidence that there is a physiological basis for the "addiction" to what is known as "runner's high." New clues to this phenomenon surfaced in the early 1970s when researchers isolated certain morphinelike compounds produced by the bodies of athletes. These compounds suppress pain and give a feeling of euphoria. They are called "endorphins" because they seem to act like endogenous (body-produced) morphine.

Exercise is followed by increased endorphin levels in some individuals, possibly accounting for the "exercise high." Because endorphins remain elevated for only a short time after exercise (30 to 90 minutes), many people feel that they are the basis of exercise "addiction," since repeated and perhaps even higher doses are required to obtain the same effect. The "addiction" may take a healthy form or a destructive form, depending on how extreme one's exercise program is.

Some studies show that high endorphin levels are also associated with an easygoing approach to life. People who don't take themselves too seriously and laugh readily increase or at least do not inhibit the production of endorphins.

Exercise is also associated with elevated HDL levels, as are giving up smoking (tobacco seems to suppress HDL), and having one or two drinks of alcohol or one or two glasses of wine per day. HDL is a "good cholesterol" that may help protect against coronary artery disease. So when it comes to raising your HDL and endorphin levels, you have your choice of joining two clubs, "Running and Jogging," or "Laughing and Drinking," or both (within limits, of course!).

The formula is simple, and the benefits are great. That's why exercise is one of the best ways to start taking charge of your life. Millions have. You'll be joining a huge community of people who share your efforts, and you'll find support everywhere.

Exercise is a wonderful way of putting your stress response to one of the uses nature intended—to propel your body into joyous physical expression.

10
Making the Most of Support and Leisure

Much more than common sense tells us that support helps when we're under stress. There is scientific evidence that in times of crisis, your social support systems help to protect you against illness. Research bears out this observation in a broad range of situations. For example, one experimental group of rabbits fed high-cholesterol diets did not develop hardening of the arteries at nearly the rate of a similar control group. The difference was support: the rabbits who had the lower rate of disease were petted, talked to, and given regular individual attention.

When we move from the world of rabbits to that of human beings, research shows that after a heart attack, men (they still have the large majority of heart attacks) who perceive their marriages as being loving and supportive are likely to recover sooner, return to work sooner, and live longer than bachelors or less fortunate husbands. And a study of blue-collar wives under extreme stress showed that those who had someone—usually a husband—with whom they could talk daily about their problems suffered less depression than wives who did not. A high degree of emotional intimacy, therefore, protected strongly against depression under stress. On the other hand, mere acquaintances, even if there were many, offered little support and therefore little protection.

In still another study, research that followed 100 men for up to 24 months after their jobs were abolished determined that those with the least social support had a tenfold greater incidence of arthritis than those with the most support. And a study of highly stressed executives reported that those who felt supported by superiors or top management showed reduced symptoms of illness.

Finally, some cultures are more supportive than others, and their health patterns benefit. Research on several groups of Japanese-Americans showed that those who retained the Japanese patterns of strong community ties, cooperation, and group support had lower rates of heart disease than those who lived in a more individualistic Westernized manner.

How Support Helps

Why is it that when we feel supported by others, our bodies seem to work better? Perhaps one answer is "adaptive energy" —when we have to generate all our support ourselves, we use energy that could be going for other purposes.

Our primary support comes from within, from the way we talk to ourselves. It is essential in managing stress to realize that we can maximize good feelings and minimize unhappy feelings on our own. But how much richer our lives are for the understanding, response, and concrete help of others. Their support helps us reaffirm our positive self-views and our connection with a larger community.

With those who support you, your personal worth is clearly established. This climate of feeling reinforces your own self-acceptance. If you are lucky, the support will go beyond passive acceptance to active recognition of your feelings and your special qualities. Receiving nurturance enhances your ability to give it, creating a cycle of support. Underlying all emotional support is the perception that someone cares about you and believes in you.

On a practical level, support groups allow you to "audition" your self-talks, so you can hear your own thoughts and decide for yourself whether they're reasonable. Support systems also give you feedback, another way to check your self-talks and their consequences.

For many, religious groups have a support function, through their principles and beliefs and through the opportunity of sharing these beliefs with others. Religion can also offer relief from loneliness and a sense of community that helps people feel they're part of something important outside themselves.

The response of support groups can be a powerful reinforcement in making behavioral changes. Formal groups like Alcoholics Anonymous and Weight Watchers have proven that peer support helps people change destructive behaviors when no other kind of help can.

I once had the privilege of observing an open meeting of International Doctors in Alcoholics Anonymous. They were young and old, men and women, dressed in pinstripes and jeans, representing all branches of medicine. Most had become doctors because they started out as idealists and perfectionists. When their worlds started falling apart, they received medical treatment in abundance. However, the help that made the difference came not from medicine but from others in the same trouble. There's nothing like the understanding of someone who's been there, someone who shares knowledge about what works, believes in the person's ability to make it, reinforces positive efforts, and recognizes success. That's support.

The same principle holds for all formal support and self-help groups and for informal support systems as well. Tapping a community of good will opens up new personal resources and enlarges your sense of your own possibilities.

Quick now, answer this question:
Do you have the emotional support you need?
If you did not answer "yes" immediately, you need to shore up your support systems. What counts is not how much support you are actually getting but how much support you *perceive* you are getting. If you do not think you are getting the support you need, it would be wise to change either your expectations or your supportive environment, or you will suffer needlessly from stress.

One way to attract support is to open up to people. Be a self-disclosing person, one who lets others know what you think, believe, and feel. By that I don't mean walking into a room and announcing that you're depressed. You don't want to burden people with constant musings about yourself. But it does help to be honest—to say you don't know when you don't have an answer, for example, or that it's been a long day and you're too tired to make a decision. You might explain why you feel touchy at a particular time, or ask a friend to spend some time with you if you feel down. You will reduce guessing by others and help them to respond appropriately. You will also build trust in yourself as a fallible person who expresses authentic feelings instead of trying to maintain a facade. In the process, you provide others with a model of coping behavior by not stewing in your own juices and by encouraging others to be open and share their feelings as well.

So go out and find the support you need. Don't wait for people to come to you. And look especially for those who think and feel as you do. If you're trying to write a book or open a small business, spend your time with people who support your ambition and goal. And do the same for them.

Giving is getting. People in the Middle East observe that the Red Sea, which is fed by several tributaries and empties into several others, has some of the most beautiful, sparkling, life-sustaining waters in the world, while the Dead Sea, which is locked into itself, can neither give nor sustain life.

Don't dam yourself up. Let your waters flow.

Leisure—Giving Yourself the Freedom to Enjoy

Researchers now believe that an accumulation of stress hormones may help suppress the body's protective white blood cells and partially disable the immune system. This link between stress and disease would explain why we feel run down after long sieges of work or stress and why we need to renew ourselves by spending time away from stressful environments. We need leisure.

Our word "leisure" comes from the old French for "license" and basically means "to be permitted." Leisure is *freedom*, the time free from work and duty, and free from the demands and control of others.

During true leisure time, you enjoy the process of doing something fulfilling without having to achieve a goal. You have positive sources of pleasure, including people, surroundings, and activities, and you have a chance to experience the moment instead of letting it go by. Life only exists in the present, and happiness comes with active participation in life. We often focus on the past and the future; leisure is one of our few opportunities to live in the present.

Leisure cannot correct continuing problems in the work environment. But it can give us the chance to renew our resources for mastering important challenges. The detachment provided by genuine leisure can create a fresh perspective when you reenter your work world. Without leisure, life lacks balance and perspective, giving stress a chance to take over.

You may think you don't have time for leisure, but you will have to make time for recovery if you have a heart attack and are fortunate enough to live through it, as I did. Don't talk yourself into waiting for the day "when you can relax" or the day "when your problems will be over." I have seen too many people wait for that day, and never live to enjoy it. Take your leisure in stride, as part of your life and not as a pot of gold at the end of the rainbow. Most good things are fleeting and transitory. Allow yourself to enjoy them. Savor them. You have the potential to make your life today as good as it can be.

Work and Play

Chances are you know how to work. But you may not know how to play.

Among my favorite writers on relationships are the physicians Marshall and Marguerite Shearer, who point out that work requires a different mental set than play. Work is planned and disciplined, with a goal that is easily measured. It is characterized by effort, concentration, steadfastness of purpose. If you run into trouble, you redouble your efforts. In work, the attitude, "I can achieve," is a useful one to have.

Play is free and spontaneous. The emphasis is on feeling, with one moment of feeling leading to the next. In play you often explore to see what you like or if you like it at that particular moment. Play is enhanced by increased emotional involvement and spontaneity, not effort. A positive mental attitude is, "I am entitled to fun. Everyone is."

It's not the activity you choose that determines whether you're working or playing; it's your attitude toward it that counts. Sustained effort toward a goal, no matter how gratifying, runs you down after a while if it isn't balanced by freedom, spontaneous feeling, and laughter. Work drains your battery; play charges it up.

Happy adults usually have something of the child within. Occasionally, play involves spending some of your earnings on things that make sense only to you. Buying your fantasy—a spur-of-the-moment trip, outrageous clothes, a sports car (even an old one)—may strike others as bizarre, senseless, and wasteful, but that is exactly the point. It's play, and it may be the very thing that justifies in your mind the long years of parenting, marriage, or wage-earning. Go ahead. Be silly. You'll have less stress.

Using Leisure to Avoid Burnout and Depression

If you go for long periods without playing, you lose spirit and vitality. Ask yourself: "When was the last time I did things I really wanted to do and really had fun doing?" Can you remember taking time to do something pleasurable for yourself even though you were loaded with obligations? Did you feel good or guilty? If you felt good, you know the value of leisure.

Our counselors often ask people who say they never have fun anymore what they enjoyed before. Then they recommend doing it again, starting immediately. If you renew experiences that were linked with happy feelings in the past, you tend to automatically promote good feelings in the present. After you've had these experiences, just recalling them can be as delightful as the experience itself. Leisure's cooling effects on stress can last when you allow yourself to reminisce.

I have learned to build "time out" of all kinds into my schedule since my heart attack. It's been essential to my health. I take frequent short vacations, for instance, and I recommend this to you. Sometimes it seems to me that the frequency of my patients' vacations is inversely proportional to the number and seriousness of their heart attacks.

You do have to plan your vacations wisely. Decide what you want—and what you need—from a trip. Sometimes what you want is an intense, fast-paced trip that involves study or competition or exploring, one that distracts from the daily pettiness of life, from deadlines or loneliness. At other times, you need a rest, a sit-down-and-stay-put vacation to refresh you from the pressures of work or family. You may need a long vacation or only a three-day weekend. You may need to spend time with a companion or you may want to be alone.

Look back at the way you've enjoyed spending free time in the past—both vacations and other leisure time—and figure out what works for you. Then, hold out for it. In vacations, as in everything else related to managing stress and enjoying life, the key is knowing yourself and acting on that knowledge.

Many of my patients say they are helped by "mini-vacations." Frequent brief vacations scattered throughout the year allow you to get away, gain perspective, and cool down, yet they don't keep you from business and professional realities for too long. This is a great help for the person who worries about the huge pile of work waiting back at the office. Such a person can better tolerate shorter vacations and smaller piles.

Whatever vacation you choose, remember the rule that stress begins as a mismatch between your expectations and what your environment can deliver. No trip can give you everything you want. Plan ahead and don't have unrealistic expectations. You may envision yourself ensconced in a cabin in the mountains, while your mate's idea of heaven might be miles of seashore. Compromise before you go and as you go, and try to be thick-skinned about whatever happens. Vacations are meant to be play, not work.

Finally, a word about separate vacations for couples. This can be a destructive use of leisure time. It's fine to take separate trips on occasion, as long as they are balanced by vacations together. It's hard to establish a loving relationship by remote control. If separate vacations are your rule, chances are that you may just go off and have a wonderful time, and your partner may just go off and have a wonderful time. Then, when you're back together, the old problems are still there—probably even worse than ever in comparison to the wonderful time you've just had. Instead of using your leisure time to strengthen and support the relationship, you are using it to support the belief that you have more fun apart than together.

It's extremely important to give yourselves leisure together to reawaken the good feelings you have about each other. Often, the seeds of love are there, but they need the right climate to bloom.

The Workaholic at Play

A special leisure problem for couples is the "workaholic" partner. Some of my workaholic patients, both men and women, transport their office work to their leisure "play." Not surprisingly, this rankles their partners. It helps to understand what is really happening beneath the surface.

Many workaholics have an overwhelming need to achieve something, somehow. They usually find their most consistent rewards at work. Too often they are faced with conflict at home about the time they spend at work. This conflict only drives the workaholic back to work, which is what he has learned to count on for consistent rewards.

Many spouses of these workaholics tell me, "We fight all the time because my husband (or wife) works so much." Look at the other side of the coin: maybe your spouse works so much because you fight all the time.

Workaholics feel more in control of their lives when they are working. From their point of view, it makes sense to prefer the office to the home. Try not to berate your workaholic spouse, insisting that he or she spend more time with you. Substitute pleasurable activities at home in the time you do have with your spouse for the conflicts that are driving him or her away. If your spouse comes to associate your leisure time together with a pleasurable feeling, he or she will be tempted to cut back on that office time.

Of course, there are times and situations when even workaholics have good practical reasons to immerse themselves in a project. The best solution is to make the time you have together worthwhile, so that on those occasions when you must be apart, you can recall the good times rather than resent the bad ones. That way you may be able to bring perspective to those times when immersion in work is more a habit than a necessity. If you can get your workaholic to experience leisure as play, he or she will be more inclined to think of it as the thing that makes work worthwhile.

Finding Time for Leisure

If you have a hard time fitting leisure into your life, or if the free time you have is not satisfying, try establishing a routine. Make sure that leisure time is given a regular place in your life. If you look closely at the lives of productive people, you'll find that they're highly organized—they make time for what they need and want to do by planning it in their schedules. Build leisure time into your plan, and then, when that time comes around, use it to play. Structure can bring freedom. At the same time, keep in mind that the creative process is unpredictable, and if you do creatively demanding work, a certain amount of nonscheduled time out is part of a cycle of regeneration. Be aware of your own natural cycle. Do what you can to maximize your productivity within it, and trust your impulses to take leisure time when you need it, without being too concerned about organizing productivity by the clock. Build regular free time into your life, and be open to it at other times when you need to let go for a while.

Ask others at home and at work to respect your free time, so you can follow through on your plans for leisure, and make that time one of pleasure, not just escape. There will be days when you want to watch whatever is on TV, but if you consistently just "pass the time," you are wasting a precious resource for self-renewal. Escape will help you turn off stress, but it will not regenerate you to meet life's responsibilities. The most satisfying leisure involves active choice. You may choose quiet activities that let you reflect and absorb the pleasures of your surroundings. It is common and healthy to feel the need for time to just be. At other times you'll want to be more active. The point is to choose, not drift, and to find out what pleases you.

You can make your leisure more satisfying, too, if you take risks with people and build up stronger social skills, so you can involve others in mutually enjoyable activities. Let other people help you have fun.

Only you can tell when your life is picking up steam because of the refueling you get from your leisure activities. Listen to your body—it will tell you if you have enough relief from stress and if you have the right combination of rest, zest, play, and variety in your life.

Too often in the fast-track society, people think of leisure as laziness or as a luxury they can't afford. They may be afraid of their own desire for leisure and refer to it as "just killing time" or "dropping out of circulation." That's unfortunate, because leisure is not a luxury but a necessity. It is a vital contribution to life and health.

11
Eating Right

We are surrounded by best-selling diet books, yet most Americans have only a very general idea of what constitutes good nutrition. Even those who are nutrition-conscious often do not get good advice—Americans spend one to three billion dollars a year on "health" foods, vitamin supplements, and fad diets, a tremendous outlay for dubious benefit and possibly harmful effects. You'll be best off if you remember three key principles of eating well: balance, moderation, and variety. Good eating habits alone don't make you healthy, but they can certainly help you keep, and even improve, your health. Eating well is one important way you can maintain a sound body and take control of your life.

The following guidelines are suggested for most American adults. (They do not apply to people who need special diets because of diseases or conditions that interfere with normal nutrition. These people may require special instructions from a trained dietitian in consultation with their physicians.)

Maintain a Healthy Weight

The question of being overweight is complex. For one thing, there's a difference between "overweight," "fat," and "obese." For another, statistical evidence suggests that being slightly overweight may actually extend your life and health. A definition of our terms is in order.

"Overweight" means being heavier than average for one's height. Fullbacks are usually technically "overweight," but they are muscular rather than fat. "Fat" means having excess body fat. "Obesity" represents the extreme in body fatness.

The average percentage of weight formed by fat increases with age, ranging from about 15 to 25 percent in men and about 25 to 32 percent in women. Excess fatness is considered to become obesity when the proportion of body fat goes up 5 percent or more above the average for one's age. But it would be a mistake to assume that the average is also the ideal; it may be common to gain weight with age, but it isn't necessarily the best thing for your health. For that reason, it is wise to consider the lower average percentages to be baseline or ideal, and obesity to be present when 20 percent of body weight is fat in men and 30 percent is fat in women.

Obesity is strongly associated with high blood pressure, heart disease, diabetes, and even cancer. But the medical problems come with obesity, not with simple overweight or being "pleasingly plump." *The health risks are at the extreme ends of the weight scale—obesity and extreme thinness*—and both may be related to the inability to handle stress.

A word about actuarial tables for height and weight. Most of these were first developed by insurance companies after World War II, when the idea was that the thinner you were, the longer you'd live. As always with conclusions that apply to large populations, insurance tables work as a group measure, but they may not apply at all to an individual. Furthermore, data from several studies (including the large, ongoing Framingham Study) suggest that those who are slightly overweight—but only slightly—live longer than any other group. Indeed, when the Metropolitan Life Insurance Company released new height and weight tables in 1983, the ideal weight for a long life was adjusted upward for the first time since 1959. The latest tables show an average increase in recommended weight of 13 pounds for men with small frames, 7 pounds for men with medium frames, and 2 pounds for men with large frames. For women, the average increase is 10 pounds for those with small frames, 8 pounds for women with medium frames, and 3 pounds for women with large frames. However, the new ideal weights, though higher than in the past, are still below the average weights of most Americans. And critics of the new tables say the prolonged life is due to advances in other areas of health care and that people are living longer in spite of being overweight.

If you are obese, you are endangering your health. If you are obese and also have high blood pressure, and if you drink and smoke, you are a keg of gunpowder waiting for the ignition that may come to you by way of sudden stress. Furthermore, obesity is in itself a source of stress, since people who are grossly overfat usually don't feel in control of either their weight or their lives. The obese person needs medical attention.

How do you know if you're "obese" and not merely "overweight" or "fat"? Let's start with the standard tables, but only as a point of discussion. For both men and women, if your weight is more than 20 percent above the top end of the range for your height and frame size and you are not unusually muscular, you are obese.

Height and Weight Standards

Following are weight tables by height and size of frame, for people aged 25 to 59, in shoes and wearing five pounds of indoor clothing for men, three pounds for women.

MEN

HEIGHT	SMALL	MEDIUM	LARGE
5'2"	128–134	131–141	138–150
5'3"	130–136	133–143	140–153
5'4"	132–138	135–145	142–156
5'5"	134–140	137–148	144–160
5'6"	136–142	139–151	146–164
5'7"	138–145	142–154	149–168
5'8"	140–148	145–157	152–172
5'9"	142–151	148–160	155–176

MEN

HEIGHT	SMALL	MEDIUM	LARGE
5'10"	144–154	151–163	158–180
5'11"	146–157	154–166	161–184
6'0"	149–160	157–170	164–188
6'1"	152–164	160–174	168–192
6'2"	155–168	164–178	172–197
6'3"	158–172	167–182	176–202
6'4"	162–176	171–187	181–207

WOMEN

HEIGHT	SMALL	MEDIUM	LARGE
4'10"	102–111	109–121	118–131
4'11"	103–113	111–123	120–134
5'0"	104–115	113–126	122–137
5'1"	106–118	115–129	125–140
5'2"	108–121	118–132	128–143
5'3"	111–124	121–135	131–147
5'4"	114–127	124–138	134–151
5'5"	117–130	127–141	137–155
5'6"	120–133	130–144	140–159
5'7"	123–136	133–147	143–163
5'8"	126–139	136–150	146–167
5'9"	129–142	139–153	149–170
5'10"	132–145	142–156	152–173
5'11"	135–148	145–159	155–176
6'0"	138–151	148–162	158–179

Courtesy of Metropolitan Life Insurance Company.

The Twenties Test

The life insurance table gives you a rough idea of where your weight falls on the acceptable scale. Now for the next test. Many people attain their "normal" adult weight in their mid-twenties. If you have had what was considered a normal weight and if you are more than 20 percent above what you weighed then, you are probably obese. To feel your best, aim at no more than 10 percent above that weight.

The Jiggle Test and the Pinch Test

Take off your clothes and look in the mirror. Give yourself the "jiggle test": jump up and down. If you see too much flesh jiggling around, you have a problem. While you are standing still, see if you can pinch an inch of flesh around your middle or wherever you gain weight most easily. More than an inch means you are carrying too much fat.

Fighting Overfat

The word in any successful diet is *gradual*. It took you a long time to acquire that excess fat, and it is not going to melt away, no matter what anybody tells you.

To lose weight:

Increase your physical activity. People who maintain a good weight are best off if they don't rely on eating the absolute minimum to stay thin. They eat enough of the proper foods to satisfy their hunger and get abundant nutrients, and at the same time they burn off calories with regular exercise. Exercising right and eating right are the healthy ways to keep your weight at the ideal level, not dieting to the point of deprivation.

Eat less fat and fatty foods.

Eat less sugar and sweets.

Avoid too much alcohol. An average alcoholic drink (a 1½-ounce jigger of 80-proof gin, rum, whisky, or vodka; a 4-ounce glass of wine; 8 ounces of beer) contains 100 calories, which can distort a diet by adding calories and crowding out needed nutrients.

Improve your eating habits. Prepare smaller portions, avoid seconds, and eat slowly. Putting your fork down between every bite of food will guarantee that you eat slowly. It takes 15 to 20 minutes from the time you have had enough to eat for the satiety center in your brain to get the message that your stomach is no longer empty. If you're still eating during that time, you can quickly add a lot of calories that you won't feel the need for in a few minutes. Using low-calorie, slow-eating foods for appetizers and salad will keep you from eating too much before the meal.

Distribute your calories more evenly throughout the day. Many overfat people eat 60 percent of their total calories at dinner and go to sleep with a leaden stomach. Exercising before dinner reduces your dinner appetite. So does eating breakfast and lunch.

Why Crash Diets Fail

For those who lose weight too rapidly, there is a hidden risk: as a survival mechanism, the body's metabolism will reset itself at a much lower caloric requirement. This leads to the "rebound" phenomenon.

If you go on a crash diet (less than 800 calories a day) for as little as three weeks, your body attempts to adjust by lowering your basic caloric requirements by about one-third. The minute you resume your normal eating habits you will gain weight faster than you ever did, because a normal intake now appears to your body to be "gorging." It may take up to a year for your body to get back to a normal metabolism, and in that time you could become fatter than ever.

Eat a Variety of Foods

You need about forty different nutrients to stay healthy. These include vitamins and minerals as well as amino acids (from proteins), essential fatty acids (from vegetable oils), and sources of energy (calories from carbohydrates, fats, and proteins). These nutrients are all found in the foods you normally eat.

Most foods contain more than one nutrient. Milk, for example, provides proteins, fats, sugars, riboflavin and other B-vitamins, Vitamin A, Vitamin D, calcium, and phosphorus—among others. But no single food supplies all the essential nutrients in the amounts you need. Milk, for example, contains very little iron or Vitamin C. To assure an adequate and balanced diet, therefore, a variety of foods is essential. The greater the variety, the less likely you are to develop either a deficiency or an excess of any single nutrient. (Variety also reduces the likelihood of being exposed to excessive amounts of contaminants in any single food.)

To assure variety, select your foods each day from the Basic Four food groups.

1. The Meat Group—meat, fish, poultry, and eggs, with dry beans, peas, and nuts as alternates. 2 or more servings each day.

2. The Milk Group—milk, cheese, and dairy products, including ice cream and other milk-made foods. 2 to 4 servings a day.

3. The Vegetable and Fruit Group—4 or more servings a day, including one citrus fruit and one green or yellow vegetable.

4. The Bread and Cereal Group—4 or more servings a day, including whole grains. By adding milk, you improve the body's ability to utilize the nutrients in bread and grains.

There are no known advantages to consuming excess amounts of any nutrient. You will rarely need to take vitamin or mineral supplements if you eat a wide variety of foods. There are, however, four important exceptions:

Women in their childbearing years have a greater need for iron and may need to take iron supplements to replace the iron they lose with menstrual bleeding. Women who are no longer menstruating should not routinely take iron supplements.

Women who are pregnant or who are breastfeeding need more of many nutrients, especially iron, folic acid, Vitamin A, calcium, and sources of energy. Detailed advice should come from your physician and dietitian.

Elderly or very inactive people may need—and eat—fewer calories and may therefore absorb fewer nutrients. It is best for them to pay special attention to avoiding foods high in calories and low in nutrients. This means avoiding fat, oils, alcohol, and sugar. People in this group may also need added nutrients.

Infants have special nutritional needs. To assure your baby an adequate diet, breastfeed unless there are special problems, delay other foods until the baby is three to six months old, and do *not* add salt or sugar to the baby's food. Tastes for salt and sugar are acquired. You will do your child a favor by minimizing the desire for sweet and salty flavors.

The food fads that have swept America in recent years neglect this cardinal virtue—variety. If you are considering embarking on an extreme diet, see your physician first. There are no free lunches and there are no miracle diets.

Eat Regular Meals, Including Breakfast

Some mornings, you feel on edge, your coordination is poor, your temperature is probably down, your blood sugar is low, and your chances of having an accident are increased. The culprit? Skipping breakfast.

A North Carolina Industry Commission study of 2,000 textile workers over a two-year period showed that 75 percent of industrial accidents involved workers who had not eaten breakfast.

If you eat dinner at 6 P.M. and skip breakfast the following morning, you will be going for eighteen full hours without eating. From the time you wake up, your body anticipates the metabolic stimulation that food provides. I can think of few worse dietary habits than a "breakfast" of coffee and cigarettes. If you get nothing else out of this chapter, you will vastly improve your eating habits simply by taking time for a real breakfast.

Note that unless you're a football player, you don't need the four-egg special, with ham, biscuits, and trimmings. Try this instead: a glass of juice and a bowl of low-sugar cereal and low-fat milk, topped with fresh fruit if you like. Or, instead of cereal, you could have an English muffin or whole grain toast with polyunsaturated margarine.

Avoid Too Much Fat, Saturated Fat, and Cholesterol

Cholesterol is an alcohol steroid that is carried in the blood by lipoproteins, or combinations of fat and protein. Saturated fats are mostly animal fats in meats and dairy products. Unsaturated fats are the vegetable fats. Safflower, sunflower, corn, cottonseed, and soybean oil are all "polyunsaturated" fats, which are more unsaturated than "monounsaturated" fats like olive oil and peanut oil. The polyunsaturated fats—the most unsaturated—are the healthiest. You can identify the saturated fats because they are harder or more solid at room temperature; the unsaturated fats are more liquid. Beef fat is solid at room temperature; the vegetable oils are liquid. Hydrogenated fats are unsaturated vegetable oils that have been artificially hardened, making them into saturated fats.

The relationship between cholesterol, saturated fats, and heart disease remains complex and controversial. The plain fact is that nutritionists and scientists have not yet learned the last word on cholesterol.

For a time, the common assumption was that high levels of cholesterol could clog the arteries that feed the heart and contribute to heart attack. However, although the correlation is strong, there is little proof of a cause-and-effect relationship between saturated fat intake, high blood cholesterol, and coronary disease. In fact, the kicker is that there is "good" cholesterol—high-density lipoproteins (HDLs)—and "bad" cholesterol—low-density lipoproteins (LDLs) and very low-density lipoproteins (VLDLs). Current theory holds that while the LDLs and VLDLs may help cause hardening of the arteries, the HDLs may actually protect against it. Normally, about 70 percent of our blood cholesterol is of the "bad" variety. All we can say for certain at this point is that it appears to be in our best interests to change the ratio so that we have a higher proportion of HDLs.

Some people have diets high in saturated fats and cholesterol and still keep normal blood cholesterol levels (140–190 milligrams). Other people eat low-fat, low-cholesterol diets and still have high cholesterol levels. People vary widely, depending on their heredity and the way their bodies use cholesterol. Moreover, dietary changes alone do not turn off the body's cholesterol faucets when unrelieved stress turns them on.

From a dietary standpoint, however, reduction in total fat, saturated fat, and cholesterol is sensible for the U.S. population as a whole, especially for people who have high blood pressure or who smoke. The total amount of fat consumed is probably a more significant dietary influence on heart disease than saturated fat or cholesterol.

People often ask, "Can my cholesterol be too low?" Once again, the answer at the moment is that considerable controversy exists. Statistically, there appears to be a correlation between low cholesterol levels and a likelihood of cancer of the colon. At this stage of our understanding, reasonable reduction of cholesterol is a worthy goal, but caution advises against extreme measures.

The same holds true of medications to reduce cholesterol. Whether or not these are appropriate depends upon factors that only your doctor can decide. My preference is to avoid prescribing them unless there are extreme hereditary blood fat problems. There is considerable medical evidence that each of these drugs carries some risk, so your doctor's advice is essential.

Cholesterol and related blood fats like triglycerides are a complex dietary issue, but you needn't concern yourself unnecessarily if your cholesterol level is a little on the high side. You're on the right track if you keep the total fat in your diet down, especially the total saturated fat. And it can't hurt to raise your beneficial HDL cholesterol to an optimal level. Several steps in the right direction are starting to exercise, stopping smoking, drinking in moderation, and learning to handle stress better.

A Word about Low-Fat Diets

Some people believe that a high-fiber, low-calorie, very low-fat (5 to 10 percent fat) diet—the Pritikin Diet is the best-known example—will reduce symptoms of heart disease and help prevent it. Although the general principle of eating foods high in fiber and low in fat, salt, and calories is a sound one for all of us, the low-fat diet fad takes this principle to such extremes that it will not work for ninety-nine out of one hundred people in normal life.

For instance, people can spend five weeks of isolation in a Pritikin diet camp and get some symptomatic relief from heart trouble, but this comes about mainly because of the supervised conditions. First, they lose a fair amount of weight during their confinement, and they are forced to exercise— two important factors in achieving relief from heart disease. Secondly, they are allowed absolutely no salt, nor any of the many processed foods that contain salt. Finally, it is well known that simply paying attention to people can improve their physical well-being.

In fact, the Pritikin type of diet is rigidly limited and hard to follow without offering anything that more balanced diets do not offer—in particular, there is no evidence that such diets reverse hardening of the arteries. Furthermore, to obtain long-lasting symptomatic relief, adherents of such diets must maintain extremely stringent habits like those learned at the Pritikin diet camp after they are no longer under direct supervision. All in all, a more balanced, more flexible diet— such as that recommended by the American Heart Association —is both easier to follow and just as effective in relieving symptoms that come from hardening of the arteries.

Ways to Win the Cholesterol War

Here are some suggestions to put your cholesterol level at an optimal ratio of HDLs to LDLs—that is, to increase your "good" cholesterol:

• Decrease the fat in your diet to 30 percent or less of your caloric intake per day.

- Decrease the proportion of saturated, or animal, fats.
- Increase the proportion of unsaturated fats, or vegetable oils.
- If you are overfat, lose weight. Most obese people have low levels of HDLs, but the HDLs will usually rise as they lose weight.
- Exercise to raise the HDLs.
- If you drink alcohol, do it moderately (two average drinks or less per day). Small amounts of alcohol actually raise HDLs.
- Stop smoking. Smoking decreases HDLs and increases "bad" cholesterol.

Here are some specific suggestions for food intake to avoid high levels of blood fats:

- Eat less meat. Substitute vegetable proteins for some of your meat meals.
- Eat red meats (beef, pork, lamb) less often and poultry, fish, and shellfish more often.
- Choose lean cuts of meat without marbling, and trim all meats well. Remove skin and fat pads from chicken and poultry.
- Avoid high-fat meats such as bacon, salt pork, sausages, lunch meats, and frankfurters.
- Eat organ meats (liver, kidneys, brains, sweetbreads, heart) only occasionally, since these are rich sources of nutrients but are also high in cholesterol.
- Prepare meats without additional fat. Cook them by broiling, roasting, baking, and boiling rather than frying.
- Prepare soups and stews ahead of time, chill them, and skim off the accumulated excess fat.
- Eat eggs in moderation. Use egg substitutes some of the time.
- Use low-fat milk, nonfat skim milk, or buttermilk made from skim milk instead of whole milk.
- Use low-fat cottage cheese and ricotta cheese. Limit the amount of hard cheese you use and select those made from part-skim milk such as mozzarella, Parmesan, and farmer's cheese.

- Limit your intake of butter, cream, hydrogenated margarines, shortening, lards, coconut oils, suet, chocolate, and foods made from such products.
- Substitute liquid vegetable oil for solid shortening whenever possible, and limit the total amount of shortening.
- Read the label to determine if a food contains a lot of fat or saturated fat.

Eat Foods with Adequate Starch and Fiber

The major sources of energy are carbohydrates and fats (proteins also supply energy, but to a lesser extent).

Carbohydrates have a tremendous advantage over fats—they contain less than half the number of calories per ounce. So a simple formula for maintaining ideal weight is to replace some fats with carbohydrates.

Complex carbohydrates are more nutritious than simple carbohydrates. The simple carbohydrates—such as sugars—provide calories but little in the way of nutrients. The complex carbohydrates, or starches—vegetables, dried beans and peas, nuts, seeds, breads, cereals, and cereal products—contain many essential nutrients. Increasing your consumption of complex carbohydrates can also help increase dietary fiber, a food element in which the American diet is low. Eating more foods high in fiber tends to reduce the symptoms of chronic constipation, diverticulosis, and some types of "irritable bowel." There is also concern that diets with insufficient fiber can increase the risk of cancer of the colon.

To eat more complex carbohydrates daily:

- Substitute complex carbohydrates for fats and sugars.
- Select foods that are good sources of fiber, such as whole-grain breads and cereals, fruits and vegetables, beans, peas, and nuts.

Avoid Too Much Salt, Or Sodium

Sodium has been linked to high blood pressure for many decades. Salt is a chemical composed of sodium and chloride. It is the sodium part of the salt molecule (40 percent by weight) that is believed to be the precipitating factor in producing disease states such as high blood pressure.

Many investigators believe Americans eat too much salt. Americans daily take two to four teaspoons of salt—20 to 40 times the amount suggested to be needed by a healthy person. This excess put salt on the cover of *Time* magazine as Dietary Enemy No. 1.

The interaction between sodium and stress is powerful, making sodium a major factor in this nation's epidemic of hypertension. The vigilance response provoked by unrelieved stress can produce excess amounts of the stress chemical cortisol, and cortisol causes the body to cling tightly to sodium. When it does, the body retains water. This triggers a chain of events that leads to high blood pressure. Also, the retention of sodium can cause the heart muscle to lose potassium, which is essential for healthy heart rhythms.

It is a high price to pay, especially when you consider there are *no known benefits to humans of excessive sodium intake.*

Up to half of sodium intake may be hidden, either as a naturally occurring part of food or, more often, as part of an added preservative or flavoring agent. However, since the news media have trained their big guns on salt, the response has been gratifying. Public and governmental pressure is forcing food establishments, the fast-food chains and producers of canned and frozen foods to lower salt use.

To cut back on salt:

- Cook with no salt or only small amounts of salt.
- Add little or no salt at the table.
- Limit your intake of salty foods, such as prepared soups, potato chips, pretzels, salted nuts and popcorn (bars always

put out free nuts and pretzels because salt makes you thirsty), cheese, pickled foods, cured meats, and condiments such as soy sauce, steak sauce, and garlic salt.

- Read food labels carefully to determine the amounts of sodium in processed food and snack items. Watch for baking powder, baking soda, monosodium glutamate (MSG), sodium nitrate, sodium phosphate, sodium ascorbate, and sodium saccharin.

- If you're hooked on the taste, I recommend substitutes. You can find them in most supermarkets.

- When you eat out, order something individually prepared and ask that no salt be used in the preparation. For salads, ask for oil and vinegar on the side and mix your own. Bring along your salt substitute.

- When you fly, request the salt-free diet. Most airlines require at least twenty-four hours' notice, but if you notify them regularly your preference will be computerized and you can regularly fly not only in a nonsmoking part of the plane but with a salt-free diet.

Avoid Too Much Sugar

The most widely acknowledged health hazard from eating too much sugar is, of course, tooth decay. From a dental standpoint, the number of exposures to sugar is important as well as the amount of sugar you consume.

Excess sugar intake also appears related to higher levels of blood fats like cholesterol and triglycerides. Some people show high blood triglyceride levels when they take in excessive amounts of carbohydrates or alcohol. These elevations are less apt to occur when complex carbohydrates are substituted for simple sugars. However, most experts doubt that elevated triglycerides are a risk factor in coronary heart disease.

Nevertheless, if you're trying to reduce the stress in your life, too much sugar is something you should learn to live without. If you eat too much sugar, your level of blood sugar rises rapidly. This can at first make you feel more energetic. Your body, however, responds to excess sugar by commanding the pancreas to release insulin, which reduces the high sugar level. This can cause your energy level to drop abruptly. If you are a hot reactor, moreover, the adrenaline of the alarm reaction can further raise the level of blood sugar by causing the release of glycogen. This stimulates the production of still more insulin to control the blood sugar level. If the body produces too much insulin, the result is drastically lowered blood sugar levels, a condition known as reactive hypoglycemia. Such extremely low blood sugar is associated with alternations in behavior, sometimes to the point of coma and convulsions. But even without such severe reactions, you don't need to provide yourself with the additional stress of an emotional roller-coaster ride.

To avoid excess sugars:

- Use less of all sugars, including white sugar, brown sugar, raw sugar, honey, and syrups.
- Eat less of foods containing these sugars, such as candy, soft drinks, ice creams, cakes, and cookies.
- Select fresh fruits or fruits canned without sugars.
- Read food labels for clues on sugar content—if the names sucrose, glucose, maltose, dextrose, lactose, fructose, or syrups appear near the beginning of the list of ingredients, then there is a large amount of sugar.
- Remember, how often you eat sugar is as important as how much sugar you eat.

Don't Be a Vitamin Abuser

More is not better and can even be dangerous when it comes to vitamins. The word "vitamin" was coined in 1911 by the Polish-American biochemist, Kasimir Funk. He was referring to organic substances that are essential for life and that we must get from food because the human body either cannot make them or can make them only in inadequate amounts. So vitamins are essential, but if you are healthy and are eating a variety of foods, *you are probably getting all the vitamins you need in your normal diet.* There are exceptions, of course, but these are decisions for your physician or dietitian.

The Food and Nutrition Board of the National Academy of Sciences sets Recommended Dietary Allowances, or RDAs. These RDAs are the daily levels of essential nutrients considered adequate to meet the nutritional needs of practically all healthy persons. You can usually safely exceed the RDA level of vitamins by two or three times, but if, like some people, you start using megadoses—a megadose of vitamins is defined as ten times the RDA—you are asking for trouble. Taking vitamins at megadose levels can poison the body.

Millions of Americans are passing the most expensive urine in the world because the body rapidly eliminates the water-soluble vitamins—B and C—when they exceed what it needs. On the other hand, it hangs onto vitamins that are fat soluble—A, D, C, and K—and that can be toxic. The problem is that fat-soluble vitamins accumulate over a long period of time and are not eliminated from the body. Overdoses can cause a number of problems:

Vitamin A, which prevents night blindness and maintains the normal condition of mucous membranes, produces toxic symptoms when five to eight times the RDA is consumed over a long period of time. Symptoms of Vitamin A poisoning are similar to those of brain tumors, including headaches, blurred vision, loss of appetite, impairment of eyesight, muscle soreness after exercise, and general drying and flaking of the skin.

Vitamin D has also been shown to be toxic in large amounts. Its function is to regulate calcium and phosphate metabolism. A Vitamin D deficiency causes rickets in children and softness of the bones in adults. Overdoses, on the other hand, increase the body's absorption of calcium, and the excess is deposited in the soft tissues, such as the heart, lungs, kidney, and brain, where it can cause organ damage and failure. Excess Vitamin D can cause loss of appetite, nausea, weakness, weight loss, vague aches, stiffness, and even death.

Vitamin E helps form red blood cells, muscles, and other body tissues, and protects Vitamin A and the essential fatty acids from oxidation. It is so common that a deficiency is seldom seen. In adults the risks of large doses are ill-defined, but megadoses can interfere with blood clotting by destroying Vitamin K.

Excess Vitamin E also impairs the formation of Vitamin A in the liver and sometimes causes gastrointestinal upsets and muscle weakness. Other complications include leg phlebitis leading to clotting in the lungs, swelling of the tissues, high blood pressure, and severe fatigue. In animals, excess Vitamin E interferes with wound healing. Note: There is no evidence that Vitamin E megadoses can slow human aging, prevent heart attacks, counter the symptoms of menopause, or maintain virility and fertility. In fact, recent research demonstrates that excess Vitamin E actually diminishes the sex drive.

Vitamin K, which is intended to aid in clotting blood, is the least controversial. It is synthesized in the intestinal tract and deficiencies are rare. There is no specific recommended dietary allowance, and it is seldom the target of vitamin fraud.

Since the body can eliminate excess amounts through the urine, megadoses of the water-soluble vitamins are not as serious a problem as the fat-soluble vitamins. However, there are some complications:

Vitamin B_1, or thiamine, can in megadoses cause extremely bad breath, or "gorilla breath."

Vitamin B_6 (pyroxidine) dependence resulting in abnormal electroencephalograms and convulsions has been observed in normal humans taking daily supplements of 200 mg for over a month.

Massive doses of *Vitamin C* interfere with anticoagulant drugs (intended to thin blood in the treatment of clotting); cause diarrhea if more than one gram per day is used; elevate oxalic and uric acid levels, leading to kidney stones; and can cause dependency, so that deficiency symptoms may occur with diminished use. A person dependent upon massive doses of Vitamin C must be weaned off the high levels gradually, or symptoms of scurvy may appear.

Vitamin C is the subject of several controversies:

Colds. Studies show that Vitamin C does not protect you from getting colds, but it may diminish the severity of the symptoms.

Cancer. At present there is not enough research to draw conclusions of any kind about whether Vitamin C does or does not protect against cancer.

Heart disease. There is no evidence that Vitamin C helps prevent or reverse hardening of the arteries.

Minerals in Megadoses Can Poison, Too

Vitamins are organic substances that are required in the diet. Minerals are the inorganic substances that are required. The seven minerals needed in larger amounts—the "macrominerals"—are calcium, phosphorus, potassium, magnesium, sulphur, sodium, and chloride. The nine essential "microminerals," or trace elements, are iron, selenium, zinc, manganese, molybdenum, copper, iodine, chromium, and fluorine.

There are problems with excessive doses of minerals. Large doses of calcium tend to cause drowsiness and lethargy. Large doses of phosphorus hinder absorption of calcium. Excess magnesium has a laxative effect. Excess iron can cause damage to the liver, pancreas, and heart, and the only way to get rid of excess iron is by bleeding. Excess zinc causes nausea, vomiting, and bleeding in the stomach. Copper, fluorine, manganese, and molybdenum are all poisons in large amounts.

Vitamin and mineral supplements are appropriate when you're on a diet of less than 1200 calories a day. On a diet this spartan, it is hard to meet the RDAs from food alone, even with the best of planning. In such cases, a regular daily vitamin that contains 75 to 100 percent of the RDA makes sense.

But in the vast majority of cases, if you eat a variety of foods from the four basic food groups designed for an optimal caloric intake, *you should not need mineral or vitamin supplements.* If you think you might have use for a vitamin or mineral supplement, consult your physician and/or a dietitian your physician recommends.

Be Prudent When Traveling and Eating Out

One of the biggest changes in contemporary lifestyle is the move of the family from the dining room table to fast-food row.

The problem with most fast-food operations is that they don't offer the needed variety, their food is often too high in fat and too salty, and their desserts are too sugary. Some are recognizing this and trying to improve things, including installing salad bars.

Here are some general guidelines for eating out:

- For an appetizer, select fruit or fruit juice, nonsalted and nonsmoked fish, or shellfish cocktail.
- As an entree, your best bets are lean cuts of meat, broiled fish, and poultry that is unsalted.
- For salads, use a low-calorie dressing or have oil and vinegar delivered on the side and mix your own salad dressing. You can also order regular dressing served on the side. Then, instead of pouring it on the salad, dip your fork in the dressing before each bite. You'll get the flavor on each bite and consume about one-third the dressing you would otherwise have eaten.
- For sandwiches, skip pickles and salty meats like processed lunch meats, ham, and corned beef and you'll miss a lot of salt.
- For desserts, angel food cake or fresh fruit is a good choice. Almost any fruit is preferable to a rich dessert.
- For beverages, try fruit juices, low-fat and skim milk, or coffee and tea in reasonable amounts. Diet soft drinks have some sodium, but not a lot.
- Ask that the bread or rolls be served with the main course instead of with the salad. You will probably eat the entree

even if you're already full of rolls—but if they arrive together it will be easier to eat all of *some* things or *some* of
all things. Once you've taken a reasonable portion, have the
remaining "common dish" items, like rolls, removed from
the table.

- Many restaurants serve portions larger than you need. When
the dish arrives, immediately cut off a quarter to a third of
the main foods, place them on a side dish and have this
removed (ask for a doggy bag if you like). Spread the
remaining food out to cover your plate if it makes you feel
better. Then take time to enjoy each bite. It's much easier
to make one initial reducing decision than to keep telling
yourself you'll leave part of the food on your plate. If you
were raised a member of the clean plate club, don't fight it.
Just be intelligent about choosing what food on your plate
you'll clean up.

- Finally, try not to overeat at a restaurant simply because
you're paying for the food!

The Flyer's Diet

Jet traveling across time zones upsets the normal routine.
Stomach upsets, including constipation and diarrhea, often
accompany long trips because of new eating patterns and
unfamiliar food. Some common sense can help head off trouble.

Don't overeat. If you will be sitting a lot rather than moving and exercising, eat less than you normally would. High-
protein meals tend to keep you awake, while high-carbohydrate
meals tend to make you sleepy. Scrape high-calorie sauces
off meats and skip the salad dressing. If you call the airlines at
least twenty-four hours before flight time, you can often get a
special meal, such as a seafood salad or a low-calorie dinner.

Don't overdrink alcohol. Most planes are pressurized above
altitudes of 6,000 or 8,000 feet, and this gives alcohol an
added punch. One or two drinks hit you like three or four at
sea level. Once you hit the ground, go light on drinking until
your body adjusts. Jet lag, disruption of normal routines, and
changed sleeping patterns may at first reduce your tolerance
for alcohol and make you irritable.

Drink water to avoid becoming dehydrated. Air cabin humidity is very low, which may make you feel dried out. Remember that alcohol is dehydrating and will contribute to this sensation. So does the caffeine in coffee, tea, and cola drinks, which are mild diuretics and cause the body to lose fluids.

If you're vulnerable to heart disease, it is especially important to *watch your salt and potassium.* Air travel across time zones stimulates production of the stress chemical cortisol, causing the body to retain sodium and lose potassium. Excess sodium can cause the heart to work harder, and diminished potassium can interfere with the smooth functioning of the heart. If you have a heart condition, drink plenty of nonsalty liquids—not alcohol—to flush the sodium out of your system, and keep your potassium up by eating bananas and citrus fruits and drinking orange juice. Order a low-salt meal in advance through the airline or your travel agent, and avoid peanuts, pretzels, and other salty snacks (carbonated drinks contain some sodium, too). Eat lightly the day before and the day of travel, and upon arrival have a high-protein meal, watch your salt for three days, and keep your potassium up. Since alcohol can also stimulate the body's production of cortisol, you should avoid combining alcohol with air travel if you're taking special care of your heart.

Finally, if you are prone to blood clots, taking a baby-aspirin once a day can help prevent the clots.

Making Yourself Do What You Want To Do

The first big step in developing healthy eating habits is understanding what they are and why. The second step is knowing how to change the habits you have and build better ones into your everyday life.

A habit that many of us find hard to change is overeating. I often try to help my patients gain control of their stresses before adding a weight loss program to the things they are trying to manage. Many people do better with a diet if they have some extra time and energy to put into learning and practicing new habits. On the other hand, many find it easier to regulate their eating than to take control of other things in their life. Success in losing weight powerfully reinforces the feeling that you are in control. Choosing when to diet has to be a personal decision.

To make it work, plan to commit significant time and energy, expect to be rather preoccupied with the process while you are immersed in it, accept that you will be hungry sometimes but that these periods will pass, reward yourself for losses as you go, and look for support from friends (choose the ones who will be sympathetic) and weight-loss groups. Finally, if you lose your momentum by going off the diet, don't succumb to guilt and go back to the old cycle of overeating.

Many overeaters experience stress as hunger. These feelings are often followed by a quick fix of overeating. It's a cycle—you become upset, you see others eating, or you encounter other stimuli that you associate with hunger. You then believe that you are hungry and you eat or overeat.

This behavior leads to another thought pattern: you feel a loss of control and inability to deal with stress. You also gain weight. This "proves" you are out of control and you promptly feel guilty. Of course, this thought pattern causes you to pile on the food, and the weight some more. This is what I call the "scale personality." When people with this pattern step on the scales the next morning, their mood is fixed for the day—guilty. This feeling of guilt and remorse hangs over some overeaters the way smog hangs over Los Angeles. They may feel so guilty they don't eat all day, and sooner or later the feeling called hunger (this time ravenous) returns, and the cycle resumes.

The route out of this vicious cycle is rejecting guilt and regaining control of your eating pattern. Guilt is the most useless of emotions. It is much more productive to use this energy for problem-solving than for putting yourself down. The crucial time to turn things around is when you have eaten something that doesn't fit your chosen eating pattern. *Don't give up* when this happens. Turn this moment into a plus, an opportunity, by going right back on the diet and giving yourself a reward (anything but food!) for persisting.

Set as your goal not only losing weight but breaking the cycle of defeat, guilt, and loss of control by not admitting defeat, not accepting guilt, and above all not accepting that you have lost control. You can regain control at any time by going back on your diet. Don't fall into the trap of thinking there's no point to it once you've gone "off the wagon." The sooner you go back on, the sooner you'll regain your sense of control and feel better about yourself.

Are you misreading your body's signals? If you associate food with comfort, a common habit, you may experience many feelings as hunger. It helps to learn the difference between fatigue, anxiety, depression, sadness, and real hunger. Figure out what else you can do to relieve these feelings besides eating. You might distract yourself or lift your spirits by spending time with others, exercising, resting, or accomplishing some task. Make a list of the things that work for you when you're down, and turn to them when you feel hungry but you don't want to eat.

Habits, Not Diets

Ultimately, diet is not the way you want to think of your weight loss program. To most people, "diet" is a four-letter word. What you are doing is changing your *habits,* so that eventually your pattern of eating low-fat, low-sugar foods in reasonable portions at reasonable times becomes the most comfortable, normal pattern for you. It happens! Once you've reached your weight goal you'll be able to eat more, but you'll know how to do it. As you reeducate your palate, you reeducate your thinking, your feelings, and your behavior in regard to food.

Changing habits is a long-term process that takes a lot of commitment. One way to reinforce yourself for hanging in there is to join a weight loss group. Weight Watchers, TOPS (Take Off Pounds Sensibly), and Diet Workshop are among those that have an excellent nutritional program and expertise in helping people stick with a diet. That's the crucial combination—good nutrition and moral support. I recommend these groups.

Of course, you can also lose weight by burning up more calories. It is dangerous and foolish to try to do this by using drugs that kill the appetite or stimulate the metabolism, such as diet pills and nicotine. The best way is to exercise. It takes 3,500 calories to produce a pound of fat, so to lose that pound you have to reduce your food and calorie intake or use up those calories in extra physical activity. You're best off doing both, with the accent on exercise for all the benefits it brings in addition to weight loss. So go back and read the chapter on fitness and resolve to start exercising. It will make you feel good about your body and yourself.

If you want to learn more about eating right, sound advice is available from your local public health department, county extension office, county or state medical society, hospital outpatient office, and the local offices of the diabetes, dietetic, and heart associations.

Once you're eating right, you'll want to take the next step and break any bad habits you might have with cigarettes, alcohol, caffeine, and pills. This deadly quartet is our next subject.

12
Managing Alcohol, Cigarettes, Caffeine, & Pills

Singer Nat "King" Cole, whose mellow voice belied a three-pack-a-day smoking habit, died of lung cancer.

Comedian Freddie Prinze, on top of the world at twenty-one, ran afoul of stress, drugs, and depression and put a gun to his head.

Alcoholism ended the congressional career of Congressman Wilbur Mills, whose brilliant handling of intricate tax and revenue issues made him for a time one of the most powerful men in Washington.

Eccentric billionaire Howard Hughes, whose research institute pioneered techniques to treat kidney disease, died in a Mexican hotel room of kidney failure brought on by addiction to the pain-killers aspirin and codeine, and by a nearly total neglect of his health.

The drug-related, stress-related medical maladies of these celebrities are symptomatic. Their ills can be found among millions of Americans.

In ways that we don't fully understand, nicotine, caffeine, alcohol, and some drugs have the ability to trigger in the brain the release of adrenaline-derived chemicals that cause a pleasurable feeling of being in control. This momentary pleasure is perceived as a means of coping with daily stress, and the need for this feeling can lead to addiction.

In moderation, some of these agents are beneficial. Tobacco is not; its toxic, or poisonous, effects on the body are well established. On the other hand, nothing is wrong with drinking a cup of coffee to wake you up in the morning so you can approach the day's work with an alert mind. By the same token, a glass or two of wine at night can make for a memorable meal—and evening. A tranquilizer can give temporary relief from acute anxiety. Properly used, coffee, alcohol, and drugs can reduce stress. In excess, however, they magnify stress to the breaking point.

Let's look a little closer at each of these common substances. Through awareness you can use all but one of them, tobacco, to reduce, not reinforce, your stress level.

Smoking

The single best thing you can do to protect your health is to stop smoking.

Since almost all the news about smoking is bad, let me give you the good news first:

Overwhelming evidence suggests that people who quit smoking will live longer than those who continue. Although some studies indicate that the longevity of former smokers will never equal that of lifelong nonsmokers, other studies actually suggest that if you kick the habit, you may outlive those who never had it! If this is true, it may be because people who quit smoking gain a sense of control over their lives that extends into other areas. Quitting smoking may be the push you need to take charge of your life.

Here are the other reasons why you should quit:

- Of the fifty million Americans who smoke, *one-third to one-half will die simply because they smoke*. Lung cancer is the most publicized fatal result of smoking, but less well known are the equally deadly effects of smoking on heart disease, especially heart attack and sudden cardiac death.
- While most people who drink are not addicted to alcohol, nicotine dependence is almost universal among cigarette smokers. It is estimated that *98 percent of all smokers are addicted to nicotine*.

- A woman who is pregnant and smokes endangers not only her own health, but also the health of the child she is carrying. The consequences of "passive smoking" upon the unborn fetus—including the breaking of chromosomes—have yet to be fully determined, but there is widespread agreement in the medical community that *pregnant women should not smoke.*

Smoking's "Deadly Duo"—Nicotine and Carbon Monoxide

Smoking does its damage primarily through the harmful effects of tars and contaminants on the lungs and of nicotine and carbon monoxide on the heart and circulatory system.

We discussed earlier how the body's alarm reaction released adrenaline and other stress chemicals, raising heart rate and blood pressure so the body can respond to physical emergencies. When you smoke, nicotine doubles, triples, and quadruples the amount of adrenaline in your circulation. This means that your heart rate quickens, your blood pressure rises, and your heart demands more oxygen. Heavy smokers require a nicotine hit every 20 to 30 minutes during their waking hours. Think of all the adrenaline this releases into the body!

Carbon monoxide, or CO, is the second half of smoking's one-two punch to the cardiovascular system. You can get CO either from your auto exhaust system or from cigarettes. In your body, CO attacks the main oxygen carrier in the blood, hemoglobin. The CO clings to hemoglobin with 250 times the tenacity that oxygen does, establishing a beachhead in your blood and preventing a normal amount of oxygen from landing. Some heavy smokers have up to 20 percent of their blood occupied by carbon monoxide.

Ironically, CO pollution in your blood can give you pink cheeks and the look of health—that's because CO-bound hemoglobin is cherry red and the capillaries carrying the hemoglobin are close to the surface of your cheeks. But the look is purely cosmetic. Carbon monoxide is the kiss of death.

While nicotine releases adrenaline into your bloodstream, speeding up your heart, raising your blood pressure, and creating demand by the heart for more oxygen, CO crowds out the vital oxygen required by the heart. Under stress, this combination can cause chaotic heart rhythms that culminate in sudden cardiac death.

Nicotine and CO also contribute to hardening of the arteries, a condition that can intensify the demands placed upon the heart. One theory holds that CO damages the inner lining of the arterial walls. Adrenaline powered by nicotine further blasts away at the delicate inner linings of the arterial walls, and it also increases the blood's "stickiness" by activating the tiny platelets that are the first stage of clotting. Nature intended the platelets to speed to injuries in the body, forming a clot to prevent loss of blood. This protective system backfires when the arterial walls become injured. The platelets rush to the arteries, forming a sticky spot that soon attracts fats and other minerals in the bloodstream, and hardening of the arteries begins.

A special warning: Women who are on birth control pills and smoke run an even higher risk of developing or aggravating hardening of the arteries, blood clotting, and heart disease.

Smoking also aggravates angina, or chest pain, related to heart trouble. Many of my patients who throw away their cigarettes find they have also thrown away their angina, or at least made it a lighter burden.

In addition to the dangers of nicotine and CO, cigarettes contain some 4,000 or so additional chemical components whose effects on the body are unknown. Scientists have no reason to think they will help your health.

Marijuana Has Risks, Too

The long-term risks of marijuana for heart disease are not yet known, simply because scientists have not yet had time to determine them. However, research has shown that in the short term, marijuana is dangerous for heart patients, cutting in half the amount of exercise they can safely undertake without angina.

Cigars, Pipes, and Filters Aren't Much Better

Cigar and pipe smokers run a smaller risk of heart disease than cigarette smokers do, for reasons yet to be determined. These may include the noninhaling of smoke, the different kinds of tobacco used, a cooler combustion temperature, and personalities of cigar and pipe smokers as opposed to cigarette smokers. However, the risk of heart disease for cigar and pipe smokers is still almost twice the risk for nonsmokers. And for those who inhale (including many who switch from cigarettes to cigars or pipes), the risk of heart disease remains approximately the same as it is for cigarette smokers.

Filters can reduce nicotine and tars, but they usually increase carbon monoxide. And smokers of low nicotine cigarettes still crave the nicotine "hit," so they are likely to smoke more cigarettes. The data are not at all clear that low-tar or low-nicotine cigarettes reduce the dangers of smoking; in fact, recent research suggests they do not. Don't be confused by advertising claims. The only way to be safe is to be a nonsmoker.

Finally, you can be seriously discomforted, even actually harmed, by inhaling smoke from those around you. The Federal Centers for Disease Control refer to it as "side-stream smoke danger." Smoke from the cigarettes of others can cause an increase in your heart rate, blood pressure, and CO intake. Not as much as if you actually smoked yourself, but certainly enough to demand relief. Clearly, there's reason to designate public areas where smoking is banned.

The Tragedy of Lung Cancer

Among lung cancer patients, 91 percent die within five years of diagnosis. The carcinogenic dose is about 125,000 cigarettes, or a pack a day for 17 years. This rule holds regardless of what brand you smoke or with what filter. If cancer runs in your family, the odds increase. If you've been a heavy smoker, it takes 12 years before you can be sure that all the cancer-causing residue is gone.

Men started smoking cigarettes on a large scale during

World War I, and their lung cancers showed up during World War II. Women started smoking heavily during World War II, and their lung cancers are beginning to show up now.

Lung cancer will shortly replace breast cancer as the leading cancer killer of women.

Studies have shown that people refuse to listen to warnings about smoking for two reasons—an unduly optimistic view of medical science ("By the time I get lung cancer, they'll have a cure") and a belief in personal invulnerability ("It can never happen to me"). Yet in America, it has often been the indomitable figure, the man who bowed to no one, who has himself been conquered by lung cancer brought on by smoking. Look at Babe Ruth, Charles Lindbergh, John Wayne, Steve McQueen. No one is invulnerable. And there is no cure.

The Methodist Hospital in Indianapolis runs a series of medical tests it calls the "Health Hazard Appraisal." Patients get a printout measuring their risk of dying within ten years, compared to the average for their age group, and an idea of how their behaviors and lifestyle affect their odds. One newspaper sent through the appraisal a 32-year-old reporter who was both a heavy smoker and a heavy drinker. These two health habits alone make him five times more likely than average to die in an auto accident. His risk of dying of cirrhosis of the liver was more than 12 times the average; of pneumonia, three times; of heart disease, five times; of lung cancer, twice the average. If the reporter had a chest cold, his doctor would give him advice and follow his progress. In fact, this man is running very serious health risks that make a chest cold look like nothing, but he is seeking no help and doing nothing about the behavior that exposes him to such increased risk of illness and death.

How Do You Quit?

The best way is not to start. Many programs are now aimed at young people to prevent smoking. We need even more.

Once someone has started, the best way to quit is to go

cold turkey. Studies show that this method is the most likely to get lasting results. Physicians can help greatly if they will only tell their patients in the strongest language possible to stop—and mean it. I have found that most patients will stop if they realize that their physician is seriously concerned about the harmful effects of smoking on their heart. (For physicians, the National Cancer Institute offers a "Helping Smokers Quit" package, available from the National Institute of Health, Building 30, Room 4B-39, Bethesda, Md. 20205.)

You don't have to go it alone. Hypnosis works for some patients. Various organizations offer group programs. Consult your local medical society, hospital outpatient department, or public health department. Or the local branch of the American Cancer Society.

Many people say they cannot quit because they become irritable or put on weight. Remember this: You are better off temporarily cranky and fat than putting your life in danger with an addiction to nicotine and CO. Besides, crankiness and extra pounds are problems you can solve. Millions of ex-smokers have solved them, and they feel great about it. They've regained their health, plus control of a problem— smoking—that used to control them.

Coffee

Since smoking and coffee drinking often go together, the health risks of drinking too much coffee have often been overlooked in the emphasis on the health risks of smoking too many cigarettes. But James Henry and Patricia Stephens of the University of Southern California School of Medicine recently concluded that "the caffeine habit should be considered together with the smoking habit, high blood pressure, and Type A behavior as risk factors for sudden death in persons diagnosed as having heart disease."

Caffeine, like nicotine, triggers the release of adrenaline. You get a caffeine hit just as you get a nicotine hit. In moderate doses, this gives you a pleasurable feeling of being on top of things and helps you to cope. However, as I have emphasized throughout this book, the continuous stimulation of stress chemicals without physical release is not good for your body in the long run. This is especially true when your physiology is already aroused by stress.

Studies show that even relatively low doses of caffeine can aggravate stress in mice. The same can happen to people. Constant smoking and coffee drinking keep you chronically stimulated. You are in a perpetual alarm reaction. The adrenaline-derived stress chemicals are always buzzing through your body. In normal moments, you are already pumped up. If a sudden crisis hits, your physical response is likely to be exaggerated because your system is starting from a higher baseline arousal point. Thus, excess nicotine and caffeine can aggravate hot reacting.

Cardiovascular damage, the most serious of caffeine's risks, is a problem for people with existing heart disease. However, millions of other Americans who are in the clutch of too much coffee report other problems as well, including headaches, insomnia, nervousness, sweaty palms, and ulcers.

The definition of "too much" is tricky because people have widely varying sensitivities to caffeine. A standard cup of coffee (not a mug, which is larger) has about 125 milligrams of caffeine. One cup can put some extremely sensitive people on the threshold of mood and physiological disturbances. Other people can drink ten cups without ill effects. The real issue isn't how much you drink, but how you feel after you've drunk caffeine.

Many people under stress never think of tracing their headaches or upset stomachs to excess caffeine or to caffeine withdrawal. But one study found that one out of four heavy caffeine users has throbbing headaches if deprived of caffeine for 18 to 24 hours. Other signs of caffeine withdrawal are inability to work effectively, drowsiness, irritability, lethargy, nervousness, and restlessness. The symptoms are relieved by a cup of coffee, a cola drink with caffeine, or a pain reliever with caffeine.

The better way is to cut out or cut down on caffeine to the

point where you do not experience symptoms. If you stop taking caffeine entirely, you'll feel the effects for two days or so, but then the withdrawal symptoms will disappear, and you'll feel better.

Carefully watch your use of caffeine if you have a family history of high blood pressure or heart disease, if you have headaches or ulcers, or if you often feel drowsy, irritable, nervous, anxious, or hyper.

Alcohol

According to a 1982 Gallup Poll, abuse of alcohol troubles one in three American families and is considered a "major national problem" by 81 percent of our population. There aren't many issues Americans feel this united about.

Before we get into the bad side of booze, let's review the possible advantages of drinking in moderation:

Drinking up to two ounces of alcohol per day seems to be associated with longevity. There is roughly one ounce of pure alcohol in the typical drink—whether this is a cocktail made with gin, rum, scotch, whisky, or vodka, or a glass of wine or beer—so this means no more than two drinks per day.

Drinking up to two ounces of alcohol per day also appears to increase the proportion of the so-called "good" cholesterol, or high-density lipoprotein cholesterol (HDL) described in Chapter 11.

Finally, drinking up to two ounces of alcohol per day, especially with friends over meals, is a good way for some people to loosen up, communicate, and add a warm glow to the day.

Although these statements may be valid, in reality few people drink to achieve longevity or to raise their HDL cholesterol. Many do use a drink to relax at the end of a long day and to socialize. Here, wine and beer are the drinks of choice. They allow the gradual elevation of blood alcohol levels, as opposed to the sudden "fix" or "hit" of concentrated alcoholic drinks, particularly those mixed with carbonated or soda water, which rapidly increases the rate at which the body absorbs alcohol. The business lunch is greatly enhanced if it includes wine with the food rather than cocktails before it. However, even wine, in large amounts, interferes with the absorption of essential body vitamins, and it contributes extra calories.

Now let's face the real problems of drinking to excess. My definition of moderation is the two-ounce-per-day *maximum*. Drinking more can certainly harm your health, and in the all-too-common extreme form of alcoholism, it can destroy your life.

The Health Hazards

- Alcohol stimulates production of the stress hormone cortisol. Excess cortisol causes a retention of sodium and a loss of potassium. Too much sodium raises the blood pressure; too little potassium, which is a muscle preservative, makes the heart vulnerable to rhythm disturbances.
- Alcohol is a diuretic. Too much dries us out (so to speak). This drying effect enhances the body's clotting mechanism, so people who drink too much run the added risk of blood clotting.
- Alcohol directly damages the heart muscle fibers. Over time it also causes the heart to become dilated and flabby, decreasing its ability to pump. Heavy drinking eventually puts you at a point of no return. The medical term for this is *alcoholic cardiomyopathy,* and it is fatal.
- Alcohol can cause cirrhosis of the liver, a fatal complication that has rapidly become the fourth biggest cause of death among middle-aged men.
- Alcohol can lead to a form of high blood pressure called alcoholic hypertension.
- Alcohol provides "empty calories" by acting nutritionally in much the same way as a few lumps of sugar.
- Alcohol, even in the smallest quantities, does temporary reversible damage to the bone marrow. If you drink regularly and consume more than a moderate amount, this damage can cause anemia.

- Pregnant women are at special risk. Drinking even small quantities during the early months of pregnancy exposes your unborn baby to risks of fetal alcohol syndrome, which may cause deformity, mental retardation, and even fetal death. Up to an ounce of alcohol a day is probably not a major risk for the average healthy pregnant woman, but ideally, exposure to any drug or toxin should be avoided during pregnancy, and you should consult your physician about drinking if you are pregnant.
- By softening the heart muscle, elevating blood pressure, weakening the heart's ability to pump blood, and provoking chaotic heart rhythms, heavy drinking greatly increases the risk of sudden cardiac arrest. As a result, excessive alcohol intake is considered a major risk factor in sudden cardiac death.

How Do You Quit or Persuade Someone You Love to Quit?

An excellent approach to managing alcoholism and problem drinking is Alcoholics Anonymous and its companion programs Al-Anon (for spouses, partners, parents, and children of the alcoholic) and Alateen (for adolescents). AA has one or more chapters in virtually every community in the nation. It is confidential, there is no charge, and members come from all walks of life. A good first step may be to start with an intensive alcohol treatment program, usually lasting for three weeks.

One champion of this approach is Betty Ford, wife of the former president, who when first confronted with her alcoholism ordered the physician out of her house. But when her husband, children, and physician persisted, she consented to the treatment that turned her life around. Today, the alcoholism and drug abuse treatment center at the Eisenhower Medical Center in Palm Springs, California, is called the Betty Ford Center for Chemical Dependency after its grateful benefactor.

As Mrs. Ford and millions of others have found, the first step to the alcoholic's recovery is awareness. Part of the very essence of a drinking problem is to deny that your drinking is a problem. Denial is a major impediment that must be overcome before anyone can start on the road to recovery. One method of dealing with it is a technique called "confrontation." The family, close friends, employer, and, occasionally, the physician confront the alcoholic under the guidance of a skilled alcoholism counselor. They tell the alcoholic that they will provide further support only if he or she accepts the spot that they have arranged for that day in an alcohol rehabilitation program. If the alcoholic refuses to go, they withdraw from all relationships with that person. Although at first glance this seems extreme, it is the only method that has consistently succeeded in forcing most alcoholics to recognize their problem before being almost totally destroyed. This process, however, should be undertaken only with competent guidance from an experienced counselor.

If you need help, call your local AA office or alcohol outreach program or your personal physician.

Drugs

If you are consistently using sleeping pills, tranquilizers, or other drugs, that is proof positive that you can benefit from applying the contents of this book to your personal life, and perhaps from seeking the assistance of a trained counselor or intervention group.

Tranquilizers

Taking tranquilizers for temporary relief of an extreme anxiety state is an appropriate use of medication. What is dangerous is attempting to control anxiety through drugs instead of looking for the cause.

The problem is that the more you use tranquilizers, the more you need and the less they work. Especially dangerous is mixing tranquilizers like Librium and Valium with alcohol. The effect is synergistic (multiplying through combination), and it can kill.

Abuse of tranquilizers often starts when a patient tells the doctor that he or she has symptoms of anxiety, and the doctor doesn't take the time to find out what the reasons are or doesn't know how to help. The easy way out—a tranquilizer—is prescribed. The patient likes this temporary feeling of control over stress. He or she extends the use of the tranquilizer and then goes on to a stronger dosage, and the vicious cycle that can lead to addiction is under way.

"Uppers"

People also get hooked on prescription drugs by starting with amphetamines, or "uppers," which, like nicotine and caffeine, stimulate adrenaline. This is a problem particularly for women who are given amphetamine prescriptions to relieve menstrual cramps or to suppress appetite in weight-loss programs.

For some people it is a short step from using physician-prescribed drugs to prescribing for themselves and blasting up with amphetamines and other uppers and crashing down with booze and tranquilizers. This burns your body up—fast.

Sleeping Pills

Sleep is not a peaceful process. Your brain waves indicate that sleep is actually a time of intense mental activity. The most critical is Rapid Eye Movement, or REM sleep—the time when you dream. Most sleeping pills have been shown to block this REM sleep. Scientists believe that dreaming, or REM sleep, is essential for you to get relief from the stresses of a complex, inhibiting society and restore your body to self-regulation and emotional health.

If this REM sleep, which can occur three to five times a night for 10–20 minutes each time, is blocked, it is possible in a few days in susceptible people to produce symptoms such as hallucination and loss of concentration. Also, many of the drugs used to induce sleep can cause lethargy and lassitude when you are awake.

It is much better to sleep physiologically than pharmacologically. The muscle relaxation techniques you learned in Chapter 8 should help if you do the exercises right before you go to bed.

Problem Drinking and Drug Abuse —Test Yourself

In excess, drugs and alcohol are truly the crutch that cripples. Ask yourself the following questions:

—When you drink or use pills, can you control how much or how many? Do you ever take more than you intend?

—Do you lie about the amount you drink or the number of pills you take?

—Since you started taking alcohol or drugs, have you seen your doctor more?

—Lately, are you spending less time in the evening and during weekends and holidays with your family and friends?

—Has your sexual activity diminished since you began taking alcohol or drugs?

—Do you drink or take drugs in order to feel comfortable at a party?

—Are you arguing more with your family, friends, and others?

—Lately, do you feel more like a loner? Are you isolated in some way?

—Do you have a pill for every purpose, for every mood, for every problem?

—Have you been using alcohol as a medicine?

—Are your children showing increasing signs of stress? Are they having behavior problems or problems with the law or problems in school?

—Do you often feel guilty after you have had something to drink or have taken drugs?

—Do you say, "I only had a couple of drinks" when you know you had more?

—Do you dislike people who allow you to drink or who forgive you for drinking or using drugs?

If you find yourself answering "yes" to many or even a few of these questions, you may have a problem or be on your way to having a problem with drinking or drugs.

* * *

Take real control of your stresses, not chemical control. If you retreat to a chemical haze, you will never be able to clearly see—and do something about—stress. Realizing that you rely on smoking, drinking, caffeine, or pills to get through the day is the essential first step in working out better ways to manage stress.

13
Relieving Stress on the Job

In America, people are identified by what they do, to the point that it often seems they are their work—in the eyes of others and even in their own eyes. It's no accident that we often introduce ourselves by telling what we do for a living. That's why losing a job, being out of the job market for a long time, having serious conflict at work, or feeling torn between work and home can threaten much more than a source of income. These job stresses can undermine one's sense of personal worth and identity. One way to keep that from happening is to keep your work in perspective and to learn ways of thinking about it that help you stay on top of job stress.

Coping with the Loss of a Job

The most obvious stress threat is unemployment. Losing a job can feel like being hit by a truck. But you can cushion the blow and increase your resilience by accepting the reality of the loss, examining your options, and building support for your new job search.

Take time to mourn the loss of your job, just as you would grieve over the loss of a loved one. Feel and express your anger and sadness, and realize that they may be with you for a while. At the same time, do what you can to get on with your life. Force yourself to consider your options and dig deeper to discover skills you might not know you have.

It is essential to engage in activities that maintain your sense of identity and self-esteem; they are closely linked to the sense of control that makes stress manageable. Volunteer work or self-help groups work for some; for others, it's time to exercise or do that project you've been putting off for years.

It's also time to seek out your friends and stay in touch with people who support you. Studies show that people who maintain social contacts are less likely to become ill than those who are loners. Human connectedness helps relieve stress. The importance of community cannot be overestimated. Interruption of social ties affects the body's defense systems, making you more susceptible to stress and illness.

Staying in motion is vital. People without activity and structure in their lives tend to suffer more than those who have things to do, especially on a regular basis. So join a dance class, try out that restaurant that specializes in East Indian cuisine, find a regular tennis partner, shop for antiques, meet your friends for lunch, catch up with the movies, work in the garden.

If you think you are in deep distress, get emotional counseling at once, either individual therapy or self-help groups, depending upon which you would be more comfortable with.

Finally, don't give up—ever—on the job search. The job that will make your life better may very well be just around the corner. Keep turning the corners.

Stress on the Job—the Road to Burnout

Next to being unemployed, working at a job you dislike is one of the biggest chronic stresses of life. And among job stresses, one of the most common unrecognized syndromes is burnout. If you look around, you'll find many friends and co-workers who suffer from burnout without being able to identify what is happening to them.

Like a disease, burnout proceeds in stages. Recognizing the symptoms puts you in a better position to gauge realistically where you stand with your job stress, and that helps you decide what to do about it.

The best analysis I've seen of this process comes from Dr. Robert Veninga and Dr. James Spradley, who identify five stages of burnout. Their description is so accurate that anyone suffering from burnout, or who is on the way to it, will be able to recognize the symptoms.

The Five Stages of Burnout

In the first stage ("job contentment") the workers report that they "love their job" and everything is going well. Adaptive energy is, however, being used, and if not replenished the individual will likely enter stage two ("fuel shortage").

In the fuel shortage stage the worker begins to complain about "tiredness" and "lack of energy" and sleep disturbances. The individual complains about his "inefficiency." [We observe] five expressions of lost productivity: jadedness, cynicism, lowered creativity, avoiding decisions and increased accidents. An executive noted: "I guess I have been hitting it too hard. I don't have any spunk. I feel jaded and indifferent." He repeatedly complained that "there are just too many things to do and not enough time to do them." He feels that he is never "caught up" which is a common feeling among individuals in this second stage.

In the third stage ("chronic symptoms") the individual is exhausted and the symptoms of ill-health can be noted. As one worker said in discussing his work related problems, "I become almost physically ill. My body aches as if I have a viral illness. I get tension headaches and am nauseated." But anger often accompanies the physical symptoms. The worker resembles a volcano always on the verge of eruption. The calm, accepting, easygoing person becomes chronically angry—often at a boss or co-worker and, at times, the anger extends to a family member.

In the fourth stage ("crisis") the symptoms become critical. Dr. Carroll Brodsky, a physician, studied burned out teachers and prison guards. The subjects had very few waking moments when their thoughts weren't riveted on their job. They thought about their problems all the time—while driving home, or watching television. They replayed their

problems, whether it be an argument with the principal or
fear of a prisoner's threats, and came away feeling, "This
job is bad for me; the problem isn't going to go away." At
times the individual wants to look for an escape hatch: "I
want to get the heck out of my job, my family, my whole
way of life."

In the final stage workers "hit the wall," often finding
themselves unable to continue. For some, there is an intense turning to alcohol and drugs for relief, for others
there is a mental or physical breakdown. And for still
others there can be serious physiological deterioration.

Take a good look at your job situation and your own
feelings and symptoms. If you are experiencing some early
warning signs of fuel shortage, do something *now* before
your symptoms become chronic.

If you are already experiencing chronic symptoms, do something *now* before you reach a crisis.

If you think you are *already* at the crisis stage, drop everything *immediately*. Do not hit the wall. You're not a marathoner
trying to finish a 26-mile race. You're running with the only
life you'll ever have. Make the necessary adjustments that
will allow you to continue working without undue stress. If
you cannot adjust to the job you're in, change jobs or quit.
It's not worth dying for.

Job Stress: Who Are the Copers?

People who have learned to live flexibly with stress are
aware of their physical and emotional state, and do not push
themselves beyond their endurance. They do not care excessively how others judge them and are committed to acting in
the ways they think best. They live by guidelines rather than
rigid rules. They like solving problems and they approach job
stress with the attitude that "there's always a way" to make
things work.

Flexible copers don't worry about job problems until it is
time to deal with them. They are able to relax and enjoy
free time, and a sense of humor helps them handle frustration and keep things in perspective. Because they have inter-

ests outside their work, other roles—whether parent, hobbyist, friend, spouse, or community volunteer—are there to stimulate them and bolster self-esteem.

In general, people who cope flexibly with job stress take a pragmatic approach that minimizes feelings of personal risk and maximizes the positive stimulation of work. One excellent way of describing and studying this approach has been developed by behavioral scientist Suzanne Kobasa, of the Graduate School and University Center of the City University of New York. The most productive and satisfied workers exhibit "the three C's":

—*Commitment* to themselves and what they are doing.
—A sense of being *in control* of their work, rather than controlled by it.
—A view of change as a *challenge* that stimulates them to grow.

The "three C's" form interlocking parts of an overall coping style that Kobasa calls "hardiness."

Commitment begins with a belief in yourself that, under stress, minimizes the feeling of threat. Committed people know not only what they are involved in, but why they chose it, and this knowledge comes from their own goals and priorities. This understanding and sense of purpose gives them perspective and the ability to judge accurately specific problem situations. Committed people also have a strong sense of connection to those who form their community of interest and involvement. They know that they can depend on others and also that others are counting on them. Aaron Antonovsky, a prominent researcher on stress and health, calls this sense of community and accountability to others the most fundamental interpersonal resource for coping with stress.

Control is the tendency to believe and act as if one can influence the course of events. People who feel in control look for explanations that take into account their own responsibility for what happens in their lives, and they feel capable of acting on their own. They can incorporate different events into an ongoing life plan, so they feel they can deal with whatever comes along.

Challenge is the view that change is normal and an opportunity rather than a threat to security. People who see change as challenge are curious and interested. Others may panic when the chips are up in the air, but flexible copers see change as a chance to make the chips come down in a better pattern. They seek new experiences, practice responding to the unexpected, explore their surroundings, and know where to turn for resources to help them cope with stress. They are mentally open and can tolerate ambiguity, so they are able to start understanding and appraising even the most unexpected events.

Kobasa's research shows that responding to stress with a sense of commitment, control, and challenge is linked with a decrease in illness. She concludes that it is especially important for health for someone to have a hardy style of coping in a period of intense stress.

Becoming a Coper

Certain attitudes and behaviors bear a special relation to work life. They include your response to physical symptoms, your attitudes toward change, your management of time, the way you work with others, and maintaining a balanced life. There is much that you can do.

Listen to your body. People who suffer from job stress may not realize what is wrong or why, especially if they are depressed. For them, the first step in feeling better is focusing on any physical symptoms and recognizing that these are stress-related. Recognizing a problem is the beginning of understanding it, and your body is often the best place to see and accept signs that there is a problem.

That was certainly true for me, but the signs had to get painfully strong before I got the message. It took a heart attack, even though my body gave me plenty of advance warning. I believe it is particularly common for men to deny the signals their bodies are sending them, because they are often trained to be stoic and don't want to appear "weak." But those who cope well with stress respond quickly to fatigue and other signs that they are pushing too hard. They are aware of their physical state without being preoccupied with it, and they take care to note and remedy physical problems.

Prepare for change by learning to expect things to change. Your way of making a living will probably be different in the future than it is now. In their best-sellers *The Third Wave* and *Megatrends*, Alvin Toffler and John Naisbitt, respectively, have shown us that the world is dramatically changing, particularly in a fundamental move from an economy based on industry to one based on the creation and distribution of information. This transition is bringing about many other changes, including high technology, a global economy, and a change in our patterns of work and careers.

It is important that we learn to look upon this change as opportunity. We no longer need to spend a lifetime doing the same thing over and over again without the chance to try something totally different. It is likely that some chapters in our lives will be more fulfilling than others. It is also likely that corporations, instead of discarding outmoded production systems and employees, will be required and motivated to retrain them. Welcoming change will increasingly become a way of life and an expected part of one's career rather than a series of obstructions, detours, and frustrations.

Even on the job from day to day or month to month, you can teach yourself to see change as normal and as an opening for opportunity. And you can initiate change if you prepare yourself for a number of outcomes. Anticipate what might go wrong—or right—in your job and think through how you will handle it. Review your potential choices and mentally rehearse how you will respond to a given change. Always have several strategies to fall back on. Risk-taking is a big plus, provided you are realistic and know what you will do if things don't work out as you hope.

Manage your time. The more stressed you feel, the harder it is to define your priorities. You can find yourself going in circles. If you have trouble getting everything done, you don't have time to manage your stresses. But if you don't manage your stresses, you have trouble getting things done.

The single most important tool you have for breaking out of this cycle is *taking* regular time every day to sit down and plan. List the things you want and need to accomplish. Think about which are the most important, according to their consequences, and assign high, medium, or low priorities to each item on your list. Then do the top-priority jobs first. The priorities will change over time, so you need to revise your list and priorities every day to determine where you put your energies. And you need to practice acting on your priorities instead of allowing yourself to be pulled every which way by people and projects that are lower on your priority list.

It's easier to stick to your plan if you like what you're doing. If you're spending a lot of time on tasks you don't enjoy, write down the things you like to do and the things you don't. Discuss them with your supervisor and see if your work can be structured so that you do more of the things you like. Generally we do best what we enjoy most. You may be surprised to find that your supervisor recognizes this and will support changes that make the most of your skills and interests.

You're lucky if you are doing work you like and believe in, but don't fall into another trap and try to be a perfectionist about it. Perfectionism is self-destructive because you've made the game impossible to win. But since you are the one who set up the rules, you can change them.

Remember the general stress management principle that what you do does not determine your value as a person. Genuine feelings of self-worth come from inside you, not from others' responses to what you do. When you keep this in mind you can let go of the fear of failure. Then you can accurately judge how much time and energy to give any project, and when to wrap it up and move on. You can accept that it will be imperfect, examine objectively the way you handled it, and learn for the future without using up creative energy worrying about your talent and competence. When you give up perfectionism, you don't give up doing a good job. You let go of believing that it's got to be perfect every time for you to feel acceptable and adequate. The result is often better judgment and better work, more productivity, and a feeling of being in control that frees you to enjoy your work.

Learn to work well with others, because your stress at work has much to do with your feelings and behavior toward the people you work with. Often we create stress by not being aware of the messages we're sending to those around us or understanding the responses we get.

Listening is one way to remedy that problem. People in authority, especially, need to remain open to listening to the concerns and ideas of others. Listening helps you understand what is happening at work and what the prospects are for future development. It is important not only to listen for information but also to be concerned with people's needs, hopes, and dreams. Becoming aware of them will help you to help them and to reach mutual goals.

It also helps you build support systems, especially when you identify certain people with whom you can share ideas and friendship. You can build a team spirit by involving others in your planning so that you are not isolated. That way, however things turn out, the group stands together. Such a support group can share stress experiences, which helps remove the feeling of shame that some people experience when they feel overwhelmed by stress and breaks the destructive perception that stress is a sign of personal weakness. And a support system can help people organize to direct attention to organizational causes of stress and the possibility of group action to solve these problems.

You also build support by delegating work, which helps you to develop and expand. If you keep everything to yourself, whatever you are doing can never become bigger or better than you are. People often say, "If I let someone else do it, I know they'll mess it up." But others have to have responsibility and make mistakes before they can be expected to do it better, to be a part of the system, and to improve it. The delegation of authority with responsibility helps others find a place in your dreams, your goals, your objectives. It will enhance the overall operation once the right chemistry develops, and morale will improve.

Giving feedback effectively is also important. When people do well they need to be told so, warmly and enthusiastically. We never outgrow the satisfaction of having good work recognized. It is one of the world's best antidotes to burnout, and one of the best incentives to renewed effort, because it helps bring out good feelings about ourselves which may become elusive in times of stress. Everyone wants to feel part of a community and yet stand out as special. Positive feedback highlights our special capabilities. The most effective positive feedback isn't generalized "good boy, good girl" kind of talk but instead recognizes the specific contribution that a person has made.

Negative feedback is just as important; we probably learn more from it, if it is done well, than from praise. Negative feedback needs to be done firmly and gently. It is often helpful to touch people when you tell them they need to do better—an arm around the shoulder as you walk down the hall or a touch on the wrist says, "I believe in you and I know we can work this out." If you are not a person who feels comfortable touching people in this situation, or if you are talking with someone of the opposite sex and do not want to be misunderstood, any nonverbal sign of reassurance, from the expression on your face to the posture of your body, can convey the same calming message.

Others can do this for you, too, if you seek out mentors who take an interest in your future. Honest feedback from an experienced person you respect gives you a perspective on yourself and the world that no other relationship can provide. And at a different stage in your life you can become a mentor. The rewards of teaching others are great. As you mature, you become increasingly capable of transferring the limelight and enjoying the role of helping others reach their potential.

A final note about relations with people on the job. We can't choose everyone we have to work with. We can maximize our good relationships and minimize our bad ones. But often we'll be stuck with one or two people who don't respond to any strategy for getting along. For these people, remember the Brain Tumor prescription: pretend the person has a brain tumor and is not responsible for his or her behavior. Some inner demon drives that person and he or she feels no control over it. It doesn't make sense to torture yourself over other people's problems that make them act irrationally. Once you realize they have a "brain tumor," you can let go and move on with your job and your life.

Put balance into your life. The life of a workaholic is not very well balanced, not very rewarding, and sometimes not very long. A career can be a source of genuine fulfillment, but it can also become an escape from other responsibilities and a retreat from personal relationships. When the career runs into trouble, the person who is wholly dependent on it has no other resources for personal satisfaction. Careers reflect a positive commitment when they form part of an overall balance of life that includes commitment to self, others, community, and activities outside of work.

To build this kind of balance, you need to build non-work time into your life every day, plus frequent special time-outs for periods ranging from half a day to a month or more. *Stop the World, I Want to Get Off* was a great musical, and doing that is a great way to reduce some of the stress in your life.

One way to "stop and get off" is by taking three-day weekends, and don't wait too long for this kind of refreshment. Do it often, realizing its importance in maintaining your health and well-being. It is not an alibi or an escape but a necessity.

Take time off during the week, too. A half-day's vacation is a good breather, as is a noon catnap or exercise break. Or go to lunch with friends to break away from the routine and give yourself a chance to laugh and visit. You'll come back with a better perspective on what you've done and what you'd like to do in order to feel that the day was reasonably well spent.

Even five-minute breaks during the day help you keep your balance. If you do not allow yourself lunch/rest/talk/walk/fun breaks, you are telling yourself that you're just a machine. But even machines need "down time"—and you need time to refuel and regain your zest and sense of choice and control in your life.

Finally, take regular vacations. Burnout is expensive for everyone. I know of one corporation that actually pays bonuses to induce its workaholic researchers to take vacations!

What Organizations Can Do

Job stress is such a problem for employee health and absenteeism that business is beginning to take the lead in finding a solution. The battle cry was sounded years ago when the chairman of General Motors noted that GM spends more on health benefits than it does on steel. Health promotion in the workplace is an idea whose time is here.

A national task force that I chair on the physician's role in the work setting attacks this problem with strategies for promoting healthy lifestyles where people work. We are trying to convince business to launch wellness programs in six key areas that contribute to stress and heart disease. The goals are to control high blood pressure, reduce cigarette smoking, control alcohol abuse, improve nutrition and control weight, increase exercise, and finally to manage stress and cool down the hot reactors.

Wellness programs are spreading with the increasing recognition that stress affects work performance and that the workplace is the easiest place to intervene in the stress cycle for large numbers of people. Such programs make good business sense. Employee assistance programs began in factories in the late 1930s to minimize losses due to alcohol abuse, and by 1965 two hundred existed. Nearly five thousand more had appeared by 1981, as it became evident that wellness programs saved employers money in reduced absenteeism and increased productivity.

The other way that organizations can prevent and reduce stress is through humane management. Today there is much talk about "corporate cultures." Observers note that, increasingly, the most successful companies rely not so much on hierarchy and structure as they do on a corporate culture rooted in humanist values, including a commitment to employee well-being and flexibility about individual needs which promote both creativity and productivity.

Thomas Peters and Robert Waterman touched a national nerve in 1983 when they published *In Search of Excellence,* a book about the success of employee-centered companies. They point out that the best-run companies recognize the human need to conform and feel secure, and, at the same time, to stand out, to make a difference, even to be heroic.

Organizations can help by building reward systems that make employees consistently feel like winners. Setting targets that people can meet—and giving them the chance to set their own targets—is one way of helping people gain a sense of control, confidence, and initiative. It helps, too, to establish informal environments that allow people from diverse areas to talk and solve problems together, rather than spending excess energy defending their turf. Others have pointed out that employee ownership, a nonhierarchical management style, sabbaticals, recreation facilities, and reorganization of the workplace to allow self-pacing all give employees greater control of their work lives—and greater commitment to the organization that responds to their needs.

Change is inevitable. For most people the question isn't whether it will happen but how they can meet it to best advantage. Change certainly has costs, but there are great benefits to accepting it and making change a personal opportunity. The same is true for stress of all kinds, including the stresses of work.

14
Maintaining a Healthy Heart

My experience as a patient has made me a better physician. Before, I was an "I say, you do" doctor. That ended when I had my own heart attack while telling people how to prevent heart attacks.

My mother used to say, "None are so blind as those who will not see." I was blind to my own case. I urge you to take this chance to really look at yours. If you have high blood pressure or have survived a heart attack, realize that you can learn how to control both conditions, as I did.

The message for rehabilitation after illness is the same as the message for prevention, or delay, of heart trouble. *You don't have to be sick to feel better.* However, to people with high blood pressure and to people who have lived through a heart attack, controlling stress may be a matter of life or death.

Holding Down Your High Blood Pressure

The two major ways to treat the person with high blood pressure are medication and motivation. You are the key to the success of both treatments.

Medication. Unless behavioral changes enable you to keep your blood pressure down, you may very well have to take medicine every day for the rest of your life. If you are on medication, you will need to continue it even after your blood pressure has dropped, or your blood pressure will go up again. Furthermore, it is essential to take the medicine every day, even if you feel well. If you feel sick, see your physician. In any case, have your blood pressure checked frequently. Better yet, check it yourself.

Like most physicians, I used to use a stepped-care approach to prescribing medicine for blood pressure control. Stepped care is a standardized form of treatment that begins with diuretics (water pills) and, if this is insufficient, adds different medicines one by one until blood pressure is controlled. However, at our clinic we are now using a new approach custom tailored to the specific causes of high blood pressure in the individual patient.

In our lab we divide high blood pressure patients—many of them hot reactors—into three broad categories: output, vasoconstrictive, and combined.

People in the output category have high blood pressure because their hard-driving hearts pump extra strongly. If caught early enough, most of these people will respond to behavioral management plus, if necessary, drugs to slow down the heart and diminish the force of its contractions. People in the vasoconstrictive category have high blood pressure because their blood vessels constrict. For them, drugs that open up the blood vessels are essential, and it is important to avoid drugs that reduce the force of the heartbeat, since in these people the heart may be dangerously weakened already. Finally, in people who have both hard-driving hearts and tightened blood vessels, it is important to prescribe drugs that correct both problems.

In all three categories—whether output, vasoconstrictive, or combined—the key to drug treatment is knowing *how* the cardiovascular system is raising the blood pressure. Measuring blood vessel resistance in addition to the heart's output of blood has enabled us to treat the causes of high blood pressure more specifically, with medication custom tailored to the individual's cardiovascular system.

Motivation. Follow-up treatment for all our patients involves what I call the "BASICS." Since you cannot carry a laboratory on your shoulders or a team of consultants at your side, it is important that you keep track of what you need to do to control your high blood pressure and to make sure that you are doing it. You are the best manager of the treatment prescribed for you. Here's how the "BASICS" work in controlling high blood pressure.

The "BASICS" of Controlling High Blood Pressure

B is the *bad behavior* you want to change, including smoking, hot reacting to stress, excessive salt intake, regular overeating that leads to obesity, skipping your medications, and being unable to relax.

A is for *autonomy*. You can take control of your health.

S is for *self-monitoring devices*. One of the most helpful things you can do is to regularly take and record your blood pressure. A diary of how your blood pressure fluctuates during the stresses of a typical week is a valuable clue to what's going on in your life. A recent study in the *Journal of the American Medical Association* reports that self-monitoring of blood pressure has been very effective in helping people with borderline hypertension recognize and regulate their high blood pressure. Many of our patients tell us it helps them "feel," or sense, when their blood pressure is rising and this enables them to bring it back down. If you do not want to invest $60 to $175 for an electronic or digital readout device, you can buy a blood pressure cuff with a built-in stethoscope for $25 to $35.

I is the *incentive* you must have to take charge of your own health and be as free of a doctor as possible. Build incentives and rewards into your self-management program.

C is for the *cues* that cause your heart rate to jump and your blood pressure to rise. You should know what things increase the strain on your heart. For example, you should know if an unpleasant phone call or a competitive situation is making your heart work as hard as it would if you were running up two flights of stairs with a 25-pound weight under each arm. If you know what makes your blood pressure jump, you can avoid it or change how you cope with the situations that make it jump. Ask yourself, "Is it worth dying for?" and you'll find that other options will start coming to mind.

S is for the *support* you need from your physician, family, friends, boss, and co-workers. Patients with high blood pressure can make important lifestyle adjustments more quickly and effectively if others support these changes.

Treating the Heart Attack Patient

Over half the people in the U.S. who have a first heart attack, or myocardial infarction (MI), survive it. Each year, 550,000 Americans die from heart attacks, but 600,000 more live to graduate from a common educational experience—the hospital coronary care unit.

If you want to see the wonders of medicine, stop by sometime and visit the coronary care, intensive care, and surgical units of a major teaching hospital. You will see an electronic Taj Mahal of medical gadgetry. Yet, despite all our marvels of technology, I have found that the most potent therapy for the heart attack victim is something much more human—the power of words.

Survivors of a heart attack have suffered irreversible damage to their heart muscle. For various reasons, parts of their heart muscle have been cut off from the vital supply of blood, nutrients, and oxygen. The result is the death of heart tissue.

A few survivors deny their illness and look forward to a speedy return to their old way of living and working, but the overwhelming majority are scared stiff by the experience. They have been hit over the head with a two-by-four, and they are ready to listen. For the first time in their lives, they may really hear suggestions that can start them thinking about their lives, developing insights about themselves, learning new ways to cope, and making necessary emotional adjustments. The days immediately after a heart attack are the ideal time for the cardiologist and family physician to talk to the patient about changing life-threatening behaviors.

Unfortunately, because of our current health insurance

policies and reimbursement systems, the physician is usually paid better for what he does to you mechanically than what he does with you verbally. Patients themselves often willingly pay more for an open-heart operation by a surgeon than for an office visit with a family physician for a talk that may save their lives. Surgery and technology play a major role in coronary care, but I always start patient rehabilitation efforts right after the heart attack by listening.

The major question I want the patient to answer is, "Why did it happen now?" Knowing the reason for a heart attack is 90 percent of knowing what to do to prevent another. When they're in the coronary care unit (CCU), patients will often tell you things about their work, their spouses, and their lives that they've never talked about before. It's remarkable how often heart attack victims will describe a series of catastrophes in the preceding six months to a year—events that left them chronically fatigued and with the feeling that they couldn't make progress, no matter how hard they tried. What really counts is how they perceived these events. Many found themselves asking, "Is that all there is?"

I not only listen to the CCU patient, I also focus in on another crucial recovery factor—the home environment. Are the spouse and family supportive, neutral, or negative toward the patient and his condition?

In the first few days after the attack, I try to get across one message: reassurance. I tell my patients, "Relax; more people die within the first twenty-four hours of a heart attack than within the next five years. You've made it through the crucial first twenty-four hours. Now it's time to plan for the next five years of your life." This helps allay the patient's first reaction—acute anxiety.

Then I talk with the patient and his or her family and set some major goals, including acceptance of the disease; knowledge of the disease (to permit the patient to make better decisions for the future); emotional support; sustained adherence to necessary changes in lifestyle; and reaching an optimal level of functioning.

In discussing these goals, I emphasize to the patient that

what counts is how hard the heart is working, not how hard the body is working. After all, immediately before their heart attacks, most victims are doing mental, not physical work.

In reflecting upon their attacks, most patients will recall going through three stages. First, there is often a chronic phase of living for years, even decades, under high stress. Many have been hot reactors to those stresses. Then there is an intermediate phase months before the attack. This is usually the joyless struggle of beating against the tide in a situation where the patient sees no chance of winning. And finally, a few days or weeks before the disaster strikes, there is often an acute emotional shock, which may be unrelated to the patient's chronic problem. As in my case, this acute emotional shock may take the form of rage with no acceptable physical outlet.

After overcoming their anxiety about their heart attack, patients usually become depressed. Fortunately, for many the depression is self-limiting and lifts when they realize they can return to a reasonable life.

One response that occurs at this point should be countered right up front. I strongly discourage my patients from thinking they've earned a Purple Heart as a casualty of life's wars. Some patients will use a self-defeating self-talk: "Now I have my Purple Heart. I've been trying to tell people I'm sick, and now they all know I am. It's okay for me to be a dependent person."

Instead, I try to encourage this self-talk: "I could have died. Now, I'm going to make the most of this second chance. I am going to take control of my life and live the way I really want to."

I tell my patients that they will be best off if they become the managers of their own health. After all, nobody knows you better than yourself.

In exploring priorities with the executives who come through our clinic, I propose the idea that material things are only the ornaments of life. Beyond a certain point, they are not satisfying. The question is: what in your life brings you real satisfaction—what stirs your creative energy? When do you feel productive with peace of mind?

Often, heart attack patients have no idea of how to go about relaxing and enjoying themselves. They do not know how to play. People who manage multibillion-dollar conglomerates may not think in terms of managing their lives so that their personal bottom line is one of maximum satisfaction. Although getting the most out of life often requires nothing more than a little common sense, as Voltaire observed, "The thing about common sense is that it is not very common."

To help heart attack patients make the most of the rest of their lives, I propose a "portfolio of coping techniques." The goal, of course, is to prevent Number Two, the second heart attack. The methods I teach are those described in detail elsewhere in this book, but adapted and especially selected for the heart attack patient's particular lifestyle.

It is my strong belief that there is no *one* thing that people can do to save themselves from stress or from a first or second heart attack. True management requires orchestrating a symphony of behavioral and coping instruments.

I give my heart attack patients advice on a wide range of specific situations that they need to think about and act on. The advice is as valid for normal living as it is for rehabilitation. The lessons learned by heart attack victims—and I am one of those victims—can help you postpone or reduce your own chances of having a heart attack.

On smoking. The heart attack patient has no choice about this insidious risk factor. One of the most important things a patient who has just recovered from a heart attack can do is quit smoking. For the short term, I will work intensively with the patient to kick the habit. But my long-term position is this: "If you don't care enough about yourself to stop smoking, I probably can't help you." One of the reasons physicians are unable to persuade their patients to stop smoking is that we often fail to make patients realize how important it is for them to stop. I am reluctant to care for the heart attack patients who cannot make this fundamental commitment to their health.

On sex. I favor the advice of cardiologist Samuel M. Fox, III, of Washington, D.C., who advises patients to resume their sexual activity, but "with a mature approach orchestrated à la Debussy rather than Wagner." For those not familiar with classical music, Dr. Fox is advising you to ease up on the throttle and work on the technique. I tell my male patients that women are usually not as impressed with sexual gymnastics as many men seem to think. Lovemaking with a partner with whom one feels comfortable and secure requires no more physical strain than climbing two flights of stairs. Now is the time to assume a more mutual role, with your partner often taking the more active part, in position as well as activity. A special warning: sex in an extramarital affair—or in any relationship that is anxiety-provoking and guilt-ridden—is usually associated with far more energy, alcohol, and fatty food. Statistically, it is far more hazardous. Once again, is it worth dying for?

On diet. I start teaching heart attack patients about nutrition while they're still in the CCU. The dietary goals: lose weight, lower cholesterol intake, and lower salt intake through eating habits that fit comfortably into one's normal social situations. The methods: Limit fat to no more than 30 percent of the diet, substitute complex carbohydrates for simple sugars, get the salt out of the kitchen, and use salt substitutes whenever possible.

On drinking. I encourage my patients to switch from martinis and hard liquor to wine and to have no more than two five-ounce glasses a day—or two cans of light beer—preferably in the evening with their spouse or friends. Definitely do not drink while exercising.

On exercise. I wait three months from the time of the heart attack before giving patients a full-blown exercise test. If they are ready to resume vigorous physical activity, I help them find an activity that they enjoy. If they actively dislike a certain exercise (let's say pushups remind a man of the Marines), patients may become so tense doing it that their blood pressure will rise excessively. My favorite: walking briskly somewhere interesting for a mile or two each day with someone I like.

On assertiveness. Surprisingly, many people who are recovering from heart attacks do not know how to assert themselves constructively. They may know how to swear and rant and be abusive, but they do not necessarily know how to speak up in an effective manner to get what they really want. Teaching heart attack patients to say what they want and to mean what they say is an important part of their recovery. There is one key word they need to learn and use: No. It can be a lifesaver.

On angina (or severe chest pains related to lack of oxygen to the heart muscle). Angina often has a strong anxiety component. Besides looking for organic causes, I look for trouble the patient may be having with a spouse, co-workers, or boss. If this is the provocative factor—as it frequently is—it is time to face that all-important question: Is it worth dying for?

Ultimately, heart attack patients will measure their recovery by how well they relate to their family and to their work. Cardiologists operate on this principle in West Germany, where comprehensive rehabilitation centers have been built to treat heart attack patients *and* their families. The West Germans are convinced that these rehabilitation programs can return heart attack victims to productive lives—including, if necessary, retraining for a new line of work—and they wonder why America didn't start a system like theirs years ago. I often wonder too.

My own heart attack has caused me to worry less and less about hardening of the arteries and disturbances of the heart's rhythms—standard physical precursors of heart trouble—and more and more about stress. They say that insight often follows insult. Few bodily insults are as powerful as a heart attack. Let yours—or the heart attack of someone close to you—open your eyes to the way you live with stress. If you've had a heart attack and been able to answer the question, Why now? then you know how to answer the next big question: Why ever again?

Epilogue:
It's Not Worth
Dying For

Today, we deal more with diseases of choice than of chance. Half of our illnesses are preventable—we know what causes them and how people can behave differently to prevent them. I believe that the challenge and reward of medicine now is to measure objectively behaviors that are health risks, to make people aware of these risks, to teach them to be productive without being self-destructive, and to motivate them to act.

My life as a physician includes patient care, research, and teaching. Today, I make unusual house calls. I travel and speak to groups representing business, labor, medicine, agriculture, education. More importantly, I listen. I learn about people's concerns, the kinds of stress they are under, and what they want to know about stress. They tell me that what I am saying about lifestyle, behavior, and stress really hits home. That's encouraging, because awareness and self-management are the most important tools of preventive medicine. The exciting thing about preventive medicine is that it can result in healing *before* the fact instead of after the fact. That is why, for me, the podium and the pen are as important to high-quality medicine as the operating table and the scalpel.

In my own case, the therapy of awareness and self-management have been lifesaving. I maintain a very busy work schedule, yet today my blood pressure is a normal

118/78. I am off all medications, my exercise treadmill test is normal, and our lab shows me to be a cool reactor.

Today, I find that I can accomplish what reasonably needs to be done during the day. Occasionally I take home some work-related reading material, but usually I use my home as a retreat from the world and a chance to renew my perspective and restore my creative energy. I take the "six months to live" approach seriously and I accept the fact that there is a limited amount that I have to do or want to do each day.

My motto is this basic rule: Don't sweat the small stuff. And the corollary: It's all small stuff. I have learned that most of the time you can't fight and you can't flee, but you can learn to flow.

Today, I depend more on myself for endorsement of what is important to me and less on the applause of "my mother's bridge club"—all the people I used to think were watching and judging my success. It took me years to realize that nobody was paying that much attention! And that even if they had been, I was cheating myself by gearing my life to them instead of to my own true needs and desires.

Today, I have learned to sense when my blood pressure is rising and to feel when I am fatigued, instead of denying what my body is telling me. If I begin to heat up, I cool myself down with muscle relaxation and constructive self-talks, and, if necessary, by leaving stressful people and situations to themselves. I no longer drive myself to achievement at all costs, ignoring the wisdom of my body. Instead, I have taught myself to say a lifesaving word—"no."

The strongest part of my "coping portfolio" is a rewarding relationship with my wife, son, and daughter. I often say that Phyllis and I have been married several times—but always to each other. We have learned how to negotiate our differences and to make changes when they need to be made. Most of my contribution has come since my heart attack; I know now in a deeper way how important love and family really are. I have found the joy of becoming more of a father to my children as well. I try to allow them to grow and pursue their own personal goals—the ones they think best—rather than burden them with my immaculate misconceptions of how the world should be. It isn't always easy, but they talk to me now about things they once might have kept to themselves, and as time passes we're getting closer.

I try to walk briskly for a mile or two each day as an enjoyable part of my preventive maintenance program, even when I'm traveling. Between planes, I put my luggage in a locker and walk all over the airport. At home, if the weather is bad I often ride my stationary cycle for twenty minutes or so. It helps keep my weight down and my spirits up.

I take other time for myself too—with my model trains, with reading, and with frequent travel. Even when these activities are related to my work, I do them in a spirit of leisure: exploring and adventuring for the fun of it.

Work, too, is a different experience. I now pursue it more in a spirit of creativity, for its importance in its own right, rather than as the deadly serious and exclusive source of my self-esteem that it once was. And although I have no close relatives to consider as family, I feel that I do have an adopted family—the medical team I work with and the many friends and advisers I have throughout the U.S. and the world.

Over the years, I have seen from every possible angle what can go wrong with the heart. I am confident that what I advocate is prudent, if not always absolutely proven. I firmly believe that whatever you truly aspire to create is worth living for, with all the vitality that comes from building a truly balanced life. Long before modern science flourished, the ancient Greeks said, "Nothing to excess." I've survived the self-inflicted wounds of excess, and believe me, no matter what the provocation or the incentive, you don't have to kill yourself to deal with it. It's not worth dying for.

Notes and Sources

Chapter 1: The Stress Epidemic
Donald Tubesing's remark likening stress to violin strings was quoted by Jane Brody in her "personal health" column in *The New York Times* of August 26, 1981. Dr. Tubesing is the author of *Kicking Your Stress Habits* (Duluth, Minn.: Whole Person Associates, 1981).

The list of emotional, behavioral, and physical signs of stress compiled by Capt. Neil S. Hibler, Ph.D., was reported by Capt. Katie Cutler in "Making the Best of Stress," *Airman* magazine, April 1981.

Chapter 2: Stress in Action: How Your Body Responds
Theories and research detailed in Chapters 2 to 5 on hot reacting and the effects of alarm and vigilance on the cardiovascular system were developed in collaboration with cardiologist James C. Buell, M.D.

The metaphor of the circulatory system as a personal Red Sea appears in "The Amazing Heart," an article in the June 1981 issue of *Your Health and Fitness,* a magazine published by Curriculum Innovations, Inc.

227

Chapter 3: The Hot Reactors
Hans Selye's books include *The Stress of Life* (New York: McGraw-Hill, 1956), *Stress Without Distress* (Philadelphia: Lippincott, 1974), and most recently for the medical community, *Stress in Health and Disease* (Boston: Butterworths, 1976).

The major book for the public by Meyer Friedman and Ray Rosenman is *Type A Behavior and Your Heart* (New York: Knopf, 1974). In a later medical journal article, "The Modification of Type A Behavior in Post-Infarction Patients," Meyer Friedman discusses their criteria of Type A behavior and the methods of rehabilitation for Type A heart patients (see *American Heart Journal*, vol. 95, no. 5, May 1979).

Jane Brody's summary of Type A behavior characteristics is quoted from her September 1980 *New York Times* News Service article, "Heart Ills Tied to Competitive Action." Copyright © 1980 by The New York Times Company. Reprinted by permission.

Chapter 4: Hot Reacting, High Blood Pressure, and Heart Attack
For a concise, informative statement on high blood pressure and the cardiovascular system, see the American Medical Association pamphlet "Your Blood Pressure."

A postscript to the story of Joe, the mobile home inspector whose heart attack ended in sudden cardiac death: Joe's brother filed a claim against the government. I was the medical consultant. Although I don't do this often, Joe's case was so compelling I decided to study it and write a medical opinion. In late 1982, the U.S. Department of Labor reversed itself and decided that Joe's death was "causally related to stress to which he was exposed in his job as a construction analyst." Joe's estate, at least, would benefit from his ordeal. Legal experts tell me this is a pivotal ruling by a federal agency, establishing legally that under certain conditions, job-related stress can kill.

Chapter 5: Are You a Hot Reactor?

Test 1 is adapted from one developed at the Stanford University Heart Disease Prevention Program. It was published in *The American Way of Life Need Not Be Hazardous to Your Health* by John W. Farquhar, M.D. (New York: Norton, 1979).

Test 2 was published as "The Social Readjustment Rating Scale" by Thomas H. Holmes and Richard H. Rahe in the *Journal of Psychosomatic Research*, vol. 11, 1967, pp. 213–218.

Tests 3 and 4 were developed by me to help my patients assess the sources of stress in their lifestyles and feelings.

Test 5 was developed for this book by Mark McKinney, Ph.D., a psychologist with the Department of Preventive and Stress Medicine at the University of Nebraska Medical Center.

Caroline Bedell Thomas, M.D., Professor Emeritus, Johns Hopkins University School of Medicine, published the monograph *Habits of Nervous Tension: Clues to the Human Condition* in 1977 as part of the Precursors Study, a research project that has followed the progress of 1300 people since they were medical students in 1946. The study has focused particularly on the psychobiological precursors of serious illness and premature death.

Chapter 6: Changing Your Self-Talks

Drs. Hermann Witte and Helen McIlvain, behavioral psychologists on our medical team, contributed substantially to the content of this chapter. Hermann Witte is responsible in particular for the ten basic irrational self-talks and their rational counterparts, the chart contrasting the effects of these self-talks, and several images and metaphors, including the thick-skinned and thin-skinned reactions to stress, the brain tumor analogy, and the view of behaviors as separate pieces in a mosaic picture we present of ourselves. Helen McIlvain explained and elaborated on the principles of cognitive/behavioral psychology and helped with examples.

Chapter 7: Clarifying Your Values
The Checkbook, Pride, Change, and Adjective Tests for clarifying values were adapted from exercises published in *Managing Stress: A Businessperson's Guide* by Jere E. Yates (New York: AMACOM, a division of American Management Associations, 1979, page 152.)

Chapter 8: Relaxing Your Body
Dr. Mark McKinney, a psychologist with our clinic, formulated the Relaxation Self-Assessment Test and the PMR Exercise tape and contributed to the ideas and information throughout this chapter. Information on breathing comes from Dr. Hermann Witte and on visualization from Dr. Michael Miner, also psychologists with our clinic.

Chapter 9: Increasing Your Fitness
Primary contributors to the content of this chapter are family physician and sports medicine specialist Dr. Morris Mellion and fitness expert Tracy Dorheim, both of our clinic. Also contributing were Dr. Mark McKinney and Marge Sailors.

A good source for further reading on the set point theory of weight control is *The Dieter's Dilemma* by William Bennett, M.D., and Joel Gurin (New York: Basic Books, 1982).

Chapter 10: Making the Most of Support and Leisure
Dr. Helen McIlvain contributed to the support section and Dr. Hermann Witte to the leisure section of this chapter.

Chapter 11: Eating Right
The major thrust and content of this chapter was provided by dietitian Phyllis Eliot. Input was also received from Glenda Woscyna, Dr. James Buell, and Tracy Dorheim.

Chapter 12: Managing Alcohol, Cigarettes, Caffeine, and Pills
Drs. Morris Mellion and Michael Miner of our clinic contributed information on alcohol, drugs, and caffeine for this chapter. For a medical review of the current issues in smoking and heart disease, see Wilbert Aronow, M.D., and Norman Kaplan, M.D., "Smoking and Cardiovascular Disease," Chapter 4 in Norman Kaplan and Jeremiah Stamler, eds., *Preventive Cardiology* (Philadelphia: Saunders, 1983).

The quotation on caffeine as a risk factor in sudden cardiac death comes from James P. Henry and Patricia Stephens in "Caffeine, Stress, and Cardiomyopathy," a paper presented at the third National Conference on Emotional Stress and Cardiovascular Disease, April 30–May 2, 1982, Myrtle Beach, S.C.

Chapter 13
The description of the five stages of burnout is from *The Work/Stress Connection: How to Cope with Job Burnout* by Robert L. Veninga, Ph.D., and James P. Spradley, Ph.D., copyright 1981 by Robert L. Veninga and James Spradley, reprinted by permission of Little, Brown and Company.

The description of Dr. Suzanne Kobasa's work on commitment, control and challenge is based on S.C. Kobasa, "The Hardy Personality: Toward a Social Psychology of Stress and Health" in J. Suls and G. Sanders, eds., *Social Psychology of Health and Illness* (Hinsdale, N.J.: Erlbaum, 1982).

Insights that helped focus my thinking on job stress appear in "Career-Related Depression," report of a symposium on stress published in 1982 by Lederle Laboratories, particularly the "Introduction and Overview" by Gene Usdin, M.D., and "Patterns of Executive Stress and Depression" by Harold M. Visotsky, M.D.

"Redefining the Role of the Employee" by Joel Kotkin and "The Eleventh Megatrend" by Connie Zweig in *Esquire,* May 1983, report in more detail on the current movement toward humanistic corporate values.

Chapter 14: Maintaining a Healthy Heart
The quotation from Dr. Samuel Fox appeared in *Health and Sickness Through Physical Activity* by Michael L. Pollock, Jack H. Wilmore, and Samuel M. Fox (New York: Wiley, 1978), p. 337.

A further bit of advice for people with heart disease or high blood pressure: consider a pet. Drs. Aaron Katcher and Alan Beck of the University of Pennsylvania, James Lynch and Sue Thomas of the University of Maryland, and Erica Friedmann of Brooklyn College have worked together on various studies concerning the therapeutic value of pets. Members of this group found, for example, that blood pressure rises when people read to each other or even read the telephone book aloud, but it can drop when they talk to their pets. Petting a dog or just watching fish swim in an aquarium lowers blood pressure, and the benefit is measurably greater for people with high blood pressure than for those with normal blood pressure. One study followed the progress of 92 patients who had been in a coronary care unit for heart attack or angina. Only 6 percent of those who owned pets died within one year of leaving the hospital, compared to 28 percent of the patients who did not own pets. The companionship of pets made a difference for both men and women, no matter how severe their condition was. Researchers note that the important difference in having a pet is being attached to it and interacting with it.

Recommended Reading

Stress, Your Heart, and Your Health

AMERICAN HEART ASSOCIATION, 7320 Greenville Ave., Dallas, Tex. 75231. Contact your state affiliate for literature on physiology and diseases of the heart, or write the national organization for literature and the location of your state affiliate.

COUSINS, NORMAN. *Anatomy of an Illness*. New York: Norton, 1979.

COUSINS, NORMAN. *The Healing Heart: Antidotes to Panic and Helplessness*. New York: Norton, 1983.

DOSSEY, LARRY. *Space, Time, and Medicine*. Boulder, Colo.: Shambhala Publications, 1982.

FRIEDMAN, MEYER, and RAY H. ROSENMAN. *Type A Behavior and Your Heart*. New York: Knopf, 1974.

SELYE, HANS. *Stress Without Distress*. Philadelphia: Lippincott, 1974.

Guides to Behavior Change

ALBERTI, ROBERT, and MICHAEL EMMONS. *Your Perfect Right: A Guide to Assertive Behavior*. San Luis Obispo, Calif.: Impact, 1974.

BURNS, DAVID. *Feeling Good: The New Mood Therapy*. New York: Institute for Rational-Emotive Therapy, 1980.

COATES, THOMAS, and CARL THORESEN. *How to Sleep Better: A Drug-Free Program for Overcoming Insomnia*. Self-

Management Psychology Series. Englewood Cliffs, N.J.: Prentice-Hall, 1977.

ELLIS, ALBERT, and ROBERT HARPER. *A New Guide to Rational Living*. New York: Institute for Rational-Emotive Therapy, 1975.

GORDON, THOMAS. *Parent Effectiveness Training*. New York: McKay, 1970.

INSTITUTE FOR RATIONAL-EMOTIVE THERAPY, 45 E. 65th St., New York, N.Y. 10021. Catalog of publications.

LAKEIN, ALAN. *How to Get Control of Your Time and Your Life*. New York: Signet, 1973.

LEWINSOHN, PETER, RICARDO MUÑOZ, MARY ANN YOUNGREN, and ANTONETTE ZEISS. *Control Your Depression*. Self-Management Psychology Series. Englewood Cliffs, N.J.: Prentice-Hall, 1978.

MAULTSBY, MAXIE C., JR., M.D. *Help Yourself to Happiness Through Rational Self-Counseling*. New York: Institute for Rational-Emotive Therapy, 1975.

WITTE, HERMANN. *Becoming Thick-Skinned*. 1983. Mimeographed manual for use with first course in workshop series, Coping Effectively with Stress. Available from Dr. Witte or from the International Stress Foundation, 8901 Indian Hills Drive, Suite 4, Omaha, Neb. 68114.

Relaxation and Biofeedback

BENSON, HERBERT. *The Relaxation Response*. New York: Morrow, 1975.

BIOFEEDBACK SOCIETY OF AMERICA, 4301 Owens St., Wheat Ridge, Colo. 80033. Tel. (303) 422–8436. Geographical directory of certified biofeedback practitioners and their specialties (many are also relaxation therapists).

BROWN, BARBARA. *New Mind, New Body*. New York: Bantam, 1975.

JACOBSON, EDMUND. *You Must Relax*. New York: McGraw-Hill, 1976.

MCKINNEY, MARK. *Relaxation training tapes*. 1984. Available from International Stress Foundation, 8901 Indian Hills Drive, Suite 4, Omaha, Neb. 68114.

Fitness

ANDERSON, ROBERT. *Stretching: For Everyday Fitness and for Running, Tennis, Racquetball, Golf, and Other Sports.* Bolinas, Calif.: Shelter Publications (distributed by Random House), 1980.

COOPER, KENNETH. *The New Aerobics.* New York: Bantam, 1970.

COOPER, KENNETH. *The Aerobics Program for Total Well-Being: Exercise, Diet, Emotional Balance.* New York: M. Evans, 1982, and Bantam, 1983.

COOPER, MILDRED, and KENNETH COOPER. *Aerobics for Women.* New York: Bantam, 1973.

FIXX, JAMES. *The Complete Book of Running.* New York: Random House, 1977.

POLLOCK, MICHAEL, JACK WILMORE, and SAMUEL M. FOX, III. *Health and Fitness Through Physical Activity.* New York: Wiley, 1978.

Nutrition

BERLAND, THEODORE, and the editors of *Consumer Guide. Rating the Diets.* New York: Signet, 1980.

BRODY, JANE. *Jane Brody's Nutrition Book.* New York: Norton, 1981.

DEBAKEY, MICHAEL E., M.D. *The Living Heart Diet.* New York: Raven Press, 1983.

HERBERT, VICTOR, and STEPHEN BARRETT. *Vitamins and Health Foods: The Great American Hustle.* Philadelphia: George F. Stickley Co., 1981.

LAPPÉ, FRANCES MOORE. *Diet for a Small Planet.* New York: Ballantine, 1971.

MAYER, JEAN, M.D. *A Diet for Living.* New York: McKay, 1975 (special Consumers Union edition, 1976).

Alcoholism

ALCOHOLICS ANONYMOUS. Numerous publications, many free or at nominal cost, available at local chapter offices.

MAULTSBY, MAXIE C., JR., M.D. *A Million Dollars for Your Hang-*

over. New York: Institute for Rational-Emotive Therapy, 1978.

NATIONAL CLEARINGHOUSE FOR ALCOHOL INFORMATION, P.O. Box 2345, Rockville, Md. 20852.

NATIONAL COUNCIL ON ALCOHOLISM, 733 Third Ave., New York, N.Y. 10017. Literature also available from local affiliates, listed in telephone yellow pages under "alcoholism."

Work

BOLLES, RICHARD. *What Color Is Your Parachute? A Practical Manual for Job-Hunters and Career-Changers*. Berkeley, Calif.: Ten Speed Press, 1972.

RUDDICK, SARA, and PAMELA DANIELS, EDS. *Working It Out: 23 Women Writers, Artists, Scientists, and Scholars Talk About Their Lives and Work*. New York: Pantheon, 1978.

PETERS, THOMAS J., and ROBERT H. WATERMAN. *In Search of Excellence: Lessons from America's Best-Run Companies*. New York: Harper and Row, 1982.

TERKEL, STUDS. *Working: People Talk About What They Do All Day and How They Feel About It*. New York: Avon, 1972.

TOFFLER, ALVIN. *The Third Wave*. New York: Morrow, 1980.

Index

A

Abdominal breathing, 123–24
Actuarial tables, 163
Adjective test, 116
Adrenal cortex, 27
Adrenal glands, 27
  benign tumors of, 57
Adrenal medulla, 27
Adrenaline:
  and alarm reaction, 27, 29, 30
  and amphetamines, 199
  in animal research, 16
  and blood sugar, 177
  and caffeine, 193
  early research on, 35
  effect on heart of, 30–31
  and nicotine, 189–90
Aerobic exercise, 137–39
  and weight loss, 138
*Aerobics Program for Total
  Well-Being, The* (Cooper,
  143
Aerospace workers, 15, 17
  sudden cardiac death in, 62
Al-Anon, 197
Alarm, 27–33
  artery damage from, 69
  and caffeine, 194
  daily frequency of, 31–32
  effect on heart of, 30–33

and high blood pressure, 57
  in hot reactors, 38
  and smoking, 189
Alateen, 197
Alcohol, 14, 187, 195–98
  and burnout, 205
  and HDL levels, 151, 171,
    173
  health hazards of, 196–97
  after heart attack, 222
  heart muscle weakened by,
    60
  and jet travel, 182, 183
  and obesity, 164
  quitting excessive use of,
    197–98
  self-test for problem
    drinking, 200
  and tranquilizers, 198
  and triglycerides, 176
  and wellness programs, 213
Alcoholics Anonymous, 117,
  154, 197
Altruistic egoism, 112
American Cancer Society,
  193
American Heart Association,
  172
American Medical Association,
  14, 228
Amino acids, 167

Amphetamines, 199
Anemia, 196
Anger, 22
  exercise to relieve, 138
  in hot reactors, 85
Angina, 56, 63, 121, 223
  and smoking, 190
Animal research, 16–17
  on support systems, 152
Anti-stress self-talks, 103,
    104, 106–10
Anxiety, 22, 122, 123
  and angina, 223
  drugs for control of, 198–99
  exercise to relieve, 138
  after heart attack, 219, 220
  in hot reactors, 85
  and hunger, 185
Aorta, narrowing of, 57
Appetite, effect of exercise
    on, 138
Aronow, Wilbert, 231
Arteries, 23
  coronary, 60
  effect of high blood pressure
    on, 56
  See also Hardening of arteries
Arterioles, 23
Arthritis, 153
Aspirin, 187
Assertiveness, 223
Atherosclerosis, see Harden-
    ing of arteries
Auto accidents, 192
Autonomy, 217

B

Barnard, Christiaan, 1
Baseball, 139, 144
Basketball, 139, 144
Beck, Alan, 232
Becoming Thick-Skinned
    (Witte), 102
Behavioral signs of stress, 19
Bennett, William, 230

Betty Ford Center for
    Chemical Dependency, 197
Bicycling, 138
Biofeedback, 122–23, 132
Biofeedback Society of
    America, 132
Birth control pills, 58
  and smoking, 190
Blacks, frequency of high
    blood pressure among,
    58–59
Blindness, 57
Blood clots, 31, 183
  and alcohol, 196
  and smoking, 190
Blood pressure, 25–27, 225
  in alarm reaction, 29
  and exercise, 136, 137
  home measurement of, 87,
    217
  in hot reactors, 38
  and smoking, 189
  and sodium, 196
  in vigilance reaction, 30
  See also High blood
    pressure
Blood sugar, 176–77
Body composition, 143
Bone marrow, effect of
    alcohol on, 196
Bowling, 139
Brain:
  effect of high blood
    pressure on, 56
  infections of, 57
  tumors of, 57
"Brain tumor" analogy,
    106–7, 212
Breads, 168
Breakfast, 169
Breaks, relaxation, 131–32
Breakthrough insomnia, 121
Breast cancer, 192
Breastfeeding, nutrition during,
    168
Brody, Jane, 37, 227, 228
Brooklyn College, 232

Browning, Robert, 118
Buell, James, 7–8, 227, 231
Buffington, Ruth, 5
Burnout, 203–5, 213
  using leisure to avoid, 157–59

C

Caffeine, 193–95
  and jet travel, 183
Calcium, 180
  loss of, exercise and, 137
Cancer:
  of colon, 171, 174
  lung, 187, 188, 191–92
  and obesity, 163
  and Vitamin C, 180
Cannon, Walter, 35
Capillaries, 23
Carbohydrates, 167, 174
  and triglycerides, 176
Carbon monoxide, 189–90
Cardiomyopathy, alcoholic,
  196
Cardiorespiratory fitness, 143
Cardiovascular system:
  functioning of, 23–27
  uncoupling of, 30
Carotid artery, 140
Casteneda, Aldo, 1
Catecholamines, 61–62
Central nervous system
  disorders, 57
Cereals, 168
Challenge, sense of, 207
Change:
  inevitability of, 214
  preparing for, 208
Change test, 116
Checkbook test, 114
Chest breathing, 123
Chloride, 180
Cholesterol, 170–74
  and cortisol, 31
  after heart attack, 222
  high levels of, 14

and sugar, 176
and vigilance, 60
Chromium, 180
Cigarettes, see Smoking
Cirrhosis of liver, 192, 196
City University of New York,
  206
Cocaine, 14
Codeine, 187
Coffee, see Caffeine
Cognitive restructuring, 96
Cold pressor test, 87–89
Cold reactors, Type A
  behavior in, 39, 49–53
Colds, Vitamin C for, 180
Cole, Nat "King," 187
Collateral blood circulation,
  136
Colon, cancer of, 171, 174
Colorado, University of, 1
Combined hot reactors,
  40–41, 44–47, 216
Commitment, sense of, 206
Complex carbohydrates, 174
Compulsions, 86
Concentration, lack of, 121
"Confrontation," 198
Congestive heart failure, 56
Conservation-withdrawal system,
  see Vigilance
Consistent behavior, 119
Constipation, 86
  fiber to relieve, 174
  when traveling, 182
Consumer Reports, 87
Control, sense of, 206–7
Cooper, Ken, 143
Copper, 180
Coronary arteries, 60
  and HDL, 151
Coronary bypass surgery, 44
Coronary heart disease, see
  Heart disease
Corporate cultures, 213
Cortisol:
  and air travel, 183
  and alcohol, 196

Cortisol (*con't.*)
  in animal research, 16
  early research on, 35
  effect on heart of, 30–31
  and sodium, 175
  and vigilance reaction, 27, 30
Crash diets, 167
Cross-country skiing, 138
Cutler, Capt. Katie, 227
Cycling, stationary, 138

D

Daily life stress test, 89–90
Dancing, aerobic, 138
Delegation, 119, 210
Depression, 122
  and exercise, 136, 138
  after heart attack, 220
  in hot reactors, 85
  and hunger, 185
  and job stress, 207
  and support, 152
  using leisure to avoid,
    157–59
  and vigilance, 31
Diabetes, 14
  and obesity, 163
Diarrhea, 86
  when traveling, 182
Diastolic pressure, 25, 26,
    90
Diet, *see* Eating habits
Diet Workshop, 185
Dissonance stage, 111
Diuretics, 216
Diverticulosis, 174
Dizziness, 123
Dorheim, Tracy, 230, 231
Dreaming, importance of,
    199
Drinking, *see* Alcohol
Drugs:
  abuse of, 14, 198–201, 205
  for high blood pressure,
    215–16

E

Eating habits, 162–86
  and breakfast, 169
  and fats, 170–74
  and healthy weight, 162–67
  after heart attack, 222
  and salt, 175–76
  and starch and fiber, 174
  and sugar, 176–77
  when traveling and eating
    out, 181–83
  variety in, 167–69
  and vitamin abuse, 177–81
  and weight loss, 183–86
  and wellness programs, 213
Edwards, Jesse, 1
Egoism, altruistic, 112
Eisenhower Medical Center,
    197
Elderly, nutrition for, 168
Electrical system of heart,
    60–61
Elia, Salim, 5
Eliot, Phyllis Allman, 2–3, 6,
    225, 231
Ellis, Albert, 97
Emergency system, *see* Alarm
Emotional habits, 97–99
Emotional signs of stress, 19
Encephalitis, 57
Endorphins, 151
Endurance, 144
Environment, taking control
    of, 117–19
Essential fatty acids, 167
Essential hypertension, 57,
    58
Exercise:
  after heart attack, 222
  for unemployed, 203
  and weight loss, 186
  and wellness programs, 213
  See also Fitness
Exhiliration, 86
Expectations, unrealistic,
    116–17

F

Fad diets, 162
Failure, programming yourself
    for, 117
Farquhar, John, 229
Fatigue, 121, 123, 225
    and hunger, 185
    and job stress, 207
    pathological, 62
Fats, 167
    avoiding excessive intake of,
        170–74
Federal Centers for Disease
    Control, 191
Feedback, 211
Fetal alcohol syndrome,
    197
Fiber, 174
Fight-or-flight response,
    22
    catecholamines in, 61
    introduction of, 35
Fitness, 134–51
    over forty, 144
    getting started on, 139–43
    goals of, 143–51
    as fun vs. hard work, 150–51
Flexibility, 143
Florida, University of, at
    Gainesville, 1
Fluorine, 180
Flyer's diet, 182–83
Food groups, 168
Ford, Betty, 197
Football, 139, 144
"Fourteen-foot risk factor,"
    17
Fox, Samuel M., III, 222, 232
Framingham Study, 163
Friedmann, Erica, 232
Friedman, Meyer, 35, 37, 228
Fruits, 168
Funk, Kasimir, 177
Future, visualization of,
    118
"Future shock," 13

G

Gainesville Veterans Administra-
    tion Hospital, 1
General Motors, 231
Glycogen, 177
Goals:
    of fitness, 143–51
    of heart attack patients, 219
    weight loss, 185
Golf, 139
Gorilla breath, 179
Guilt, 184
Gurin, Joel, 230

H

Handball, 139
Hardening of arteries, 23
    adrenaline and cortisol in, 30,
        31
    and exercise, 136
    and low-fat diets, 172
    and smoking, 190
    and Vitamin C, 180
Hardiness, 206
Headaches, 22, 52, 121
    and caffeine, 194, 195
"Health" foods, 162
"Health Hazard Appraisal," 192
Heart:
    effect of alarm and vigilance
        on, 30–34
    effect of exercise on, 136
    effect of high blood
        pressure on, 56
    effect of smoking on, 189
    functioning of, 23–27
    rhythm disturbances of, 196
Heart attack, 56, 215
    and smoking, 188
    support and recovery from,
        152
    treatment after, 218–23
    See also Sudden cardiac
        death

Heart disease, 14, 192
  and air travel, 183
  behavior linked to, 35
  and caffeine, 194, 195
  and cholesterol, 170
  hypertensive, 56
  and marijuana, 190
  and obesity, 163
  and smoking, 188
  traditional risk factors for,
    14–15
  and triglycerides, 176
  and Vitamin C, 180
Heart muscle:
  effect of alcohol on, 196
  effect of vigilance on, 60
Heart palpitations, 123
Helplessness, 15, 17
Hemoglobin, 189
Henry, James P., 193, 231
Hereditary factors in high blood
    pressure, 57, 58
Hibler, Neil S., 19, 227
High blood pressure (hyper-
    tension), 14, 23, 121
  alcoholic, 196
  and caffeine, 193, 195
  causes of, 57
  contribution of alarm and
    vigilance reactions to, 30
  controlling, 215–18
  and dietary fats, 171
  essential, 57
  hot reacting vs., 43–44
  and obesity, 163, 164
  physical effects of, 55–57
  relaxation therapy for, 129–31
  and sodium, 175
  and stress, 57–58
  susceptibility to, 58–59
  treatment of, 59
  and wellness programs, 213
High-density lipoproteins
    (HDLs), 170–73
  and alcohol, 195
  and exercise, 137, 151
Holmes, Thomas H., 229

Hopelessness, 15, 17
  in self-talks, 108
"Horribilizing," 52, 107, 108
Hot reacting, 35–92
  and blood sugar, 177
  and caffeine, 194
  combined, 40–41, 44–47
  control of, 216, 217
  defined, 37
  and exercise, 136–37
  and heart attack, 220
  and high blood pressure,
    43–44, 55–59
  output, 40–43
  relaxation therapy for, 129–31
  and sudden cardiac death,
    59–62
  tests to determine, 65–92
  vasoconstrictive, 41, 47–49
  wellness programs for, 213
How Are You Reacting to
    Stress? (test), 75–85
Hughes, Howard, 187
Hunger, stress experienced as,
    184
Hydrogenated fats, 170
Hypertension, see High blood
    pressure
Hypertensive heart disease,
    56
Hypertrophy of heart, 60
Hyperventilation, 123
Hypnosis, 132
  for quitting smoking, 193
Hypochondria, 52
Hypoglycemia, reactive, 177

I

Ice hockey, 138
Immune system, 30
In Search of Excellence
    (Peters and Waterman),
    214
Incentive, 217
Increased activity, 86

Individual therapy, 203
Infants, nutrition for, 169
Insomnia, 121
  and caffeine, 194
Insulin, 137
  and sugar intake, 177
Intellectual insight, 110
Invisible entrapment, 2, 17
  and vigilance, 31
Iodine, 180
Irrational self-talks, 98,
  102–9
Irritable bowel, 174
Iron, 180
  supplements, 168
"Is That All There Is?"
  syndrome, 17
Isometric exercises, 139

J

Japanese-Americans, 153
Jet travel, 182–83
Jiggle test, 166
Job stress, 203–14
  and burnout, 203–5
  coping with, 205–13
  organizational programs for
    relief of, 213–14
Jogging, 135, 138
Johns Hopkins University
  School of Medicine, 85,
  229
*Journal of the American
  Medical Association,* 217
Jumping rope, 138

K

Kaplan, Norman, 231
Katcher, Aaron, 232
Kidneys, 23
  diseases of, 57, 187
  effect of high blood pressure
    on, 56

Kobasa, Suzanne, 206, 207, 231
Kotkin, Joel, 232

L

Labor, U.S. Department of, 228
Lederle Laboratories, 232
Lee, Peggy, 17
Leisure, 155–61, 226
  to avoid burnout and
    depression, 157–59
  finding time for, 160–61
  for workaholics, 159–60
Librium, 198
Life-Assessment Test, 70–72
Life-Event Test, 67–69
Life Stress Lab, 8, 86
Lifestyle changes, 59
Lillehei, Richard, 1
Lillehei, C. Walton, 1
Lindbergh, Charles, 192
Lipoproteins, 170
Listening, 210
Liver, cirrhosis of, 192, 196
Low blood pressure, 26–27
Low-density lipoproteins (LDLs),
  170, 172
Low-fat diets, 172
Lung cancer, 187, 188,
  191–92
Lungs, 23
Lynch, James, 232

M

McIlvain, Helen, 229, 230
McKinney, Mark, 229, 230
McQueen, Steve, 192
Magnesium, 180
Manganese, 180
Marijuana, 190
Maryland, University of, 232
Maultsby, Maxie, Jr., 97
Meat, 168
Meditation, 129, 132

Megatrends (Naisbitt), 208
Mellion, Morris, 230, 231
Mental arithmetic test, 89
Mentors, 211
Metabolism:
  and crash diets, 167
  effect of exercise on, 137
Methodist Hospital (Indianapolis), 192
Metropolitan Life Insurance
      Company, 163
Milk, 168
  nutrients in, 167
Mills, Wilbur, 187
Miner, Michael, 230, 231
Minerals, 167
  megadoses of, 180–81
Minnesota, University of, 1
Molybdenum, 180
Money, choices in how to
      spend, 114
Monounsaturated fats, 170
Mossey, Jana, 96
Muscle-to-fat ratio, 138
Muscle tension, 22
Muscle tone, 138
Muscular fitness, 143
Myocardial infarction (MI),
      218

N

Naisbitt, John, 208
National Academy of Sciences,
      Food and Nutrition Board
      of, 178
National Cancer Institute,
      193
National Institutes of Health,
      36
Nausea, 86
Nebraska, University of, 1
  Medical Center, 7, 229
Negative feedback, 211
New Aerobics, The (Cooper),
      143

New York Times, 37
Nicotine, 189–90
Nietzsche, Friedrich, 7
North Carolina Industry
      Commission, 169

O

Obesity, 14, 162–64
  and high blood pressure,
      57, 217
Output hot reactors, 40–43,
      216
Overweight, 162, 163

P

Painkillers, 14
Palpitations, 123
Pathological fatigue, 62
Pennsylvania, University of,
      232
Perfectionism, 104–5, 209–10
Peters, Thomas, 214
Pets, 232
Philosophic effort, 86
Phosphorus, 180
Physical signs of stress, 19–20
Pinch test, 166
Planning, 119
  job-related, 209
Platelets:
  effect of adrenaline and
      cortisol on, 30
  effect of smoking on, 190
Play, 156–57, 221
Pneumonia, 192
Pollock, Michael L., 232
Polyunsaturated fats, 170
Positive feedback, 211
Potassium, 180
  and cortisol, 31
  in flyer's diet, 183
  loss of, 60, 61, 175, 196
Precursors Study, 229

Pregnancy:
    alcohol during, 197
    high blood pressure during,
        58
    nutrition during, 168
    smoking during, 189
Prinze, Freddie, 187
Pritikin Diet, 72
Programming for failure, 117
Progressive muscle relaxation,
    123–28
Proteins, 167, 173

Q

Quest for Fire (film), 113

R

Raab, Wilhelm, 35
Racquetball, 139, 144
Rahe, Richard H., 229
"Raison d'être," 113
Rapid Eye Movement (REM)
    sleep, 199
Rational Emotive Therapy, 97
Reactive hypoglycemia, 177
"Rebound" phenomenon, 167
Recommended Dietary
    Allowances (RADs), 178,
    180
Recreational drugs, 14
Relaxation therapy, 120–33
    abdominal breathing in,
        123–24
    biofeedback in, 122–23
    breaks for, 131–32
    progressive muscle relaxation
        in, 124–28
    and recognition of stress
        cues, 132–33
    "reminder stimulus" in,
        131
    supervised, 132–33
    visualization in, 128–29

Religion:
    support from, 154
    and values, 112
Research and development
    plan, 118
Risk-taking, 208
Rosenman, Ray, 35, 37, 228
Rowing, 138
"Runner's high," 150
Running:
    competitive, 144
    in place, 138
Ruth, Babe, 192

S

Sailors, Marge, 230
Salt:
    excessive intake of, 57, 217
    in flyer's diet, 183
    reducing intake of, 175–76,
        222
    retention of, 60
Saturated fats, 170–74
Scale personality, 184
Selenium, 180
Self-help groups, 154
    for unemployed, 203
Self-hypnosis, 129
Self-talks, 95–111
    case example of, 99–102
    constructive, 225
    and emotional habits, 97–99
    for heart attack patients, 220
    irrational, 98, 102–9
    and support groups, 153
Selye, Hans, 35, 112, 228
Sex hormones, impact of
    cortisol on, 30
Sexual activity after heart
    attack, 222
SHAPE program, 50
Shearer, Marshall and
    Marguerite, 156
Shortcomings, acceptance of,
    107–8

Shoulder breathing, 123
Shumway, Norman, 1
Sickel cell anemia, 59
Side-stream smoke danger, 191
Sighing respiration, 142
Simple carbohydrates, 174
Simple Stress and Tension
 Test, 65–66
Simplification, 119
"Six-months-to-live" test, 115–16
Skiing, cross-country, 138
Sleeping pills, 198, 199
Sleeplessness, 22
Smoking, 14, 35, 188–93
 and dietary fats, 171
 and HDL levels, 151, 171,
  174
 and heart attack, 221
 and high blood pressure,
  217
 and obesity, 164
 quitting, 192–93
 and wellness programs, 213
Sodium, 175–76, 180
 retention of, 196
 See also Salt
Southern California, University
 of, School of Medicine, 193
Spasm of blood vessel, 31
Speech, stylistics of, 51
Spradley, James P., 204, 231
Squash, 139
Stamler, Jeremiah, 231
Stanford University Heart
 Disease Prevention Program,
 229
Starch, 174
Stationary cycling, 138
Stephens, Patricia, 193, 231
Stepped-care approach, 216
Stop the World, I Want to
 Get Off (musical), 212
Stress, 13–21
 animal research on, 16–17
 body's response to, 22–34
 cause and effect of, 14–17
 early warning signs of, 19–20

experienced as hunger, 184
 and high blood pressure,
  57–58
 management of, 20–21,
  91–92; see also specific
  techniques
 testing response to, 86–91
 See also Alarm; Hot reacting;
  Job stress; Vigilance
Stress Clinic, 8
Stress cues, 132–33, 217
Stress of Life, The (Selye), 35
Stressful Attitudes Test,
 73–75
Stretching exercises, 145–49
Stroke, 56
Sudden cardiac death, 48,
 59–62
 and alcohol, 197
 case example of, 62–64
 and catecholamines, 61–62
 and smoking, 188, 190
Sugar, reducing intake of,
 176–77
Sulphur, 180
Support, 152–55
 for high blood pressure
  patients, 218
 job-related, 210
 for unemployed, 203
 for weight loss, 185–86
Sweating, 123
Swimming, 138
Systolic pressure, 25, 26, 90

T

Technology:
 impact on everyday life of, 13
 and physical response to
  stress, 22
Tennis, 139, 144
Tension, exercise to relieve, 138
Testosterone, 30
"Thick-skinned" reaction to
 stress, 96

Third Wave, The (Toffler), 208
Thomas, Caroline Bedell, 85, 229
Thomas, Sue, 232
Thoreau, Henry David, 119
Thrombus, 31
Time:
  for leisure, 160–61
  management of, 208–9
  values and use of, 114–15
  wise use of, 119
Time magazine, 175
Toffler, Alvin, 13, 208
Tombstone test, 112–14
Tooth decay, 176
TOPS (Take Off Pounds Sensibly), 185
Trace elements, 180
Track and field, 144
Tranquilizers, 14, 198–99
Traveling, prudent diet for, 181–83
Treadmill test, 86–87
  before starting fitness program, 140
Triglycerides, 171, 176
Tubesing, Donald, 20, 227
Twenties test, 165–66
Type A behavior, 35–38
  and caffeine, 193
  in cold reactors, 49–53
  in hot reactors, 39–40
  and self-talks, 96
  summary of, 37
Type A Behavior and Your Heart (Friedman and Rosenman), 35
Type B behavior, 36
  and self-talks, 96

U

Ulcers, 22
  and caffeine, 194, 195
Uncoupling, 30
Unemployment, 202–3

"Uppers," 199
Upset stomach, 121
Urinary frequency, 86
Usdin, Gene, 232

V

Vacations, 158–59, 213
Valium, 14, 198
Value clarification, 112–19
  adjective test in, 116
  change test in, 116
  checkbook test in, 114
  and expectations, 116–17
  pride test in, 116
  "six-months-to-live" test in, 115–16
  and taking control of environment, 117–19
  time test in, 114–15
  tombstone test in, 112–14
Vasoconstrictive hot reactors, 41, 47–49, 216
Vegetable oils, 167
Vegetables, 168
Veninga, Robert L., 204, 231
Very-low-density lipoproteins (VLDLs), 170
Video games, stress testing with, 89
Vigilance, 27–34
  in animal research, 16
  chronic, 34
  and cholesterol, 60
  effect on heart of, 30–34
  and high blood pressure, 57
  in hot reactors, 38
  salt retention caused by, 60, 175
Visotsky, Harold M., 232
Visualization, 123, 128–29
  of future, 118
Vitamin A, 178
Vitamin B$_1$, 179
Vitamin C, 179–80
Vitamin D, 178

Vitamin E, 178–79
Vitamin K, 179
Vitamins, 167
    megadoses of, 177–80
    supplements, 162
Voltaire, 221
Volunteer work, 203
Vomiting, 86

W

Walking, 138
Warming up for exercise, 144–45
Water pills, 216
Water retention, 175
Waterman, Robert, 214
Wayne, John, 192
Weight, healthy, 162–67
Weight lifting, 139
Weight loss, 166–67, 183–86
    amphetamines for, 199
    and exercise, 138
    after heart attack, 222
Weight Watchers, 154, 185
Wellness programs, 213

West Germany, 223
Wilmore, Jack H., 232
Witte, Hermann, 102, 229, 230
Work, 156–57, 226
    See also Job stress
Workaholics, 159–60, 212
Woscyna, Glenda, 231

X

Xylocaine, 5

Y

Yale University, 96
Yates, Jere E., 230
Your Health and Fitness (magazine), 23, 227

Z

Zinc, 180
Zweig, Connie, 232